HUMAN GROWTH, BEHAVIOUR AND DEVELOPMENT

SAGE was founded in 1965 by Sara Miller McCune to support the dissemination of usable knowledge by publishing innovative and high-quality research and teaching content. Today, we publish more than 850 journals, including those of more than 300 learned societies, more than 800 new books per year, and a growing range of library products including archives, data, case studies, reports, and video. SAGE remains majority-owned by our founder, and after Sara's lifetime will become owned by a charitable trust that secures our continued independence.

Los Angeles | London | New Delhi | Singapore | Washington DC

HUMAN GROWTH, BEHAVIOUR AND DEVELOPMENT

ESSENTIAL THEORY AND APPLICATION IN SOCIAL WORK

ALASTAIR GIBSON AND NEIL GIBSON

Los Angeles | London | New Delhi
Singapore | Washington DC

Los Angeles | London | New Delhi
Singapore | Washington DC

SAGE Publications Ltd
1 Oliver's Yard
55 City Road
London EC1Y 1SP

SAGE Publications Inc.
2455 Teller Road
Thousand Oaks, California 91320

SAGE Publications India Pvt Ltd
B 1/I 1 Mohan Cooperative Industrial Area
Mathura Road
New Delhi 110 044

SAGE Publications Asia-Pacific Pte Ltd
3 Church Street
#10-04 Samsung Hub
Singapore 049483

Editor: Kate Wharton
Production editor: Katie Forsythe
Copyeditor: Roza I. M. El-Eini
Proofreader: Philippa Emler
Marketing manager: Tamara Navaratnam
Cover design: Lisa Harper-Wells
Typeset by: C&M Digitals (P) Ltd, Chennai, India
Printed and bound in Great Britain by Ashford
Colour Press Ltd

Library of Congress Control Number: 2015935203

British Library Cataloguing in Publication data

A catalogue record for this book is available from
the British Library

ISBN 978-1-4739-1273-1
ISBN 978-1-4739-1274-8 (pbk)

At SAGE we take sustainability seriously. Most of our products are printed in the UK using FSC papers and boards.
When we print overseas we ensure sustainable papers are used as measured by the Egmont grading system.
We undertake an annual audit to monitor our sustainability.

CONTENTS

LIST OF FIGURES

ABOUT THE AUTHORS

Alastair Gibson graduated with an MA in History before becoming frustrated as a hospital administrator and deciding to move into the more challenging and rewarding practice of social work. He worked in Aberdeen and Gateshead in a variety of health care social work settings and then taught at Robert Gordon University (RGU). Developing his enthusiasm for interprofessional practice, he was a founder member of the Centre for the Advancement of Interprofessional Education (CAIPE) and helped develop shared training for social work, health, education and police trainees. He has thoroughly enjoyed teaching Human Growth and Behaviour as well as being Course Leader of the BA (Hons) Social Work by Distance Learning before retiring in 2009. He is now an independent practice teacher.

Neil Gibson graduated with a BA in Communication and worked in the media, travel and tourism before re-entering education and obtaining an MSc in Social Work. He has worked in residential childcare, substance use, care management and adult protection before joining the social work teaching team at Robert Gordon University where he currently works.

ACKNOWLEDGEMENTS

I would like to thank Joyce Lishman for her support and companionship in furthering my knowledge of psychosocial theory. In addition, thanks to the many students whose motivation and desire to learn have been a further inspiration. Finally, thanks to Maureen for tolerating my antisocial fixation on a computer screen for the past year and to Coen for keeping me active and entertained.

Alastair Gibson

Thanks to the students who have crossed my path when teaching Human Growth and Behaviour for making me think about the best way to describe these complex theories. Thanks to Ian Jeffries for reading and critiquing sample chapters, and thanks to Kirsi and Coen for all the support.

Neil Gibson

We would both like to thank Kate Wharton, Katie Norton and Katie Forsythe at Sage for their encouragement and enthusiastic support.

INTRODUCTION

In this book, we are hoping that you will find a clear explanation of the main theories which are delivered on social work courses under the headings of 'human growth and behaviour' or 'human growth and development'. These theories are psychodynamic and psychosocial, which means that they address the conscious and unconscious parts of an individual's personality, but also address the individual's relationships with other people. Experience has taught us that the understanding of individuals is a complex matter, and that there is no simple, straightforward approach which provides an easy answer. To apply social work interventions without making a holistic assessment of personality may result in negative outcomes for the service user and a sense of failure or frustration for the worker. The theories that we address in this book reflect this complexity, and we shall try to make them as clear as possible in the written word.

With greater understanding of the theories, you will hopefully develop more confidence in incorporating them into your practice. One of the potential dangers is that social workers apply these theoretical approaches mechanistically, as if 'one size fits all', whereas the message we wish to convey is that of understanding the uniqueness of each individual with whom you may work. Therefore, in addition to providing an explanation of theories, we also intend to demonstrate how these theories can be applied to social work or social care practice by providing case examples.

We understand that you may wish to skip over this Introduction to get to the actual content, but please read on for a few more minutes in order to find out how best to use the book.

First, we are going to concentrate on the psychosocial: we are not going to go into psychological or sociological theories in any depth, but we shall direct you to further reading throughout. Second, we are going to attempt to show you how theories overlap and complement one another: in assessing people's needs, you are putting together a jigsaw and these various theories are your jigsaw pieces. Third, we hope to show you that, while these theories provide broad knowledge and understanding, the individual's unique set of experiences determine how these theories can be applied, and it is fundamentally important that we apply theory to the individual's circumstances and do not try to fit the individual to the theory.

You will find the book arranged in four parts. Part 1 will address the importance of early childhood in the formation of personality and behaviour, looking at the emotional needs of a child and the potential implications of the care received by a child on future behaviour and development. The three chapters in this first part all focus on how the young child develops in relationship with other people, from the immediate primary carers to a widening range of contacts with extended family, neighbours, friends and others. Chapter 1 considers the importance of attachments and bond formation; Chapter 2 considers the framework of Erik Erikson's Life Cycle, which sees personality development as a succession of expectable stages; and Chapter 3 introduces Object Relations Theory, which applies a psychodynamic approach to understanding the individual. In Part 1, we draw parallels between these three key themes, which we see as the basic psychosocial 'toolkit' for practice.

Part 2 follows the same pattern. We continue to discuss Attachment, Life Cycle and Object Relations theories, but we move on chronologically to older childhood, adolescence and young adulthood. Chapter 4 considers how earlier attachment patterns impact on relationships as we move from the dependence issues of childhood to the responsibilities of adulthood. Chapter 5 considers the importance of identity formation, the implications of unresolved emotional factors from young childhood and the significance of adult relationships as opposed to adolescent relationships. Chapter 6 develops the Object Relations theoretical approach by considering how personality development from childhood may affect our capacity to form positive adult-to-adult and adult-to-child relationships. While our primary aim is to help you better understand these key theories, we shall be acknowledging their contexts within a sociological and environmental perspective and shall direct you to further reading on these areas.

Part 3 deliberately has the same format as Parts 1 and 2 and moves on to adulthood and older age. Attachment is too often applied only to young childhood, and, in Chapter 7, we consider how attachment styles impact on adult relationships, including those adults who are carers or who are cared for. Chapter 8 considers Erikson's final two stages of his Life Cycle Theory and the links between the emotional outcomes of earlier stages on the older adult, as well as the link between adult experiences and the emotional demands of old age. Chapter 9 considers to what extent issues from childhood which impacted on young adulthood can be strengthened at this point in life or whether they limit an individual's capacity to develop emotional maturity. Object Relations Theory provides insights into themes of dependence, interdependence and rejection, which are very relevant to this stage of life.

Finally, Part 4 moves away from the chronological framework and addresses the principal challenges which face individuals in their everyday lives. Chapter 10 considers transitions that occur throughout life and will look in detail at how successfully or unsuccessfully we cope with change. In considering change, the chapter will also focus strongly on the individual's experience of loss, including loss as bereavement. Chapter 11 will consider the individual within the context of family, looking at family structure, family systems and psychodynamic influences and questioning whether there can be such a thing as a 'normal family'. Chapter 12 acknowledges that much emphasis has been placed on understanding how difficulties or problems may arise throughout the book and considers how individuals may develop resilience to cope with their lives and tolerate frustrations. Chapter 13 will provide evidence from direct practice about the efficacy of the theories explored in this book as qualified social workers explain and illustrate which theories they have found useful and how they have applied them.

In each chapter, you will find case examples, further reading and exercises on critical thinking. We hope that you enjoy reading the book and that you find it helpful.

PART 1

CHILDHOOD IN THE EARLY YEARS

Over the following three chapters, we shall consider the baby and the very young toddler. We shall discuss how relationships between the child and the child's carers are hugely important for the child's present and future development. The formation of attachment patterns and the development of affectional bonds are discussed in Chapter 1; the importance of a positive balance of care provision, based on Erikson's Life Cycle Theory, is discussed in Chapter 2; and the significance of meeting a child's emotional needs for dependence and consistency, based on Object Relations Theory, is discussed in Chapter 3.

1 ATTACHMENT – BONDING AND BRAIN DEVELOPMENT

An understanding of attachment theory and behaviour is absolutely essential for effective social work practice. This chapter will look at the work of Bowlby, Ainsworth and more recent theorists to understand the foundations of attachment and identify the various styles of attachment.

The chapter will begin by clarifying the concept of bond formation and will explain how this differs from attachment theory, before going on to look at the basic concepts of attachment and why they are so useful within social work and social care practice.

It is important that any worker understands what a secure attachment should consist of, so focus will be given to this attachment style to begin with, before going on to look at the insecure attachment styles, namely anxious/ambivalence, avoidance, and disorganised. Examples will be given to illustrate some of the typical behaviours exhibited within each style.

The chapter will then look at recent developments in neuroscience which recognise the importance of attachment styles on brain development. Throughout the concluding sections, links will be made to social work practice to demonstrate how this knowledge can be used within assessment and interventions.

By the end of the chapter the reader should:

- Know the difference between 'bonding' and 'attachment'
- Understand how relationship-building begins
- Appreciate the importance of a secure attachment style
- Know the difference between the three insecure attachment styles
- Recognise the potential for neurobiological impact
- Begin to think about how to apply this knowledge in practice

BONDING

'Bonding' is a general term used to describe the process of forming an emotional connection with another person. As human beings, we will form many bonds with many people throughout our lifetime, and from the moment that we are born we begin the first of these bonding processes with our mothers. In maternity wards all across the country, the first experience of the outside world that a baby will encounter is skin-on-skin contact as the midwife encourages the mother to place the newborn across her chest so that the baby can hear the comforting sounds of her heartbeat. But this was not always the case in maternity hospitals – even in the mid-1980s, the practice of skin-on-skin contact to encourage bonding at birth was seen as a radical move (Brody, 1983) – and 20 years previously, babies were wrapped in swaddling cloth and placed in cots as soon as they were born.

There is now a realisation that bonding with a baby begins long before the skin-on-skin experience. From the moment a pregnancy is discovered, the bonding process is initiated – parents will begin to develop hopes and wishes for the developing child, they may possibly give the 'bump' a name, and an emotional connection begins. The bonding process can be affected by a number of factors, including the mental and physical health of the parents, the development of the fetus, how much planning there was in the pregnancy, and even how active the fetus is in the womb and its response to external stimulus.

Critical Thinking

In essence bonding is the first relationship with the developing child and makes up the foundation blocks for attachment. In 'normal', healthy relationships, the bonding process has a good chance of developing in an appropriate manner, but some pregnant mothers and their partners might not be able to bond in a straightforward way.

- How might bonding be affected with mothers who are going to put their child up for adoption when it is born?
- How might the lack of pre-natal bonding affect foster carers and adoptive parents?

When the child is born, it is not concerned with bonding to form an emotional bond, it is simply looking to survive, and to do that, nature has provided the newborn with innate responses to seek out the person holding them, turning their head towards the face of the person and seeking with their blurry vision (Christiano, 2008). Later, the developing infant will also equate bonding with the psychological feeling of security and protection, and for approximately the first eight weeks of life a baby will experiment with various facial expressions, verbal gurgles and crying to attract the attention of their caregivers. Often, these facial expressions are reinforced through the act of mirroring.

LEARNING THROUGH MIRRORING

'Mirroring' is the process of reflecting back to a child so that they can learn about the nature of their behaviour and the impact it has on other people. Winnicott (1971) identified the concept of mirroring when he wrote about the importance of affirming need in a child. Within a caring relationship, the verbal and non-verbal cues given off by a child will be picked up by the carer and an appropriate response will be given – if a child smiles, the response is usually a smile back; if the child cries the response will be to comfort, either by giving food, giving affection or changing a dirty nappy. By meeting the need of the child in an appropriate manner, the primary carer will be letting the child know that they exist, they are worthy of attention and that their actions result in a reaction from the carer – from this, the child learns about their actions through observation, much like looking at a reflection, hence 'mirroring'.

When mirroring is a positive experience, this will impact on identity formation and the developing infant gains a sense of their 'true self' (Becket and Taylor, 2010). However, if mirroring is inadequate and the needs of the infant are not met, or even ignored, then a 'false self' can also develop. This false self is a form of defence mechanism which pushes the unpleasant feelings associated with unmet need into the unconscious, and the infant becomes preoccupied with trying to guess how the primary carer is going to act.

Critical Thinking

Mirroring is a natural phenomenon which occurs between infant and primary carer and is a vital part of learning for the child. A number of factors can impact on the mirroring process and, for mirroring to be effective, the primary caregiver must be emotionally available. Consider how mirroring might be affected by the following issues:

- Mental health issues
- Substance use issues
- Relationship issues

Discuss what other issues might impact on the mirroring process.

Winnicot (1971) also recognised that no parent or caregiver could meet a child's needs 100 per cent of the time, but he did suggest that parenting had to be 'good enough'. If mirroring is done empathically, then a parent should be trying to see the world from the perspective of the developing infant while affirming emotional expressions. They can also help the child to understand the names of the emotions, and to reassure the infant that these are normal feelings to be experiencing. It is also never too late to begin the mirroring process, with patience, explanation and affirmation; a child will be able to adjust perceptions of themselves based on feedback from the mirroring process. Where a child might think that they are 'stupid' because they cannot immediately master a task, mirroring appropriately can help them understand that a task is difficult and will take time to master, thus normalising emotions.

Defence Mechanisms

Reference will be made throughout the book to defence mechanisms. The term, 'defence mechanism' has become part of everyday language: this psychological expression stems from the work of Sigmund Freud, who believed that the behaviour and action of every human being is influenced by a biological drive, but that humans ultimately want to maintain a homeostasis. This desire for homeostasis is influenced by the three-way struggle between the 'id', 'ego' and 'superego'.

The id relates to the unconscious part of the mind. Primitive needs drive actions (such as hunger, safety, shelter) and will impact on behaviour. It is here that unpleasant memories and emotions are suppressed, and which can also impact on behaviour. We can view the id as defining our 'nature'.

The superego works for the id and tries to meet the needs of it by using morals and values to acceptably satisfy it. An individual learns how to act appropriately through interaction with family and friends, as well as the wider society, and we can view the superego as our 'nurture'.

The ego is the mediator between the id and the superego, but ultimately works to protect the id. If the superego is unable to satisfy the id, then the ego has to deal with the consequences. A common outcome of an upset homeostasis is the emotion of 'anxiety' and it is up to the ego to manage this, often by deploying 'defence mechanisms'. Common defence mechanisms include:

Repression – 'forgetting' unpleasant memories by pushing them out of the conscious mind. These repressed memories are at risk of surfacing at a later date through emotions and behaviours, and can be directed at people who have nothing to do with the original cause of the memory.

Splitting – when dealing with contradictory emotions, a person might begin to see others as 'all good' or 'all bad' and compartmentalise relationships into these categories. If needs are met, then the relationship is good. If needs are not met, the relationship is bad.

Projection – characteristics of the self are externalised and attached to another person. This helps to remove unwanted personality traits from the unconscious by viewing other people as at fault.

Sublimation – satisfying the needs of the id with a substitute object, for example by using sports to deal with aggressive thoughts.

Displacement/Transference – strong emotions are directed to an alternative object or person, not the one who originally created the emotion.

Rationalisation – failing to recognise the true cause of actions and behaviours and justifying them through more acceptable reasons.

Denial – the mind refuses to acknowledge the reality of the situation because the truth is too painful to handle.

Regression – reverting to an earlier stage of development because the mind feels happier there. Behaviours and actions will manifest which are suggestive of an earlier developmental stage.

ATTACHMENT – WHY IS IT IMPORTANT?

Human beings are social animals, and to function within a society we need the ability to form relationships to build bonds. We cannot avoid forming relationships – relationships are forced on us from the moment we are born, but it is the quality of these relationships that can dictate so much behaviour, and explain so many of our actions and reactions to situations.

Whereas bonding is concerned with the emotional tie between the child and the primary caregiver, attachment focuses on the quality of the relationship as a result of this emotional bond.

Knowledge of attachment theory underpins assessment and can assist social workers in recognising risk and protective factors for young children. Attachment theory can help us understand why some children cling to their carers while others confidently settle with anybody who shows an interest in them. The theory can also help us understand why parents react to their children in certain ways, and can also explain marital fit, reactions to loss and change, and how clients might adapt within the therapeutic relationship offered from a social work service. Howe and Campling (1995) also highlight the importance of recognising attachment patterns within our own behaviour in order to help us understand other people's behaviour which can, at times, appear to be unpredictable and inexplicable, and warn that failure to comprehend attachment theory within relationships places the worker in danger of cutting themselves off from key elements of practice.

In the 1950s, John Bowlby (2008) proposed that the quality of the affectional bond between a child and their primary caregiver had a profound psychological impact which lasted for life. He explained that a child needs security while they develop; the more secure the child feels, the safer they will feel to explore the surrounding environment and consequently learn and develop in a positive manner – when the quality of the secure base is affected, the feeling of safety that the child needs is also affected. Bowlby (1969) identified three areas in which a developing child interpreted the environment: first, the child forms ideas of how the physical world behaves; next they learn about how their mother and significant others behave within this physical world; and, finally, they learn about how they are expected to behave. The combination of these three elements means that the child will establish an opinion on how each should interact with the others, and Bowlby referred to this as the 'internal working model'. Early critiques of Bowlby's work stated that he was too focused on blaming the mothers for poor attachment styles, but studies on attachment theory since the 1960s have placed emphasis on the carers, rather than the mother.

Fahlberg (2012) identified the concepts of 'arousal-relaxation' and 'positive-interaction' which she describes as exchanges between the child and the primary caregiver. The quality of these interactions will have a direct impact on the attachment relationship. If the caregiver is correctly attuned to the signals given off by the child, then appropriate responses will be given to behaviours such as crying, smiling and other forms of body language.

Attachment theory recognises that a child will form an attachment with a person who interacts with them, despite the quality of the interaction. Attachment relationships are not solely based on who feeds and changes the child, but also on who communicates with the child through daily interactions and play. Even if a child feels ignored, unwanted or even at risk, an attachment will be formed. Mary Ainsworth et al. (2014) further developed Bowlby's ideas by looking at insecurities that the child experiences when the secure base does not provide a high level of safety and security. She developed an experiment called the 'Strange Situation', wherein she looked at the reactions of a child when the primary carer was present, then when they were absent and the child was left with a stranger, and then when the primary carer returned (see box below). This resulted in a classification system for attachment styles: 'secure', 'anxious/ambivalent', 'avoidant' and 'disorganised' (which was later added by Main and Solomon, 1986).

Summary of Ainsworth et. al's (2014) 'Strange Situation'

Ainsworth observed that infants would naturally try to seek out the security of their primary attachment figure (which is usually the mother) at times of fear, stress or uncertainty. She devised an experiment to look at the infant's reactions to strangers that consisted of seven steps:

1. Mother and child play together in a room filled with toys.
2. A stranger enters the room (usually a researcher), talks to the mother, and attempts to interact with the child, too.

3. At a given signal, the mother then exits the room, leaving her child and the stranger together. The stranger continues interacting with the child.
4. The mother re-enters the room and the stranger departs. The mother will comfort the child.
5. The mother will again leave the room, leaving the child alone with the toys.
6. The stranger enters the room and tries to comfort the child (if required). If possible, the stranger will leave the room again.
7. The mother returns (and the stranger leaves if still there) and continues to interact with her child.

From the reaction of the child, the attachment classifications of 'secure', 'anxious/ambivalent', 'avoidant' and 'disorganised' have been arrived at. These are explained below.

Before looking at the specific attachment styles, it is important to consider when attachments form in relation to the development of a child. Schaffer and Emerson (1964) conducted a longitudinal study, observing the attachment behaviour of 60 babies over an eighteen-month period. They proposed that for the first two to three months, a child will demonstrate indiscriminate attachments as behaviours are designed to illicit the attention of potential caregivers. This stage is often referred to as 'pre-attachment' and suggests that babies can be left in the care of a variety of people without causing distress to the infant, as long as basic needs are met.

From the age of around three months, the infant will become a bit more discerning in its preference for proximity to the primary carer. It can begin to recognise familiar and unfamiliar people and may show more of a response towards the primary caregivers and demonstrate this in body language, such as following with their eyes and clinging to the carer.

At six months old, attachment becomes more clear-cut and the infant has strong preferences towards particular people. These preferences are based on feelings of security, protection and comfort, and behaviour is geared towards obtaining these. Behaviour is also dictated by obtaining proximity with the primary carer and the infant will protest when the primary carer leaves (separation anxiety) and will also show signs of distress around strangers. The infant should now begin exploring the environment on the understanding that they can return to the secure base of the primary carer to seek comfort.

After nine months of age, the infant will have formed multiple attachments and will be showing signs of increased independence, and by around two years old, attachment styles should be evident as the child now views the primary carer as a separate person and has formed a relationship accordingly.

WHAT IS SECURE?

Social work and social care places an emphasis on facilitating change for the better. Within attachment theory, the best situation that can be hoped for is that a child will experience a secure attachment.

Ainsworth et al. (2014) observed that a securely attached infant will happily explore their environment but will always return to the primary carer when feeling upset or scared. The infant will get distressed when the primary carer leaves the room (and the infant is left with the stranger), but will be easily comforted when the primary carer returns and will express happy emotions and be comfortable being in physical contact with the carer. In their experiment, they observed that some infants were able to be comforted by the stranger but showed a definite preference for the primary carer. The main characteristic of a securely attached infant is that it will seek comfort from the primary carer and express preference for being in close proximity with the carer.

A secure attachment means that the child is able to express itself appropriately without fear of being reprimanded and without having to supress any needs they may have. If a child can freely express itself, then this is a sign that the carer is allowing the child to have age-appropriate autonomy and it is able to explore the environment, knowing that it can return to the carer when they need to. It means that there is a healthy sense of independence between carer and infant and suggests that communication from the carer is sensitive, warm and appropriate, and that there is a sense of fun in the relationship.

From small observations into attachment styles we can get a considerable insight into the caring relationship. If an attachment is secure, then we can assume that there is a healthy secure base for the child to explore from, the child has a strong sense of trust in themselves and others (see Chapter 2), and that this will facilitate the building of resilience in later life (see Chapter 12).

Professionals using attachment theory need to understand this ideal as this is what we can encourage parents and carers to work towards. If communication is supportive, warm and consistent, if there is a healthy sense of trust and autonomy, and if the carer is available when needed, then attachment should be secure.

Case Study

Karen

A social worker went on a home visit to see a foster carer who had been looking after Karen, a 15-month-old girl, since she was 8 months old. Karen had been removed from her mother due to issues of neglect. She had been settling in well with the foster family, but this was only the second visit from this particular social worker.

The social worker and foster carer sat in the living room while Karen crawled around on a play mat, occasionally pulling herself up to her feet and toddling around for a few short steps. During the meeting, the foster carer left the room to get some drinks from the kitchen. While out, Karen began to become unsettled and started to babble in an agitated manner, eventually bursting into tears. The social worker picked up Karen to give her a cuddle but Karen wriggled in her arms. The foster carer came back through and the social worker handed Karen to her. Karen buried her face into the foster carer's neck who spoke softly to her and stroked her back and Karen eventually stopped crying. After a couple of minutes, the foster carer placed Karen back onto the play mat and she continued to interact with her toys.

From this brief incident, the social worker thought about the 'Strange Situation' experiment and ascertained that Karen was displaying a healthy, secure attachment with the foster carer.

WHAT IS ANXIOUS/AMBIVALENT?

Within the 'Strange Situation' experiment, some children exhibited an unusual reaction when they were reunited with their primary carer. When the primary carer initially left the room, the infant became distressed. The stranger was unable to comfort the infant, but even when the carer returned to reassure the infant, the infant still did not calm down and seemed to exhibit anger and frustration towards the carer. It was further noted that even before the carer left the room, the infant showed little interest in exploring the environment and playing with toys and always seemed to be keeping a close eye on the carer to make sure they were in close contact. Towards the end of the experiment, the infant showed virtually no desire to return to playing with the toys and remained anxious about the fact that the carer might depart again.

When a child displays an 'anxious/ambivalent' attachment style (also known as 'resistant/ambivalent'), we can assume that the care they are receiving is inconsistent. The child has learned that there is no predictable pattern for receiving attention from the carer, and instead they must remain focused on the emotional availability of the carer and make a bid for attention when appropriate. Sometimes, the carer will be able to respond appropriately to the needs of the child, but at other times they may respond by ignoring or shouting at the child for expressing need, therefore the child is never quite sure what response they will get. Fonagy (2003) describes the anxious/ambivalent child as being clingy and Gerhardt (2006) attributes this to the fact that the child, instead of supressing emotions, carries these emotions close to the surface so that they can engage with them at short notice to attract attention from the carer. These emotional outbursts tend to seem exaggerated but are simply a strategy that the child has developed for engaging with the carer. As a result, an anxious/ambivalent child does not properly learn to regulate these emotions and relies on others to manage these outbursts, resulting in a low sense of trust in themselves, but in a high sense of trust in others, leading to 'learned helplessness'.

It is not unusual for attachment styles to be repeated throughout families, and often a child's attachment style can be an indicator of the parents'/carers' own experience of being raised, too – this being simply a case of history repeating itself. If the carer carries an anxious/ambivalent attachment style into adulthood (see Chapters 4 and 7 for more detail), then it is likely that they will be needy and preoccupied with how other people view them. This will be transferred into the parenting role and the parent may get an unconscious reward from feeling needed by a desperate child.

As Winnicott (1971) pointed out, parenting should be 'good enough' and there will inevitably be situations where a parent/carer cannot be 100 per cent attentive to the needs of a child, but with anxious/ambivalent children the care is consistently unpredictable. Within social work, we might see this in a number of service user groups. If a service user has an addiction to a substance or behaviour, this might make them unavailable (both physically and emotionally) for periods of the day/week. If someone has a number of caring responsibilities, it might mean that they are not always available for the child and may be preoccupied with other demands on them. Therefore, it is important that we do not view carers who foster anxious/ambivalent styles as 'bad'. Obviously, a secure attachment is the ideal, but an anxious/ambivalent style is simply a survival strategy that the child has adopted to ensure that they can attract a response when available, and, quite often, in later childhood, the child exhibits a 'parenting' role towards the carer as a means of fostering interaction (Byng-Hall, 1998).

To assist a move from anxious/ambivalence towards a secure style, the carer should be encouraged to think about their communication styles with the child. Attachment is reliant on the quality of time spent, not just the quantity of time, so carers should be encouraged to set aside time where they give the child their full attention, spend time explaining things to the child, help them identify feelings and emotions (through mirroring verbally and non-verbally), but also to be aware of times when they are emotionally unavailable and recognise this within themselves so that they can attempt to protect the child from any negative effects of this.

WHAT IS AVOIDANT?

Where anxious/ambivalent children are unsure about the consistency of the relationship with their carer, avoidant children are more definite in their assessment and realise that the carer is emotionally unavailable for most of the time and cannot really be relied on to meet their needs.

Ainsworth et al. (2014) observed that avoidant children (also known as 'detached/avoidant') showed no distress when the carer left during the 'Strange Situation' experiment, they showed no preference between the carer and the stranger, no emotion when the carer returned after separation, and remained engaged with their toys throughout the experiment. In some instances, the child would actually avoid interaction with the carer on return and gazed elsewhere so as not to make eye contact.

An avoidant child has learned that it is not a good idea to express need. This might be because it results in an adverse reaction from the carer – possibly upsetting or angering them – and the child feels that it is better to supress need in order to protect the carer from adverse emotions. As a result, an avoidant child may appear calm and controlled from the outside, but internally the child is dealing with accelerated heart rates and feelings of anxiety which they would usually seek assistance from the carer to correct and return them to the comfort zone, but as they learn that this is not going to be forthcoming from the carer they try to supress these feelings (Gerhardt, 2006).

In later chapters, we will look at how psychoanalytic theories sit alongside other theories used in social work such as psychological and sociological perspectives, but at this stage it is important to consider the impact of society on attachment theory. Certain societies and cultures encourage independence in children from a very early age (which is not the same as 'autonomy' – see Chapter 2), others might place more importance on material possessions and prefer to spend free time engaged with their latest piece of technology rather than play with the child, while many also have to place careers at the forefront of daily routines which means that when they return home they are exhausted and the child may possibly be in bed already – all may impact on the quality of time spent with a child and the focus of attention when with the child. These three scenarios are offered up, not as a criticism of parenting, but as recognition that we are products of the societies we live in and will impact on how we form relationships. In the UK, statutory maternity leave will cover 52 weeks, which starts when a woman leaves work before birth – this means that many parents have to place their children in nursery placements as early as nine months old in order to return to work and are therefore reliant on the nursery staff to develop the attachment style throughout the day – compare this to other European countries such as Finland, Germany and Poland who offer statutory maternity leave until the child is three years old.

Critical Thinking

Emotional connection underpins the quality of the attachment relationship, but our emotions can be affected by numerous factors. Consider how emotions (and the consequent attachment relationship) will be affected by the following factors:

- Mental health issues
- Size of family/number of siblings
- Parental relationship issues
- Substance use

From your own experience of being parented, can you think of any other significant factors you faced when growing up that impacted on the emotional connection between you and your parental figures?

Perry (2001) recognises 'dissociative adaptations' in avoidant children, wherein a child will give up attempting to gain attention from their primary caregiver because of the continued absence of appropriate attention and will in turn disengage from the external world and begin to live within their internal fantasies, often described as 'daydreaming'. Avoidant children will also lose themselves in play more readily than secure children, but with continued absence of emotional engagement with the primary carer, the child may become rebellious and develop low self-image and self-esteem as they feel that they are not worthy of their carers' attention.

Similarly, as with anxious/ambivalent children, the avoidant attachment style should not be seen as 'bad' – it is merely a survival strategy for the child and may get them through life quite successfully. Certainly, an avoidant child will grow up with a lot of trust in themselves, but very little trust in other people and may view need in others as a weakness.

WHAT IS DISORGANISED?

Of all the insecure attachment styles, disorganised attachment causes most concern. Identifying definitive characteristics of this style is difficult due to the unpredictable nature of the reactions that a child might display if they have a disorganised attachment. At the core of attachment theory, as with the majority of psychoanalytic theories, is *anxiety*, and the manner in which we address anxiety is learned through our interactions with other people. Anxious/ambivalent styles and avoidant styles are strategies which a child develops to deal with anxiety, but with disorganised attachment there is no clear strategy for dealing with anxiety and, as a result, this builds and builds within the child. This can be attributed to the reaction that the child receives from the primary carer when expressing need.

If the reaction that a child receives from the primary carer is completely unpredictable, extreme, violent or illogical, the child will struggle to identify a need with an outcome as there is no continuity. One moment they might get a hug when displaying certain behaviour, the next they might get struck for the same action. The detached attachment style suggests extreme fluctuations of behaviour from the caregiver but is not always a predictor of violence or abuse – Shemmings and Shemmings (2011) state that it can predict maltreatment, but may not necessarily correlate with it. Crittenden (2008) believes that not all parents who have been abused themselves (and consequently developed a detached attachment) go on to be abusers, suggesting that 70 per cent will not harm their own children, but 30 per cent have the potential to do so and this is why detached attachment styles deserve so much focus within social work.

Reactions that a child might exhibit within an experiment like the 'Strange Situation' are often termed as 'bizarre'. The child might freeze, roll into a ball, express distress when being comforted, or cling while leaning away from the carer with the rest of their body. There is no consistency to the reactions and this goes hand in hand with the internal workings of the child who does not know which action to employ for a safe reaction.

As well as signifying abuse, exhibition of a detached attachment can also signify depression or emotional disturbance within the carer and may be linked to traumatic events in the carer's life which have not been appropriately dealt with (such as loss, death or abuse – see Chapter 12). As a result, the carer is unable to provide the basic needs of protection and safety for the child – the child seeks safety, but the very person it should feel safe with is also the person who is creating a feeling of danger and distress in the child – the natural instincts are to run away to a place of safety, but this place of safety is causing the harm. It may be that the carer is disconnected from the experience of providing care and may be frightened by the experience and responsibility. There may be transference (see 'defence mechanisms' in the box at the beginning of this chapter) onto the infant and hostile feelings may be directed towards it. Carers may also be unable to see things from the infant's point of view and use their own logic to interpret an infant's actions – it is not unusual for carers who experience this to state that they feel that their child hates them. Young infants need to feel safe and have not developed the ability to recognise complex emotions like hate, but the logical reasoning of this is lost within the illogical chain of reactions caused by a detached attachment style; to the carer, their belief that the infant hates them is very real, and the result is that the reaction that the carer has towards the child's needs can be unpredictable and cause the infant to experience 'fright without solution' (Hesse and Main, 2006). As a result, the developing infant will have a low sense of trust in itself, and a low sense of trust in others, too.

HOW DOES THIS AFFECT THE BRAIN?

Recent developments in neuroscience now recognise the importance of attachment theory on brain development in young children. Obviously, we do not expect social workers to be experts in neurobiology, but there are some concepts that help our understanding of the importance of attachment theory within our professional practice. It is now recognised that the brain develops in a neurosequential manner and that the experiences we have as we are growing up help the brain to mature and neurological connections to be made so that we can rationally deal with issues as we face them (Gaskill and Perry, 2012).

At the top of the brain stem, we find the limbic area of the brain and this is the part that is responsible for arousal and emotions within the body. It is also the area that manages our basic instincts, in particular the 'fight or flight' response. This is regulated by the sympathetic and parasympathetic nervous system that will release cortisol into the body to regulate brain and body functioning to increase or decrease breathing and heart rates, to relax or tense muscles and to manage our internal organs. When functioning normally, the sympathetic system produces cortisol to help us when aroused or stressed and respond quickly, and the parasympathetic system will help us at times when the body is at rest and aid feelings of being soothed. Babies cannot soothe themselves, so they learn from the responses of their carers – if a baby cries because of feelings of anxiousness, the normal response will be for the carer to hug, kiss and verbally soothe the baby – the sympathetic system will be calmed by the parasympathetic system, cortisol will tell the body that everything is safe, and the baby will relax (as with a secure attachment style). However, if the baby is not taught how to calm down and left in a state of high arousal, then the sympathetic system keeps producing cortisol that tells the body that quick actions are required and the baby cannot relax (as with the insecure attachment styles) (Bernard and Dozier, 2010). This system also has a built-in self-defence mechanism – if the sympathetic system is becoming overwhelmed by the production of cortisol, then the parasympathetic system will flood the brain with chemicals to immediately relax the system, but as a result the body freezes, a reaction familiar to some of the 'bizarre' responses seen in a disorganised attachment.

Learning from the primary carer also assists the development of the cortex, which is the area of the brain that facilitates our understanding of the outside world and, in particular, the development of the prefrontal cortex and the orbito-frontal cortex located behind our foreheads. As infants, the right side of the brain develops significantly as it is responsible for visualisation, aesthetic appreciation, creativity, intuition and holistic thinking. The orbito-frontal cortex makes complex links with the right side of the brain and helps us to manage our emotional responses and ensure that they are appropriate in any given situation. This part of the brain is not something that nature develops itself, it has to be nurtured and will not actually mature until around three years old – if ignored, the orbito-frontal cortex will not develop and higher social capacities, such as thinking, reasoning, and empathising, are lost (Schore, 2000; Schore, 2001; Gerhardt, 2006).

Self-regulation is learned through feedback from others, and the sympathetic and parasympathetic system is only one of many systems within our biological make-up that depends on equilibrium (Gerhardt, 2006). Certainly, social learning theory comes into play here, but clearly the impact of poor attachment extends beyond behaviour and has a significant biological impact, so we need to recognise the importance of the psychoanalytic impact on the developing child and the consequent impact on biology. The long-term consequences of poor attachment and the disequilibrium of the chemical balance within our brains can be linked to an inability to form logical summations to emotional responses, which can lead to poor mental health and a negative effect on the internal organs leading to poor physical health.

HOW DOES THIS HELP SOCIAL WORK?

In this section, we have introduced the reader to the basic concepts of attachment theory and how observations at an early stage can lead to the identification of relationship issues and the ability to address these. The secure attachment style is the ideal and, chances are, if social work intervention is required within a children and family setting, a secure attachment will be absent from the family environment, but knowledge of this style can inform the worker about what the ideal should be and can assist in the work they undertake. As we explore attachment across the lifespan in future chapters, it will also become apparent that the worker themselves can offer that secure base that has been absent in the family environment.

Assessment tools within social work now incorporate questions based on ascertaining attachment styles, and knowledge of the insecure attachment styles can also inform interventions. We have looked at the 'Strange Situation' experiment but as children get older, more tools become available to identify attachment styles. Use of a stem story is not uncommon, wherein social workers will start a story and ask the child to say what happens next. The story will build in intensity and the purpose is to ascertain how the child reacts to stress and anxiety, and how they view their familial relationships. Workers may also use a semi-structured interview as the child gets older and, once defined, a knowledge of attachment theory can assist work with carers to give them information about what they are doing, the effect this is having on the child, and how they may relate differently. Potentially, a little bit of information for the carers at this stage can stave off serious problems in the future.

Knowledge of the impact on trust is also useful when delivering interventions. If a child is avoidant, they will have a high sense of trust in themselves and low trust in others, so the social worker is going to have to overcome this obstacle by employing tactics within the intervention to let the child feel that they are the master of the task and that the social worker is learning from them. A consideration of control within the intervention for anxious/ambivalent children is also important as they have a low sense of trust in themselves and a high one in others, which can lead to 'learned helplessness', therefore attention must be constant but not domineering and the social worker must reassure the child that they are being kept in mind at all times. Outlining boundaries and routines is important in all cases. Continuity and predictability becomes increasingly important for disorganised children as they will have a low sense of self-worth and may react in extreme ways to the slightest provocation. Exploring feelings and emotions is advisable but this will only be successful if the social worker builds up a relationship of trust and security with the child.

It is important to stress that attachment styles can change over time. As we get older, we become involved in many more relationships and we learn to adapt through these interactions, but our first relationships are so crucial in giving us the ability to engage appropriately in these future relationships, and also for our brains to comprehend the world around us.

2 ERIKSON – THE INITIAL STAGES

Having established the importance of attachment formation in childhood, we turn to another theoretical perspective which takes a different approach, but which reinforces the significance of our relationships with family and wider society in shaping our personality and subsequent behaviour.

By the end of the chapter the reader should:

- Understand the importance of early childhood in shaping personality and behaviour
- Be aware that both positive and negative experiences are important in shaping a healthy personality
- Understand the significance of the word 'versus' in Erikson's theory
- Understand the factors which describe the influence of nurture on individual development
- Appreciate the importance of the care provider at this stage of childhood development

---

Erik Erikson (1965) identified eight stages of development in the human lifespan which he termed 'crises', and, essentially, the crises refer to the individual's ability to cope with the expectable experiences associated with their physical and cognitive development, with the formation and development of relationships and with the ability to interact and cope with the structural expectations of society. This is a classic psychosocial theory based on psychodynamic theory. It follows the initial work of Sigmund Freud (1933) in acknowledging the conscious and unconscious parts of the self, but it places a strong emphasis on the importance of the external world as an influence on the individual's conscious and unconscious emotional and behavioural development. You will note that each stage identified by Erikson contains the word 'versus' between a positive and negative outcome: that illustrates Erikson's view that each stage is characterised by competing experiences, some good, some bad. A positive outcome is a positive balance of good experiences over bad. You should note: a positive outcome is not related to 100 per cent good experiences.

> ## Critical Thinking
>
> Consider how Erikson's assessment that a favourable balance is the psychologically healthy outcome of each stage and to what extent there are similarities with Winnicott's suggestion that 'good enough parenting' is what a young child needs.

STAGE 1: BASIC TRUST VERSUS BASIC MISTRUST

The first of the life crises is babyhood, the point at which we totally depend on others to meet our physical and emotional needs. Here, Erikson closely overlaps with the attachment theorists in Chapter 1, highlighting the critically important quality of the relationship between the baby and the primary carers. He also emphasises the ego, as identified by Freud (see Brown, 1961; and Fyffe, 2014) as the conscious aspect of ourselves, and Erikson recognises that it copes, with varying degrees of success, with the life crises which we all experience. An ego which is emotionally strong will enable the individual to deal constructively and positively with events, while, on a sliding scale, an ego which is more fragile will experience more difficulties. In the previous chapter, you read about ego defence mechanisms which unconsciously protect the ego from anxiety-provoking situations, and these integrate with Erikson's theory. Particularly important in the first few years of life are the ego defences of introjection and projection.

It is not advisable to place an exact age boundary between each of Erikson's stages, because each individual develops physically and cognitively in different ways, but instead we should consider what the significance of each stage is. Babyhood is that point in our lives when we have to rely on others to have all our needs met: we cannot move ourselves, feed ourselves or clean ourselves without help. However, Erikson points out that, at this point in our lives, we also have to *feel* the goodness of affection and love. A positive outcome at this stage of our lives does not solely depend on our physical needs being met, but it also depends on the quality of the interaction between primary carer and baby. If the carer feels love towards the baby, if the carer can be sensitive to the baby's needs and can put the baby's needs before their own, this is likely to be transmitted through comforting touch and holding, warm and affectionate eye contact and encouraging and soothing verbal communication. All these behaviours from the carer have an impact on the baby, and this is the key message of all the theories we cover in this book. Freud's concept of the 'id' is seen as less relevant, because clearly the baby is in a more complex relationship with carers and not simply an organism existing simply for self-satisfaction.

With only limited powers of communication, which develop over this stage, with no concept of time or capacity to reason, a baby is a human being who has only intense feelings. This is where we apply our understanding of introjection and projection. Psychodynamic theory describes how a baby internalises the feelings he or she has and this process of taking feelings inside oneself is the defence mechanism of introjection. Good feelings, arising from the positive quality of care given, are taken inside and form the bedrock of our personality. We feel good about ourselves and good about those people who are external to ourselves. This is what Erikson means by the term 'basic trust', and the word 'basic' is used deliberately to describe the strong, fundamental nature of this feeling: what we feel as babies forms the basis of our personality throughout life. Bad feelings, those feelings which cause anxiety and distress, have to be dealt with by our developing ego. Remember: at this stage in life, a baby cannot quantify or rationalise. There are no slight discomforts or mild inconveniences, just simple bad feelings which must be got rid of, and these are projected onto the external world. People become the holders of these bad feelings, which, for the baby, results in a feeling of 'basic mistrust'. The external world cannot be relied upon.

In Erikson's first stage, we hope that the baby acquires a positive balance, but this implies that the baby must also experience some of the negative aspects of care. If a child or young person were to grow up having had all their needs met, had never experienced any distress or frustration, they could be totally trusting. Imagine how dangerous that would be. However, it is fairly easy to understand how in everyday circumstances a loved baby acquires some essential mistrust. A baby cries for food, the carer responds immediately by getting the feed ready, and the whole process takes only a few minutes before the baby is contentedly sucking. However, in those few minutes, this baby, much loved and well cared for, has felt the rage of bad feelings: these bad feelings are projected onto the outside world as the origins of basic mistrust. The discomfort of a wet nappy, the spasms of colic, being wakened suddenly by a loud noise and many other routine events in the overall context of a loving home may also serve to provide the required negative balance.

The negative balance will outweigh the positive if a child has fewer good feelings to introject and more bad to project. A carer who feeds a child, changes nappies regularly and generally meets the physical needs may not have the feelings of warmth and love towards the baby. As a result, the baby does not get held or cuddled, and, as we have seen from attachment and bond formation, feels the badness of neglected emotional needs. If we also factor in aspects of chaotic caregiving, carers who are self-absorbed, carers who neglect or carers who abuse, we may begin to understand how the balance of basic mistrust may outweigh the more positive balance. We cannot stress enough how powerful and influential these experiences are in shaping the individual's personality, and, later in the chapter, we shall provide examples to illustrate this.

STAGE 2: AUTONOMY VERSUS SHAME AND DOUBT

Feelings continue to be intense at this stage, but the baby is becoming a toddler and the focus of emotional development reflects the tremendous newfound physical ability to move and control muscles and to develop more interactive communication.

Fundamentally, the outcome of toddlerhood is the basis of our self-esteem: a positive balance will result in a basic feeling of self-worth which will be a strong element of our personality throughout life, and a negative balance will result in varying degrees of self-doubt or caution which can influence our behaviour throughout life. Psychologically, the feelings which are generated by the experiences that we have as toddlers are still rooted in our unconscious minds, and the defences of introjection and projection are still dominating our development.

This second stage can begin towards the end of the first year or between ages one and two, depending on when the baby moves from total dependency to self-propulsion. At this point, the toddler has exciting new experiences to enjoy, can decide what to do, can explore the immediate environment as never before possible: the carer has to cope with this, has to decide what is allowable and what is not, and has to decide what is safe and what is not. For both carer and toddler, this is a stage involving a potential battle over who controls who. As Erikson (1965: 263) wrote, 'under normal conditions, it is not until the second year that he [the infant] begins to experience the whole critical opposition of being an autonomous creature and being a dependent one'.

Critical Thinking

Try to remember your earliest memory. Can you remember anything about being a baby? Can you remember the excitement you felt when you first began to crawl, or the sheer pleasure of the first steps you took? Can you remember exploring the house and the reactions of your parents or carers? I'd be very surprised if you can remember, and, for most of you, it is unlikely you remember anything other than a snapshot-style isolated memory within the first two to three years of life.

Consider carefully what this means. Significant, possibly huge, events took place in your development, and these created strong feelings, none of which you can consciously remember. Yet they were part of you and remain part of you.

For a positive balance at this stage, the toddler needs to feel the goodness of being able to do things unaided, such as crawling, walking, playing with simple toys, drawing on paper, drawing on the wall, playing with the electric plugs and so on. Now, you will readily appreciate that while some activities are generally acceptable and uncontroversial, others listed are more contentious and downright dangerous. An infant cannot, in order to survive, have complete autonomy. This stage is characterised by the dynamics of setting boundaries, boundaries which permit a toddler to choose what to do and enjoy doing it but which protect a toddler from harm. Those of you reading this who are parents will readily recognise that this is one of the most difficult parts of parenting; those of you who are not parents will probably be aware of toddlers you like (because they are polite and friendly) and toddlers you do not like (because they are wilful, noisy and demanding). The toddler who has no boundaries and who has freedom to choose is not necessarily the lucky one. Complete autonomy at this stage, just like total trust at the previous stage, does not result in emotional, psychological or physical well-being: to believe one can do anything is life-threatening, to believe one can do what one wants makes one antisocial and/or shameless.

The potential long-term effects of this stage depend considerably on how boundaries are imposed. Some carers do not mind if a toddler makes a mess when playing, while some are so clean and tidy that they become angry if a spot appears on a carpet or wall. Some carers are encouraging, while some carers have a low tolerance of the expectable demands and needs of young children. Each of us will have had our own unique set of experiences and responses as toddlers which will have uniquely characterised the basic sense of self that we have. Some of us will be fortunate to have had a positive balance, having had the freedom to do what satisfied us, the support of loving carers and the protection of sensible boundaries which we came to accept. We feel inherently good about ourselves, and, as life progresses, while we encounter problems or upsets along the way, we feel able to deal with them for better or worse because we have an inner unconscious feeling of self-worth. Some of us may have had a more mixed experience, some positive but as many experiences of being criticised, prevented or punished. While we can get by in our lives, we never quite believe that we are competent, deserving of praise or able to undertake some activity. Some of us may have had too much experience of the negative aspects: too rigid a boundary-setting or no boundary-setting, too much criticism or punishment of our actions as toddlers. We have no self-esteem, have great difficulties with aspects of control or order, and spend a lot of energy either challenging authority or trying to establish some kind of satisfying boundaries.

Erikson identified the negative balance at this stage as shame *and* doubt, and so far the examples have concentrated on doubt. The development of muscle control extends also to the sphincter and anus, and Erikson developed his theory building on Freud's anal stage (Brown, 1961). Toddlers can now choose where and when they urinate and defecate, and carers are faced with the task of toilet training. Carers handle this stage of development in different ways. Some will approach this task in a rigid, behavioural, training approach, some will delay until the child is older, some will approach it in an easygoing but responsive style. Once again, the crux of this life crisis depends on how this aspect is dealt with, and on levels of stress which are felt and conveyed by the adult carers. By building anxiety in the child through chastisement, expressions of disgust, over-zealous concentration on making a child use a potty, a carer instils the sense of shame in a child. Once this is internalised, the developing infant may become unconsciously influenced by a deep-rooted fear of creating a mess or a deep-rooted desire to resist control by others, and future behaviour may be influenced, again unconsciously, by an excessive desire to create a mess or disorder or by a considerable fear of creating a mess or disorder. We shall consider the potential implications of this for practice later in the chapter.

STAGE 3: INITIATIVE VERSUS GUILT

The third of Erikson's stages of development in young childhood coincides with the developing cognitive abilities of the toddler as he or she becomes a child. For more detailed information on cognitive development you should refer to Ffyfe (2014). Essentially, the child has become more aware of consequences of actions, and the positive balance at this stage is still very dependent on the responses of those closest to the child, including, as ever, the carers, but now also significant others with whom the child has contact, which include playmates. We are also still at an age where we consciously remember only a little of all that happened, so once again there is likely to be a significant element of unconscious influence from this stage.

The toddler stage of autonomy versus shame and doubt was characterised by a strong desire to do things, and positive feelings of being able to do resulted in strong feelings of being happy with oneself, of being able and optimistic about one's abilities. The growing cognitive development which takes place from around three years of age, using either Piaget's (1926) biological model or Vygotsky's (1962) environmental model, increases the child's ability to understand the consequences of actions. So, if we characterise a positive balance from the toddler stage as 'I can do', a positive balance at the third stage, Erikson's initiative, is 'I can choose to do'. Whereas the negative balance of the second stage was a very basic feeling of shame and doubt, the negative balance at the third stage is a rather more complex feeling of guilt: our choices went wrong and, whatever the unfortunate consequences, we caused the unhappy outcome. At this point of development, as the child becomes more aware of consequences, successful activities with happy outcomes help build the third major part of our personality bedrock: first, basic trust, you (the external world) are OK; second, autonomy, I am OK; and, third, initiative, we are OK. A negative balance at all three stages could result in a personality very unsure of the reliability of others, very unsure about how to cope and very limited in social relationships.

This stage of development is very much about setting up the beginnings of self-identity in direct relationship with others, and the beginnings of confidence and comfort in social interaction. It also demonstrates the dynamic, interconnected relationship between the stages in Erikson's life cycle framework. A child moving into this stage with a generally positive balance from the two previous stages will be in a stronger position emotionally to cope with the expectable aspects of the initiative-versus-guilt life crisis. He or she will have an optimistic approach to being with others and will have an inner self-confidence to sustain successful interactive play with other children and adults.

Critical Thinking

Compare the theoretical message which derives from our interpretation of Erikson's life cycle theory with the messages from attachment theorists in Chapter 1. Note how, in both theoretical perspectives, the importance of the interactions between the child and those around the child are seen as critical to the formation of the individual's personality.

If you observe children at play, you may notice that, between the ages of one and two, children may seem to play together, but they are primarily playing for themselves, albeit keeping a close eye on other children whose play they may mirror or copy. However, from around three years, the potential for interactive play grows; the developing brain can begin to appreciate that there may be rewards in sharing, and, equally, there may be punishments for not sharing. A child's positive balance of initiative is more likely to develop the more the opportunity for interactive play exists, but, in applying this theory, we must always put the child in the context of his or her environment. Take, for example, the following hypothetical situations: on the surface, Grant is in a favourable position, he is growing up with two parents in a middle-class area in a house with a large garden and play parks in the locality. Shona, on the other hand, is apparently less favoured, growing up in a small flat with no garden and with one parent. However, Grant's parents are houseproud, excessively tidy and restrict Grant's play activity to one room with preselected toys. Shona's parent is creative and encouraging, giving Shona lots of choice around activities. While such socioeconomic disadvantages may create difficulties, it is unwise to make assumptions based solely on this, and, in this simple example, Shona is the one likely to come through with a stronger sense of initiative.

Fantasy, make-believe and magical thinking are all part of play activity at this stage and play is a very important part in the child's emotional development (Paley, 2004). Piaget (1926) described children as egocentric at this stage, reinforcing the significance of events at this age in shaping our personalities. Erikson linked his thinking about this stage to the works of Freud and, in particular, the Oedipal complex and sexual development with Freud's concept of genital awareness (Brown, 1961). Working in the field of social work or social care, we are unlikely to need a pure Freudian approach in our work with service users, but Erikson's interpretation does give us useful material. Common to these theories is the proposition that relationships are very intense at this time. Children have strong feelings about who they want to be close to, and whether you accept the Freudian view that a boy fantasises about possessing his mother, and a girl her father, or not, children do have a strong need to gain the special attention or affectations of a key adult in their lives. 'There is a relationship-seeking energy at this age which needs to find some kind of outlet in people of the same and opposite sex' (Gibson, 2007: 80).

Given the intensity of this energy, events which impact on relationships take on a very significant importance. The birth of siblings can interfere with an existing carer–child relationship, promoting feelings of rivalry and jealousy, which can be even more painful if punished or criticised by a loved carer. A child's preference to be close to one particular carer may provoke a hostile reaction from another primary carer, creating a sense of badness and guilt in the child. On an even more serious level, the loss, through death or separation, of a sibling or carer may be conceived by a child as his or her fault, the fantasy-thinking and egocentricity being so powerful at this stage. Such feelings have to be rendered unconscious through defence mechanisms, but in the unconscious part of personality they remain an influential part of personality and can have long-term effects on interpersonal relationships throughout life.

Essentially, at this stage, the more the child feels the continuing affection of the primary carers and the more a child enjoys play and recreational activities, the more positive is the balance of initiative. As in the two previous stages, some experience of the negative balance, guilt, is necessary for the acquisition of a sensitive, balanced personality.

STAGE 4: INDUSTRY VERSUS INFERIORITY

In psychodynamic theory, the first three stages have been critical in the development of personality and the shaping of behaviour, simply because of the repression required to help us cope with the intensity of the childhood experiences. This stage is associated with a child's early experience of the demands of formal education, but be careful about applying a fixed age to this stage. Depending on their experiences within their unique environment, some children will be emotionally ready to meet this stage at five or six years, but others may still be more engaged with the demands of initiative versus guilt at that age.

Critical Thinking

Again, think back to your experiences at primary school when you began formal education (not preschool or nursery). How much can you remember of both happy and unhappy experiences?

Normally, our memories are better able to cope with what happened at this stage than with the more intense experiences of the earlier stages. Psychologically, this is viewed as an emotionally 'quieter' stage, and Freud called it the 'latency stage' (Brown, 1961) because the strong drives became temporarily dormant in these years before the onset of adolescence.

The life crisis at this stage is identified by Erikson as 'industry versus inferiority', the positive balance of industry being the ability to acquire knowledge, to be able to work alongside other children and to be successful in meeting the requirements of the education system. Although school is a primary focus at this stage, it is not the only one. Masten and Coatsworth (1998: 216) point out that 'successful children remind us that children grow up in multiple contexts – in families, schools, peer groups ... teams, religious organisations, and many other groups – and each context is a potential source of protective as well as risk factors'. Some children will obtain a positive balance of industry from school experience and validation from teachers or other adults, while some will obtain a positive balance from strength, sporting ability, sense of humour and other personal traits and validation from peers. When we try to understand and assess a service user's situation, an awareness of the wider cultural and social environment is needed before we can draw any conclusions about the priority value we might attach to any of these factors.

During these primary school years, we can better understand the significance of the earlier stages and how outcomes from the three preceding life crises impact on this, the fourth stage. Perhaps, in relation to the crisis of industry versus inferiority, the most significant could be the crisis of autonomy versus shame and doubt. While Erikson identified the negative balance as inferiority, not everyone who experiences poor marks, criticism or punishment during these latency years will necessarily acquire a feeling of inferiority, or, indeed, an inferiority complex. Someone with a positive balance of autonomy feels, without being consciously aware of it, confident and at ease with himself or herself, and has an inner self-esteem which forms part of the bedrock of personality. While quite possibly affected in the short term by negative feedback from others, a child with this inner self-belief is better placed to come through adversity at this stage with potentially little long-term negative impact. If that child has also an inner confidence in people, arising from a positive balance of basic trust, it is more likely that he or she will be able to engage with others to seek appropriate help and support, and, with a positive balance of initiative, will have the confidence to relate constructively and make appropriate choices.

Critical Thinking

Cross-refer to Chapter 12, where factors which promote resilience are discussed. Think about the importance of attachment figures and how the positive balances as identified by Erikson correspond to the positive aspects of attachment behaviour.

However, the child who has acquired a more negative balance may struggle for the opposite reasons: they have less trust in others, less belief in themselves and little confidence in wider social interaction. It is possible to speculate that a child with a strong negative balance of shame and doubt may struggle at primary school, even if capable of meeting educational standards because there is poor self-esteem. There are many you may know, and you may be one of them, who can never accept praise or positive feedback because they never quite believe they deserve it.

Case Study 1

Jane is working in a voluntary organisation which provides a planned programme over 12 weeks to support young people in their late teens to think constructively about employment and to gain some work experience. The young people have been low achievers at school, have had behaviour problems at home and at school and have been identified as difficult by other support services. The project is designed to help those who have left formal education, but have no employment, by a mix of group and individual activities designed to build confidence, self-esteem and social skills.

Initially, Jane and her colleagues must select participants who have been referred by social or educational agencies, or have self-referred because acquaintances or family members have recommended the project. In selecting the young people, a combination of procedural and questioning assessment models are used (Bolger and Walker, 2014) to try to determine the past history and the present personality strengths or deficits of the young people in order to assess their readiness to participate in a challenging programme.

In applying the information above to practice the linking to the Erikson framework can be highlighted as follows:

Assessing the balance of basic trust versus basic mistrust: How likely is the young person to respond to advice you may give, to accept adults as responsible or reliable and to be able to rely in group activities on the support of peers? One of the most difficult aspects of applying this theory is the exact determination of the balance of this first stage when the significant formative events took place many years earlier and are not, by and large, remembered. The worker is therefore making an assessment based on information from other services and a subjective response to how the young person presents at interview. Some young people with a strong balance of basic mistrust may come across as withdrawn, uncommunicative and unreliable: for them, years of mistrust in others have shaped behaviour to protect them from the desire to trust. People are so unreliable in their inner world that they have come to behave in such a way that people are driven to reject them, which confirms their inner feeling. People are unreliable: look what happens when I do the things I want to do: people don't want to know me = self-fulfilling prophecy.

Assessing the balance of autonomy versus shame and doubt: How likely are the young people to be able, as the project moves forward, to take personal responsibility for their actions, to tackle new tasks, to accept praise and encouragement and to cope with constructive criticism? To what extent are they either overly affected by feelings of doubt to the extent that their self-confidence is minimal, or feelings of shame which have caused a fear of exposing themselves, both physically and emotionally? Some, who experienced unhappy life events at the toddler stage, may have unresolved issues of control which makes them compulsively resist any attempts by others to place limits on or order in their lives. Inasmuch as we identified the self-fulfilling prophecy of basic mistrust, we can make the same link to shame and doubt. Unconsciously, the young person has internalised a feeling that he or she is no good at anything. Instead of trying to improve, they adopt antisocial behaviour which gets some reward from the approval of some of their peers. However, the antisocial behaviour gets the expected criticism and possibly punishment from adults and those in authority, which confirms to the young person his or her inadequacy = self-fulfilling prophecy.

Assessing the balance of initiative versus guilt: How able is the young person to deal with new tasks, to identify what has to be done and to put into practice new ways of coping? How able is the young person to interact with others in a broadly socially acceptable way, including with younger people, peers and older people? In the project which Jane is part of, these are important issues because the young people, in order to come through with positive outcomes, will be expected to work together with peers and to work for potential future employers. Again, information to complete this assessment will probably come from other agencies which have had contact with the young person, as well as from a subjective assessment based on the dynamic of the interview.

Assessing the balance of industry versus inferiority: Did the primary school experience provide any significant positive experiences or any significant negative? If we have indications of early life stage difficulties or problems, to what extent might positive primary school experience have helped create a more positive balance? By the same token, what might have been the effect of significant negative experiences at this stage? As we indicated earlier in the chapter, it is probable that the effects of the first three life crises are likely to have a deeper impact than this fourth stage.

Case Study 1   Continued

Jamie, who is 17, joins the programme. He grew up in a family setting which was very conflicted. His mother left when he was weeks old, his father tried to look after him with the help of his immediate family, but within his first year, Jamie was placed in foster care. Between the age of one and two, Jamie returned to his father and his father's new partner. However, this relationship broke down acrimoniously, and Jamie returned to foster care around the age of three. When his father began another relationship, Jamie returned to the family at four years old, but the relationship lasted

(Continued)

(Continued)

only two years. At this stage, Jamie's father said that he would be able to look after Jamie on his own, with the back-up of family members. Jamie's school years were constantly problematic, and he drifted through his teenage years with a group who became well known locally for petty crimes, heavy drinking and general antisocial activities. He still lives with his father, who still enters short-term relationships with other women and shows little interest in what Jamie does. At the assessment process, Jane acknowledges there are risks in taking Jamie on, which are indicated by the potentially strong balance of negative outcomes from the early life crisis stages, but feels that it was worth trying to help him before his life takes an even worse turn.

Jamie and Jane have a great deal of one-to-one contact during the first six weeks of the project, mainly because Jamie's behaviour on the programme continues to cause concern. He says that he wants to find a job, wants to find someone he can live with and wants to get a flat. However, he comes in late on most days, some days he fails to appear, he is withdrawn and fairly unresponsive in group activities and, despite being offered two weeks of work experience in a job that he wanted, he left after the first morning. The employer has said that there will be no second chance.

In her many conversations with Jamie, Jane builds a clearer picture of his personality. Underneath the frustrating, rude, swaggering adolescent exterior is a very frightened young man who has little confidence in the ability of adults to be reliable, little self-belief in his ability to do much for himself and very few social skills. At first, he talks reluctantly with Jane, but as the weeks go by, more openly. However, as his general behaviour does not improve and his attendance remains inconsistent, Jane and her colleagues reluctantly decide to discontinue Jamie's involvement, because he has repeatedly broken his side of the project contract. Such a move is really a last resort for the project, because the staff realise that this could be interpreted by Jamie as yet another rejection, reinforcing the self-fulfilling prophecies that people are unreliable and that it is not worth trying, because you cannot do it.

> *Is Jamie therefore bound to fail?* Jane, recognising that there are major issues of trust and self-esteem, has assessed that before Jamie is able to take part in an age-appropriate set of activities, he has to begin to believe in others and his own self-worth. Building on the relationship that she has begun to establish, she contracts with Jamie to meet at an agreed time on a regular basis, and arranges initially to collect him: the aim is to talk about returning to the project at a later point. Given Jamie's lack of trust, it is important to sustain the contact initially, which is why Jane collects him. As trust builds, and some autonomy develops, Jamie, hopefully, will take more responsibility for attending the meetings. There is no guarantee of success, but there is more hope for the future.

Case Study 2

This is based on a factual case.

An 18-year-old woman was attending a mental health support project for both individual and group support. She had strong bouts of depression and found it virtually impossible to make or keep friends, to the extent that it was becoming increasingly difficult to contemplate work or study.

The support worker talked regularly with the young woman about the events of her life and, during the course of this, one event began to repeat itself in the conversations. When she was about four or five, she could not remember exactly but she thought she had just begun school, she went with her parents to visit her grandparents. During the visit, her grandfather became ill (subsequently she was told he had had a heart attack), an ambulance was called, and, probably trying to shield her from the stress and tension, her parents asked her to go to the front gate and look out for the ambulance. The ambulance appeared on the street, she remembered waving to indicate that it should stop, but the ambulance driver, trying to find the address but not seeing any visible numbers, waved back and kept on driving, before realising where he should be and turned back to the house. Her grandfather was dead by the time the ambulance arrived, there was a lot of distress in the house, and the young woman remembered how she thought it was her fault that the ambulance didn't stop when it first appeared on the street. Such was the intensity of her subsequent guilt that she had repressed it into her inner world, where it sat, creating a belief that to love someone strongly was bad, because her love could cause someone to die.

As the young woman started and continued talking about this, she began feeling some kind of insight into what might have caused her to feel the way she did. A psychosocial approach to intervention might produce a positive outcome at this stage, as an individual, having achieved some kind of satisfactory insight into feelings which had not been part of her conscious self, might be able to resolve these feelings with a worker's support. However, if the thought processes continued to harbour feelings of guilt that she could have done more, a cognitive behavioural intervention might be more appropriate. For more information on these interventions, we recommend that you read Lindsay (2009).

OUTCOMES OF ERIKSON'S STAGES 1–4

- A positive balance of basic trust: a baby who is generally happy and interactive with others: smiles in response to smiling faces, laughs and gurgles when playfully stimulated.
- A negative balance of basic mistrust: more passive responses: watches carefully: less response to playful stimuli.
- A positive balance of autonomy: confident in play, confident in communication: derives a lot of pleasure from activities.
- A negative balance of shame and doubt: plays with difficulty: attention-seeking or finds it hard to settle down to do things: frequently criticised.
- A positive balance of initiative: plays comfortably with others: shows confidence in relations with close family members.
- A negative balance of guilt: less successful in play: pushy or withdrawn in relationships: tends to get into trouble more often.
- A positive balance of industry: settles into formal education well: displays in varying degrees of positivity confidence in the world, confidence in self and good relationship qualities: plays well and makes friends.
- A negative balance of inferiority: struggles at school: in some degrees less sure of others, lacks confidence in self or develops non-approved methods of sustaining recognition: may find more superficial relationships with other struggling children.

3 OBJECT RELATIONS THEORY – MEET MY NEEDS

In this chapter, we are still focusing on the childhood years to consider another psychodynamic theory which can be of considerable help to our practice.

By the end of the chapter the reader should:

- Have a deeper understanding of the importance of early childhood
- Understand how positive and negative feelings are dealt with by the very young child
- Be introduced to new definitions of stages of development
- Understand what is meant by 'split personality'
- Become aware of how splits affect your own behaviour

Object relations theory developed from the Freudian origins of psychoanalytic theory, but has more direct relevance to our practice because it considers the individual's inner emotional development as a part of more complex emotional relationships with other people. If you have come straight to this chapter from the previous one, you may recognise that exactly the same point was made about Erikson's theory, and it can be argued that Erikson is an object relations theorist. However, our experience in social work education has shown that it is difficult to understand what the theory actually is: as Brearley (2007: 92) writes, 'The term "object relations" … is unfortunate as it implies something impersonal, whereas the opposite is the case, as the central focus is on what it means to be human.' In addition, because there are very intricate psychological differences between various strands of object relations theorists, and because there is a great deal of psychological jargon in these debates, it has been very difficult for students of the subject to form a clear picture from the available literature. In this and subsequent chapters, we hope to present you with as straightforward an explanation of this theory as possible, which we consider to have very significant potential for application to practice.

The theory we shall present derives from the work of W.R.D. (Ronald) Fairbairn (1952) and J.D. Sutherland (1989), who were major figures in the development of psychiatry in Edinburgh, Scotland, during the mid-twentieth century. This chapter will attempt to summarise the considerable work undertaken by these theorists and show how we may understand the importance of childhood in shaping personality and behaviour from yet another perspective.

First, objects are people. The term 'object' is used because, in psychoanalytic theory, a baby relates initially to only part of a whole person, for example the eyes, the smile, the breast and so on. Only gradually does the baby begin to put all the parts together to recognise the whole person. For the sake of putting this theory into practice, simplify the jargon by substituting the words 'people' or 'person' when you see the word 'object'.

Second, this theory rejects the Freudian 'id', which regarded the baby as driven by instinctive basic drives to obtain pleasure or satisfaction. When we are born, our ego, that is, our conscious self, is whole, and, to put it simply, from the very beginning we want to love and to be loved. Our drive in life is to make connections with human beings (Sutherland, 1980).

Third, as with attachment and life cycle theories, our experiences of being cared for as babies, toddlers and young children are critical. We internalise the feelings which derive from our experiences into an unconscious part of our self (ego), and this process of internalising is called 'splitting' in the terminology of object relations theory. These splits in our self can influence our behaviour throughout life. Using this definition, we could say that everyone has a split personality: the term does not apply solely to the commonly expressed term used to describe violent mental disorder.

Fourth, there are three broad stages of emotional development: infantile dependence, a transitional stage and then mutual dependence. Let us look at these more closely.

THE OBJECT RELATIONS THEORY STAGES

Where Erikson's framework identified more specific stages, the object relations approach considers the broader aspect of our emotional needs in life, and the first need, based on the drive to love and be loved, is to be able to depend on primary caregivers to meet our needs in early childhood. At this point, the child's sense of self, i.e. his or her ego, is emotionally unable to cope with the everyday demands of life. This is the stage of 'infantile' dependence. Every child needs someone on whom they can depend to keep them safe, help them develop and respond to their emotional needs. In other words, every child has a need to love and to be loved. In putting forward this theory, object relations theorists are arguing much the same as Erikson did in putting forward his theory of the importance of acquiring a positive balance of basic trust and autonomy, and much the same as attachment theorists in putting forward the importance of positive attachment experiences and bond formation.

Middle childhood, including the adolescent years, is described as the 'transitional stage', because, essentially, the child is moving from what should have been the comfort of dependency towards the adult stage of mature dependency. This transitional stage involves the changing pattern of relationships: the loosening of the possibly intense relationships with primary caregivers, the broadening of relationships with others and the formation of new intense relationships with others. Depending on experiences in early childhood and events which take place in middle childhood, this stage may for some be reasonably straightforward, but given its nature, for many it is likely to be something of a roller-coaster ride with highs and lows, and for some it may be very challenging or incredibly difficult.

Critical Thinking

Have you heard the expression 'transitional object'? This is usually applied to something comforting from childhood which we have held on to, an object that has emotional value to us. For example, some of you will have soft toys (despite the fact that you are adults), some of you will have a treasured toy or something that belonged to a parent which you have kept since childhood, and some of you will take great satisfaction from putting something in your mouth, be it a cigarette, a bottle or just sucking a pen.

These may reflect the unconscious anxious feelings you had as you made your way through the transitional stage of your life and the comfort you derived from certain things in helping you cope. Take time to think about any childhood related objects or ways of behaving which are still in your life. How important are they? How easy would you find it to part with them?

Adulthood is seen as the stage of 'mature dependence'. This is an interesting phrase, because we often describe the aim of adulthood as 'independent living', when, in fact, emotionally healthy adulthood is more interactive. In object relations theory, 'mature' means the capacity to give something to a relationship, and 'dependence' means the capacity to get something from a relationship. The success of the third and final stage of adulthood is therefore based on the establishment of mutual relationships, which implies being able to relate in an appropriate way, based on mutual giving and receiving.

HOW WE SPLIT OUR PERSONALITY

As soon as we are born, our ego is formed. It is then shaped by our experiences and by how well our primary carers meet our needs. If they behave in a way which shows that they love us, and which we feel good about, our ego forms strongly in that we feel a coherent, congruent response from those we want to love in return. However, as we have already seen from the two previous chapters, it is virtually impossible to meet even the best-loved child's needs all the time. As we wrote about basic trust, a child does need to experience some unmet needs in order to have a healthy balance of basic mistrust, so delayed gratification in feeding, nappy discomfort, delayed response to crying and other everyday small events have a meaning: to, very simply, if the baby is unhappy, the baby does not feel loved. We can't stress enough at this stage that these are unconscious feelings, we have no capacity to think or say these things, they are basic, gut, primitive feelings which are felt and internalised.

As soon as the young child experiences any feeling which threatens the basic drive to love and be loved, he or she has to get rid of it from the conscious self, because such a feeling provokes anxiety. This is where we begin to split our personality. Our ego is our self, but in recognition of the fact that our self contains aspects of which we are consciously aware as well as unconscious aspects of which we are generally unaware, object relations divides the ego into three parts:

1. Central Ego = Conscious, aware part of self.
2. Libidinal Ego = Unconscious part of self which experienced some good feelings, but not enough to feel completely satisfied, leaving us wanting more = 'needy child'.
3. Anti-libidinal Ego = Unconscious part of self which experienced bad feelings, needs were punished, leaving us afraid to show or express our own need or vulnerability, or to tolerate need or vulnerability in others = 'punitive child'.

In each and every one of us exists a conscious self, and parts that are, to varying degrees, needy and/or punitive. To what extent the unconscious needy or punitive parts influence our personality and behaviour depends on how much unsatisfying or punishing behaviour we experienced when we were young children at the stage of infantile dependence. So, if we were occasionally frustrated by having to wait for feeds while hungry, or if we did not always get a cuddle from carers when we were upset, or if we were occasionally criticised for any activities, we may have experienced generally loving care but, crucially, not all the time. Even in the happiest of overall experiences lies the potential for some split off negative feelings, which create an inner neediness. On the whole, as we move into middle childhood and adulthood, our central ego will not be unduly influenced by a small, needy, libidinal ego, but in situations where our central ego struggles to cope, the unconscious split part may begin to influence our behaviour. Our needy, libidinal part of our self may temporarily dictate how we behave towards others.

The same potential for splitting is true where we have been shouted at, physically punished, or deliberately ignored or belittled by primary carers. We split off the negative feelings of hurt or anger or of being unloved, which become punitive feelings stored in our anti-libidinal ego (Figure 3.1). These unconscious feelings produce a fear of dependence which derive from a childhood feeling that need must be bad, because need gets punished. The more we were frustrated or punished in childhood, the stronger the unconscious splits, and the stronger the unconscious splits, the more they are likely to influence behaviour and overwhelm the central ego. If the childhood splits are particularly strong, the conscious, aware part of our self is likely to be only partially able to cope appropriately with adult life because of the dominance of an unconscious inner needy/punitive child. Behaviour in adulthood will, therefore, be dominated by unmet childhood needs and emotions.

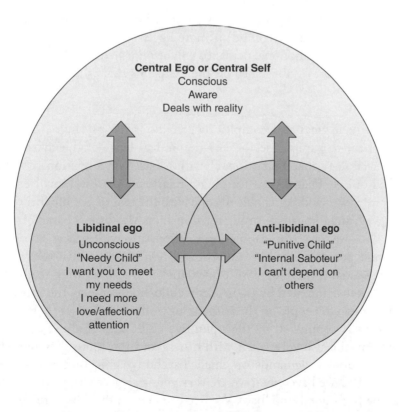

Figure 3.1   How we split ourselves: object relations theory

Because the split feelings in our selves derive from our experiences while being dependant on primary carers, we also have to split the 'bad' parts from them. In order to believe that we are lovable and in order to love the carer, we may have to get rid of the feeling that they do not love us. In the same way that we split our own ego above, we split the other person, and this is the more complicated part. The splits that we apply to others also become internalised in ourselves and can affect relationships for the rest of our lives.

The three ego divisions described above are accompanied by three splits to the external person, who are our primary carers in the first instance. These are:

1. Ideal Object = the real person. In a healthy relationship, our central ego (our conscious, aware self) relates to the whole person, accepting the reality that the person has good and bad points, parts we like and parts we do not like = the ideal object.
2. Exciting Object = someone I want who will meet my needs and take all my problems away. Our libidinal ego (needy child) is more likely to be drawn to another person on this basis, seeing only those aspects which attract us, and not the whole person = exciting object.
3. Rejecting Object = someone who has got it in for me or is out to hurt me. Our anti-libidinal ego (punitive child) is more likely to identify this in others, and anyone who makes emotional demands will be punished as will anyone who fails to provide support or assistance on the occasions that it is sought = rejecting object.

We could write at great and complex length about the psychological processes, but we shall try to paraphrase the key theoretical basis of the dynamic of ego splitting. Psychological and emotional health is based on a relationship of central ego to ideal object. That means forming a relationship which involves knowing ourselves pretty well and being able to cope with the realities of life in a reasonably successful way; and it means forming relationships with others based on who they really are. Thus we form friendships and relationships with others, accepting that we have good points, as well as not so good points, and so do our friends and partners. Essentially, therefore, we can relate to people as they really are. The more a person is dominated by their needy child/libidinal ego, the more they are likely to be drawn to people on the basis of how others will meet their needs. The more a person is dominated by their punitive child/anti-libidinal ego, the more they avoid emotional involvement with others and the more they punish those who make emotional demands on them. Psychodynamic theory acknowledges the difficulty that we have when we are very young in accepting that our primary carers can be both 'good' and 'bad'. We need to believe that they are good and so we split the badness off.

As we move into adulthood, our personalities comprise a mix of ego balance, illustrated in Figure 3.1, with a mix of relationship splitting as indicated in Figure 3.2.

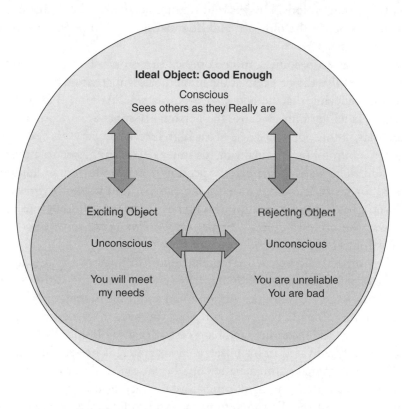

Figure 3.2   How we split other people: object relations theory

Let us try to illustrate how this might apply to a situation which could happen to anyone. Some years ago, before the criminal scams at ATMs became common, one of the authors put his debit card into an ATM in Paris. The card remained in the ATM, and despite the 'helpful' assistance of another customer, the card could not be retrieved. We shall now look at the author's behaviour and apply object relations theory to interpret it.

He recognised that there was a problem, but at this stage did not see any evidence of a crime. His central ego recognised that he should report the incident to his own bank, which he did, to cancel the card and request a new one. Thus far, his behaviour was rational and appropriate. Central ego was functioning well. One week later, home again, his new card arrived and he went to an ATM for cash. It was very early in the month, his pay should have been in the bank and he expected to see a balance of about £2000. What he saw was a debit balance of £600 and, on the balance slip, a list of regular withdrawals over the past week. His central ego was still functioning as he readily recognised the anxiety and panic in himself, and he continued to behave rationally by phoning the bank's helpline to question these transactions. He was told that a mistake had been made, the bank had not put a stop on the old card and he must now go in person to the branch to resolve the issue.

Now, he began to become a more complex person psychologically. He set out consciously to resolve the problem at the branch, knowing that he had been a victim of crime and believing that he had justice on his side. At least that was what his central ego was telling him. Because the personality splits are unconscious, he was not aware that, at this point, because of his high level of anxiety, his central ego was no longer in control. His libidinal ego, his inner needy child, was in a more dominant position as he went to the bank expecting to be comforted and, importantly, reimbursed for his suffering. As a result, the bank official he met with was not the 'ideal object' (that is, the real person who had a number of different jobs to do that day) but was the 'exciting object' (the person who we relate to in the expectation that they will meet our needs and solve our problems).

The bank official said he needed a police report to confirm a crime, and, despite the fact the crime was committed in a foreign country, sent the author to the local police station. Before he went, the author asked about his money, or lack of money. An overdraft was offered. That was not what the author wanted or expected: he wanted sympathy, understanding and hard cash. Because his unconscious splits had now become fully activated in his upset, anxious state, his needy child had wanted an exciting object to make things better, but, because he did not get that, his punitive child now identified the bank official as a 'rejecting object' who was causing pain and further distress. To the author, the bank official was whatever expletive you would care to insert.

By now, the author, who still believed he was coping (that his central ego was working well) had arrived at the police station and was very much under the control of his unconscious split ego parts, needy (dominant) and punitive (ready to intervene if needy is frustrated). The author explained his problem to the reception clerk at the police station using the fragile small part of central ego which was currently functioning. The clerk said that they could not help because the crime was foreign, and was immediately seen as the enemy, a waste of space, a bad person. The author's punitive child was in control and the clerk was a rejecting object, not a real human being. From behind, however, a policewoman had overheard and disagreed with the clerk. She said that they could help and that their Fraud Squad could deal with such a situation. The author's needy child was back in control: he had never met this policewoman, but he loved her immediately, as an exciting object. He had not a clue as to what she might really be like as a person, but at that moment she was an angel. Now dominated by his libidinal ego, he asked, in a small boy voice, if she would phone the bank and tell them. She agreed. His punitive child would really have liked her to shout at them, but his stronger needy child was just happy she was making his life easier.

Hopefully, this illustrates how we can get through life reasonably well, but when faced with difficult situations which affect our emotional balance, we can become temporarily dominated by splits in our personality of which we are generally unaware. Even when we do become aware of the splits, we cannot always control their impact. Trying to control his punitive child and re-establish a stronger central ego, the author channelled his emotions into a letter to the chief executive at the bank's headquarters. The punitive child was complaining, but the central ego wanted the bank to be aware and put procedures in place. The CEO responded with a personal letter, promising to investigate and subsequently providing feedback on the investigation, an apology and financial recompense with a little extra. The author has never met the CEO, but when that individual was eventually sacked by the bank and had his knighthood taken from him for causing the banking crisis which ruined many people's lives, the author still could not help feeling sorry for him. He was still the exciting object who had made the author's life better, even if he had made millions of others' lives worse.

For some people, however, because of the more negative early life experiences, the splits may be stronger and may tend to dominate the central ego on a more regular basis. You may know people who are anxious to please others, who take on helping or caregiving roles very readily or who become dependent or clingy in friendships or relationships. Where this becomes uncomfortable, it may be because of a dominant libidinal ego, an unconscious need to love and be loved. As people who work in a caring profession, we need to be as aware of our own motivation as possible, and consider the extent to which our own needs are being met in helping others. You may also know others who are very self-contained, who give little of themselves away and who appear to have a need to be in control. This may be evidence of a dominant anti-libidinal ego, an unconscious fear of commitment or dependence stemming from the splitting off of painful experiences in childhood at the stage of infantile dependence.

Critical Thinking

Winnicott (1960, 1974) coined the term 'good enough' to describe the mothering, now broadened to parenting, which a young child needs. Consider how good enough parenting might be the same as Fairbairn's 'ideal object'. Winnicott also coined the term 'false self', and consider to what extent people present outwardly only a part of themselves. Sometimes, that part is the unconscious needy or punitive self. Is it possible to present your real self outwardly at all times?

(Continued)

(Continued)

You might also like to think about the similarities between the needy and punitive splits in our ego and the results of the work of Ainsworth et al. (2014) on attachment behaviour as described in Chapter 1. How closely might the libidinal, needy ego resemble anxious attachment and the anti-libidinal, punitive ego resemble avoidant attachment?

APPLICATION TO PRACTICE

Shirley is a 19-year-old mother of four-month-old Michael. She lives with her 18-year-old partner James, Michael's father, in a small flat. She has been attending a paediatric clinic because of Michael's feeding problems and apparent gastric upsets, and Alan, a Child and Family Support Team worker, is working with the family.

Alan's initial assessment is that Shirley is chaotic in her approach to Michael, sometimes showing great affection and sometimes showing extreme frustration. She is feeding him formula milk and cannot seem to understand that she has to follow instructions in making up the feeds. She thinks that Michael will get more sustenance if she puts more formula in the mix than the recommended amount. When Michael is crying or squirming or refusing to suck, Shirley describes him as 'getting at her', claiming that he is deliberately winding her up. Her relationship with her partner James is also stormy, but Shirley is desperate to keep him with her, and despite their frequent arguments, cannot bear the thought of being without him. He is rarely present when Alan visits, but when he is, James is clearly dominated by Shirley's personality, handles Michael with care and sensitivity but does not appear to want to or be able to take a more assertive role. Shirley has no support from her mother or father, who separated when she was a baby. She was brought up by her mother, but she and her siblings were frequently placed in short-term residential care during childhood.

An object relations approach to the assessment would raise the following questions:

- How strong is Shirley's central ego, and James's?
- To what extent do they have the capacity to learn and to modify behaviour accordingly?
- How influential are the libidinal and anti-libidinal splits in their personality?
- Both adults are also teenagers. How able are they to be 'mature dependent' and to what extent are they still resolving issues from the transitional stage?

Clearly, Shirley's central ego is a potential source of concern. When he is content, Michael is loved like a doll, cuddled and kissed. However, more often, when he is discontented he is shouted at and seen as an enemy trying to make Shirley's life a misery. These are indications that Shirley is ranging from needy child/libidinal ego to punitive child/anti-libidinal ego in her relationships with Michael, and, similarly, with James. As the dominating carer, Shirley is receiving more attention from Alan. As an adult carer, it is vital that she relates to Michael on a central ego to ideal object basis: in Michael's case, he is four months old, totally dependent and psychologically driven by a need to love and be loved. In Shirley's case, she has to relate to Michael as a completely dependent child, putting his needs first. However, given that Shirley's dominant unconscious splits are influencing her behaviour, it could be said that she is still preoccupied with her own needs, and that instead of being able to relate to Michael as the dependent ideal object, her relationship towards him veers from seeing him as the exciting object one minute and as the rejecting object the next. James has a slightly stronger central ego, and is able to recognise that their care of Michael could be done differently. However, emotionally his libidinal ego is very dominant and he needs Shirley as much as she needs him. His anti-libidinal ego does not appear so strong, and he shows little sign of aggressive or punitive behaviour.

This illustrates the dilemma for the caring professions. At what point does Michael's welfare become so threatened that he is at physical risk, and what level of emotional risk can be tolerated. If Shirley and James cannot learn to manage Michael's feeding, his health is threatened. While intervention to help the parents might be attempted in a task centred model (Humphrey, 2014) or a cognitive behavioural model (Allan, 2014), for either of these to have a realistic chance of success, Shirley and James would require sufficient personality strength to assimilate information and modify behaviour with the available support of a professional. If their unconscious splits, both needy and punitive remain dominant, the probability is that they will not have the capacity to modify because they remain too preoccupied by each other and cannot relate to Michael's need for dependence on them.

The dominance of the childhood splits in the adult behaviour point to experiences in their own childhood where their own needs were either frustrated, neglected or punished. In such a situation, their capacity to offer care and nurture is limited by the absence of learned experience or emotional experience, and they need to be able to begin to feel better about themselves before they are reasonably able to devote sufficient attention to the real needs of Michael and see him as a whole person, the ideal object. For this to come about, intervention might require a relationship-based approach (Phung, 2014), with sensitive inclusion of more structured approaches at appropriate points in the intervention.

If we now fast forward four years, Michael, supported and monitored by health and social services, has come through his early years with minor, common physical ailments, but there are continuing concerns about his general development. His parents' behaviour towards him remains unchanged, because intervention focused on monitoring and advice-giving. No single worker has maintained continuity of contact, so Shirley continues to regard any health or social worker as a waste of space: her anti-libidinal ego regards them as rejecting objects. Critically, however, Michael has been splitting his own feelings from his central ego. He has a strong anti-libidinal ego deriving from the shouting, the forced feeding and the rough handling from his mother. He has a fairly strong libidinal ego deriving from the cuddles and praise that he received from his mother and father on those occasions that he was making their lives easier: frustrating, because he had a taste of feeling good, but not enough to leave him feeling satisfied. His central ego, which believes he is loved and which loves his parents, is a very small part of himself, probably easily dominated by his anti-libidinal and libidinal splits. In a further power struggle, his anti-libidinal ego (his inner punitive child) tends to dominate his libidinal ego (his inner needy child).

Michael begins attending nursery at the age of three, but his behaviour gives cause for concern. He is aggressive towards other children and cannot settle to play for any length of time, although he loves hearing stories. Over the past year, his aggressive behaviour becomes more pronounced, and the nursery staff reach a point where they cannot contain his behaviour and, in effect, Michael is expelled from nursery. Michael's behaviour is dominated by his anti-libidinal ego: he has internalised the feeling that his needs for affection are bad, that to be vulnerable results in pain and that other people are unreliable. The good feelings he gets at story time are not sufficient to challenge the inner splits of punitive child identifying others as rejecting objects. Of course, some of his behaviour is based on social learning (Bandura and Walters, 1963), but the deeper, internalised feelings described by object relations theory are the source of deeper concern. If Michael had a reasonably balanced personality, with a stronger central ego, he might be capable of learning how to play with behavioural interventions. However, he, like his mother and father, needs a relationship-based intervention to prevent his descent into a stigmatised, antisocial existence. At this point, intervention might have more positive outcomes if the focus remains on family interaction and does not isolate one individual as the scapegoat (Brodie and Swan, 2014).

Later in the book, we shall look at resilience and the potential for Michael to benefit from constructive relationships. Gilligan (2009) has pointed out that children may be helped by empathic contact with significant adults, such as teachers. The risk for someone such as Michael is that he becomes identified as a 'problem' and that all action is aimed at controlling him rather than understanding him. To develop positively, he needs to love and be loved, and he needs to have the opportunity to receive continuity of affection from an understanding adult who can tolerate his antisocial behaviour. 'Tolerate' does not mean accepting or approving, but it does mean sustaining an affectionate relationship. If such an adult enters Michael's life, there is hope. Michael might then have the opportunity to strengthen his central ego by beginning to accept that people are neither all bad nor all good, but, in reality, a bit of both.

Critical Thinking

A criticism of psychoanalytic and psychodynamic theory has been that it places too much emphasis on the individual as the 'problem'. In covering the theory of object relations and recommending its application in practice, we are not suggesting that you apply it in isolation. We must never lose sight of the context or the environment in which people live: but we must also never lose sight of the uniqueness of individuals as they deal with or are affected by their environment. There is evidence from sociological research of the impact of living in poverty and of the power of networking (Yuill and Gibson, 2011). Consider how the individual's response to stress and anxiety as described in this chapter might be affected for better or for worse by wider structural or environmental factors.

The impact of object relations theory begins from birth and the splitting of personality is most active in the early years of childhood when feelings are intense. The importance of adult behaviour towards children is enormous at this stage, and the impact of these interactions remains within us, influencing our behaviour and our relationships for the rest of our lives.

PART 2

FROM CHILDHOOD THROUGH ADOLESCENCE TO BECOMING AN ADULT

Over the following three chapters, we move into the adolescent and young adult parts of our life. Chapter 4 will consider how the pattern of attachments formed in childhood affects our relationships and behaviour as we move from being a child through the changing relationships and challenges of adolescence, where the need for healthy attachment is a significant part of being able to cope. Chapter 5 considers Erikson's life cycle theory and the emotional crisis of adolescence which leads to the changing responsibilities and expectations of young adulthood, where attachment patterns influence the quality of relationships. Chapter 6 will discuss the psychological Object Relations theory and the transition from childhood dependency through a transitional, adolescent stage to the emotional responsibilities required in adulthood. All three chapters focus on the responsibilities of adults to meet the emotional development needs of children.

4 ATTACHMENT – NEW RELATIONSHIPS ON OLD FOUNDATIONS

The focus of the next 3 chapters will be to look at the effect of psychoanalytic theories on an individual's journey through school, into adolescence and on to early adulthood. Each theory will be looked at in isolation, but it is important to see these theories as tools in your toolbox so that they can all be considered during assessment and throughout intervention. It may be that you can see evidence of all of the theories applying to one individual, and there will be crossover into each approach, but they are presented separately here so that you can think about each one in more detail.

By the end of the chapter the reader should:

- Understand how attachment theory helps us relate to our environment
- Gain a fuller understanding of and consider the four main attachment styles
- Have a perspective on psychodynamic theories by considering how these fit into the array of other theories available to social work
- Be aware of Bronfenbrenner's socioecological model to explain interactions, relationships and influences

---

As we have seen, attachment is influential in early development, but we do not stop forming relationships as soon as we leave infancy: quite the opposite. We also enter new environments, become exposed to new experiences, and develop a sense of awareness that there is a big world beyond the front door of our family homes. Our attachment styles develop as we grow, and these styles can dictate how we behave and interact with the wider world. In this chapter, we will look at these interactions by moving through the stages of school, adolescence and then into adulthood. We shall begin by giving a recap of the attachment styles and also strongly recommend you cross-reference the information given in this chapter with Chapters 5 and 6.

A SUMMARY OF ATTACHMENT STYLES (FROM CHAPTER 1)

Secure attachment:

- The child feels that there is a secure base to explore from, and a safe haven to return to.
- Communication from the carer is empathetic, consistent, warm and attuned to the needs of the child.
- The child feels safe in expressing needs and emotions.
- The child develops trust in itself, and trust in others.

Anxious/ambivalent attachment:

- The child generally feels safe, but the availability of emotional connection with the carer is inconsistent.
- The carer is preoccupied for the majority of the time and finds it difficult to be emotionally attuned all of the time.
- The child can be quite explosive in their emotional outbursts as they feel that they need to exaggerate feelings to get attention, and they need to gauge when their carer is going to be available to meet their needs.
- The child can develop 'learned helplessness' and has low trust in themselves, but high trust in others.

Avoidant attachment:

- The child generally feels safe, but the availability of emotional connection with the carer is absent for most of the time.
- The carer finds it difficult to be emotionally attuned to the child and can be distant and dismissive towards the needs of the child.
- The child learns that there is no point in trying to get the carer's attention as it can be a fruitless pursuit. The child supresses their emotional needs in order to protect the carer from unpleasant feelings.
- The child becomes very reliant on themselves, developing a high sense of trust in their own behaviour and actions, but a low sense of trust in others.

Disorganised attachment:

- Generally, the child lacks feelings of safety and security due to the unpredictable nature of the care given. The child often wants to flee from the 'secure base' and dreads returning to the 'safe haven', creating a sense of disequilibrium.
- The carer has issues when trying to be emotionally attuned to the child's needs and can be volatile within their reactions. This might be due to traumatic issues in their past.

- The child cannot develop any sense of continuity or predictability. The child ends up feeling stressed without an appropriate outlet for these pent up emotions.
- The child finds it difficult to trust their own emotions and actions, and equally difficult to trust other people.

THE INTERNAL WORKING MODEL

In Chapter 1, we introduced the internal working model which Bowlby (1969) believed was vital for a developing child to be able to begin to understand what to expect from relationships and, consequently, how to behave. The internal working model is responsible for the definition of the self and the organisation of expectations, feelings and attitudes. Howe and Campling (1995) explain that the internal working model can be influenced by a number of relationships when a child is young, but the older a child gets, the more organised these expectations will become, and instead of being shaped by relationships, everybody will eventually begin to shape new relationships themselves based on the information from our own internal working models – expectations of ourselves and of others, and how to coordinate interaction between the two.

As well as mirroring, Winnicott (1971) recognised the importance of 'holding' within the didactic relationship between carer and child. He described 'holding' as being the experience of meeting dependence, but also fostering independence by being emotionally available for the developing child. This involves feeding, changing, physical contact and being attuned to the demands of the child. As the child grows, the carer will gradually move away from the child, but come back and reassure the child that separation is normal and healthy. Winnicott also believed that it was not just the job of the primary carer to 'hold' the developing child, and that when school begins the environment there should also 'hold' them and be attuned to their needs at that stage. He extended this to include the general environment which the child grows up in, the people they come into contact with and the society they function in, too. Indeed, it is the aspect of 'holding' that assists the therapeutic relationship between social worker and service user.

Critical Thinking

Therapeutic alliance

If there is one quality that defines a successful social work relationship it would have to be the ability to form a 'therapeutic alliance' with the service user. This alliance is underpinned by the core values of social work, namely upholding dignity and

(Continued)

(Continued)

well-being, respecting self-determination, being holistic, identifying strengths, being non-judgemental and being empathetic (British Association of Social Workers, 2014). As social workers, we are providing a safe space for our service users to explore change. When we initially meet a new service user it would be normal for them to have mixed feelings about receiving social work support. They may feel relieved in some respects, but within society it is often seen as a sign of weakness to admit that you need help and assistance, and this can often be reflected in the initial contact.

As a starting point, we often need to help service users work towards self-acceptance before tackling some of the wider issues that present a problem. To do this, we need to listen, engage with communication skills to encourage information sharing and show that we understand how the issues are impacting on the life of the service user (without being condescending or slipping into sympathetic – rather than empathetic – responses).

In effect, we are recreating the 'holding' environment that Winnicott (1971) identified as being important for successful development. Within the relationship, the service user needs to feel able to talk about issues in a safe environment, feel that someone is listening to them and appreciating that these issues are a problem for them, and then feel that there is common ground when identifying a way forward. The empathetic social worker will use reflective listening skills to summarise where discussions are at and this helps the service user recognise that emotions have been recognised and named, just as a carer would do when 'mirroring' within the 'holding' environment. This creates a secure base for the service user to return to in order to explore ongoing changes, and we can describe the attachment relationship within the therapeutic alliance as 'earned secure' in that it is a temporary attachment style that recreates the qualities of Bowlby's (2008) secure attachment.

By the time a child enters school there should be understanding within the attachment relationship which allows the child to recognise that compromise is required within the didactic relationship. The child should be relatively autonomous but with an understanding that the primary carer is available when required – through negotiating plans for a child's return from school which 'guarantees' that the carer will be there on the child's return and will assist in the formation of autonomy and the avoidance of anxiety (Parkes et al., 2006). At school, the child comes into contact with teachers, authority and peers, and these interactions all assist in the formation of social experiences. Alongside these interactions, cognitive developments will also impinge on the internal working model.

It has already been noted that psychoanalytic theories cannot be viewed in isolation, and for a full appreciation of where they fit into the wider scope of social work theories it is useful to consider the work of Urie Bronfenbrenner as this also helps in understanding the impact on the internal working model. Bronfenbrenner (1986, 1992; and Bronfenbrenner and Bronfenbrenner, 2009) recognised the importance of relationships on human development, but believed that for a true understanding of a person the relationships in and between five distinct subsystems had to be considered. Nobody develops in isolation, and, so far, the theories we have looked at consider interactions between the child and the primary carer predominantly, but Bronfenbrenner believed that the environment, as well as society, played an important part in identity formation. He proposed that individuals are nested within a microsystem, which, in turn, is nested within a mesosystem, an exosystem, a macrosystem and a chronosystem (Figure 4.1).

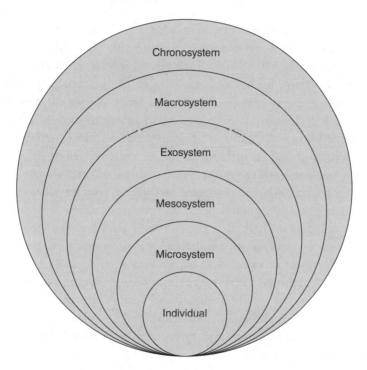

Figure 4.1   Bronfenbrenner's socioecological model

Microsystem

The 'microsystem' is the first level within Bronfenbrenner's model and would refer to members of various groups that the individual has direct contact with. This would include family members, school friends, peers and other members of the community who come into direct contact with the individual. All of these relationships within the microsystem will have an impact on how the individual functions within the other systems. Bronfenbrenner highlights the importance of the microsystem in helping a child learn about the world around them, a lot of which is dependent on trust and how a child forms impressions of this through the relationships they are involved in, and the formation of healthy attachment styles certainly contributes to healthy development within the microsystem (Brazelton and Greenspan, 2001). As we get older, the microsystem becomes wider and will encompass workmates and intimate partners, and because Bronfenbrenner stressed the bidirectional nature of interactions between each system, we become instrumental in defining the environment within the microsystem and contribute to the construction of the environments.

Mesosystem

The 'mesosystem' is the environment in which the microsystem functions and extends beyond looking at relationships between the individual and one other person. It factors in the situations which foster interaction between all parties within the microsystem, for example looking at the influence of school and, in turn, how that is impacted on by experiences from within the family group. It recognises that individuals do not function in isolation and will be influenced by other 'groups' within the community – no relationship functions in isolation and every interaction will be influenced by our experiences of interactions with others within the community. When relationships interact in the mesosystem, it brings people from the microsystem into direct contact with each other in situations that might not regularly occur and provides a new learning experience for the individual. The individual at the centre of Bronfenbrenner's model might experience a certain set of values and behaviours with one family member, and a completely different set of values and behaviours with another, estranged, family member, but when these two different family members come together the individual can witness how these behaviours and values interact by watching these two people interact. As a child grows and develops, it will come into contact with new experiences within the microsystem but can learn how to act within these as they transition through life.

Exosystem

The 'exosystem' is the level which contains factors that impact on the life of the individual, but usually indirectly and by affecting people within the microsystem, in turn, will affect the individual. These factors within the exosystem are usually beyond the control of the individual at the centre of Bronfenbrenner's model but will be influential. Examples of these factors might be the parental workplace – the child might have no experience or knowledge of what goes on within the workplace but, if it is a stressful environment, the chances are the parent will carry these stresses home and this will impact on the child. Mass media is also one of the elements that exists within the exosystem and can shape attitudes and beliefs of those within the microsystem. Usually, we can view the factors within this level as being a positive or negative influence on the development of the individual at the centre of the model.

Macrosystem

At the outer fringes of the model we find the 'macrosystem' and this is where the cultural aspects of our society lie. Within this level, we will also find the effects of government in social policy and legislation which impacts on everybody in society. Elements to consider within the macrosystem would include ethnic background, religion and social class. The values and beliefs that stem from these elements feed into every aspect of our life and will underpin our actions and relationships.

Chronosystem

Finally, the 'chronosystem' considers the age and stage of the individual and factors in natural life transitions – for example, moving from nursery school into primary school, or primary school into secondary school – but will also consider biological transitions and significant events within the life of the individual. Some of these transitions may well be unplanned, such as the death of a significant family member or the divorce of parents, but Bronfenbrenner believed that they needed to be considered within the context of the development of the individual at the centre of his model.

Critical Thinking

Take time to consider your own social ecological model. Place yourself in the centre and work out through each level and consider the following:

Microsystem: Who are the important people in your life who influence you?

Mesosystem: How are significant people connected?

Exosystem: Can you identify factors that impact on the lives of people in your microsystem?

Macrosystem: Consider your ethnicity, religion, social class and belief system. How do politics influence you at this level?

Chronosystem: Are you satisfied with this picture? How might it change in five years' time?

Bronfenbrenner's model offers an overview of relationships as we grow and develop, and an understanding that psychoanalytic theories will be impacted upon by psychological theories (modelling, social learning theory, operant conditioning and so on), peer influence, family systems and sociological theories. Psychoanalytic theories only give us an insight into how we manage internal thought processes, anxieties and relationships, but should always be seen as part of a wider theoretical jigsaw.

EARLY CHILDHOOD/SCHOOL

Toddlers will challenge parental authority and push boundaries, and this is not unique to one particular attachment style, but attachment styles will still be evident when observing the interaction between child and caregiver on reunion. As a toddler advances in age, the development of attachment goes hand in hand with other developments the child experiences, which will include cognitive, biological and linguistic growth. Dunn (1993) draws parallels with adult relationships when looking at the developing qualities of the carer–child relationship at this stage and believes that qualities valued in later relationships begin here, such as humour, communication skills and mutual understanding. Security still remains a vital component of the child's internal working model, but skills develop because of the interaction with the primary carer and this will facilitate the interpretation of the world around them, helping them make sense of their relationships with various systems from Bronfenbrenner's socioecological model.

In early childhood, Thompson (in Cassidy and Shaver, 1999) believes that the more secure the attachment style, the less problematic the behaviour of the developing child will be, even suggesting that the 'terrible twos' may not be so terrible if the attachment is secure. The secure child will demonstrate qualities which will include enthusiasm for new experiences, a willingness to take on-board guidance from the caregiver and will have fewer outbursts as a result of frustration or aggression. Empathic attunement develops as the child recognises that they are being noticed by other people; they have a name, feelings are understood and acknowledged; and with this realisation comes the recognition of other people around them – as knowledge of the self develops, so will knowledge of others, and with this should come empathy. Other researchers have identified that secure children at primary school age form friendships with ease, they are interested in learning, they have positive interactions with nursery/preschool teachers and their peers, and they are more resilient (see Chapter 12). Schore (2001) also notes that securely attached children are more able to deal with problematic situations which may cause stress or excitement because of the ability to self-modulate – in essence, because the primary carer has provided a secure base and a safe holding environment, the child has learned how to regulate emotions and how to soothe themselves by controlling emotional and physical responses. As a child grows, it develops the capacity to use learned experiences and observations to 'think about' situations, rather than 'act out' situations, and therefore develop appropriate responses. Without appropriate 'holding' by the carer, these responses will not be learned and will have to be experienced.

The qualities attributed to securely attached children have a positive impact on the self-image of the child. With insecure attachments, we have the opposite pattern and behavioural issues may manifest. As we stated in Chapter 1, at the heart of an insecure attachment lies anxiety, and it is this emotion that young children with insecure attachments have to deal with when entering new environments, like preschool and nursery. Any new experience like this can provoke anxiety in a child with the securest of attachment styles, but when compounded by existing anxiety due to non-response of the carer (avoidant), or unpredictability of reactions (anxious/ambivalent), or even violent reactions (disorganised), a child is sent into a heightened state of arousal which they will need to manage themselves without the capacity of self-modulation. This can often lead to an inability to deal internally with emotional strife, so behaviours become externalised and can manifest in violent and aggressive outbursts towards the carer or peers, non-compliance with preschool staff, inhibitions towards other children and adults, and can demand a lot of attention from support staff within educational environments. On a very basic level, insecurely attached children will often look unhappy in the presence of the primary carer and show very little interaction with them (Malekpour, 2007).

Self-image is also damaged within insecurely attached children and this can have a lifelong impact. By the time a child starts school, the signs of insecure attachments can manifest in different ways. Avoidant children can have difficulties asking their teacher for help and can appear very self-dependent. There is a fear of rejection, so it becomes easier for the child to avoid relationships with peers and teachers, and they can often lose themselves in the tasks at hand. With children who are anxious/ambivalent there is a preoccupation with trying to maintain the attention, and presence, of the primary carer and this can often result in absences from education as the child feigns illness for attention. While at school, there may also be 'attention-seeking behaviour' in order to gain the focus of the teacher, and hold their attention – with an anxious/ambivalent child, negative attention still results in a feeling of being noticed and being held in mind. At the extreme end, a disorganised child has a deep mistrust of relationships and will try to protect themselves at all cost. They believe that no one will understand them and do not like to be presented with challenges as this can invoke feelings of helplessness, shame and humiliation, so the slightest provocation can trigger reactions. The answer, for many, is to try to take control through power, and this power is often achieved through aggression towards their peers and teachers.

Clearly, these attachment styles will impact on peer relationships; if aggression is used to exert power, then bullying prevails, but, conversely, insecure attachments can also result in a vulnerability to peer pressure. This will compound anxiety further and impact on the internal working model as it constructs views of relationship-forming across different areas of Bronfenbrenner's socioecological system which can lead to long-lasting mental health issues, such as depression.

Case Study

Part 1

James came across as a quiet child. He kept himself to himself, walked to school by himself, played games on a mobile device at break times and walked home alone. He was teased at primary school because he often attended in unwashed clothes, and he often arrived at school without having had breakfast.

His teacher, Miss Baxter, became concerned about James's state of dress and about his general disengagement within the classroom. When Miss Baxter asked James questions in the classroom he would remain silent and stare blankly at the front of the room. He was assigned a classroom support assistant who tried to work with James on his reading and writing skills, and he was even sent for assessment to see if he might be dyslexic, but no concerns were noted other than that he was a little bit slower than his peers to develop his skills. They did note that he enjoyed art classes and was quite content to paint and draw when tasks were given out.

Using her knowledge of attachment styles, Miss Baxter thought that James might be displaying qualities which could be attributed to a child with an avoidant attachment style. She knew that, if this was the case, James would be guarded about forming relationships and might feel intimidated if she asked him questions directly, so she used his interest in painting and drawing as an opportunity to speak with him.

This interaction worked well as James was able to talk to Miss Baxter while not making direct eye contact. He was able to engage in a task which he felt he was good at and could use some of his drawings to express what was going on in his life. Many of his pictures were underpinned by his feelings of isolation and loneliness and he explained that both of his parents were out at work most of the time so he was not seeing much of them at home.

Discussion points:

- What course of action would you recommend Miss Baxter takes next?
- Can the school set up anything to help address avoidant attachment?
- How could you, as a social worker, work with the parents to address issues?

ADOLESCENCE

Adolescence has been described as 'the second major "window" of opportunity and risk in development, next only in significance to early childhood development'

(Moretti and Peled, 2004: 551). It is a time of transition, but also of physical, emotional and cognitive development that brings together a multitude of changes at the same time. The production of dopamine will fluctuate during adolescence, only levelling out to stable levels seen in mature adults at about 16 years of age; strategic thinking and abstract thought develops as the prefrontal cortex matures and the adolescent should move from having very concrete, set ideas, to appreciating that there are other perspectives; and puberty will result in hormones influencing behaviour (Moretti and Peled, 2004; Allen and Land, 1999).

Parkes et al. (2006) believe that this is a period where the adolescent will relinquish parental attachment and seek attachments with others. They believe that this stems from feelings experienced by the developing adolescent in which they view their carers as being flawed as human beings. This is not as negative as it sounds because the adolescent now becomes aware that the secure base they have relied on may not always be there, and their carer will not always be able to provide it due to frailty, illness or issues that are out of their control (think about issues that might arise in Bronfenbrenner's socioecological model within the exosystem and macrosystem). If the attachment relationship has been secure, then the adolescent should have built up a sense of autonomy and self-confidence, giving them the ability to form new relationships, using their internal working models to assist the direction of relationship formation, and be able to view their carer as someone they love, someone they feel connected to, and someone they will be honour-bound to link to emotionally, but will no longer be reliant on for security.

However, it is not as simple as the carer taking a step back from the relationship and letting the fledgling adolescent leave the nest – a continuing secure attachment with the caregiver, as well as an emotional connection, are vital to the successful transition from adolescent into adulthood (Ryan and Lynch, 1989). Within secure relationships, conflict and argument is normal. In early adolescence, an individual is still trying to deal with conflicting thoughts and feelings about themselves and their relationships, but as prefrontal cortex maturation leads to more abstract thought, problem-solving skills improve. However, during this process, new ideas and boundaries will be tried and tested, bringing the potential clash with the authority of the carer. Within secure relationships, it should be possible to deal with these arising issues through goal-corrected behaviour (Bowlby, 1979, 2008). This entails adjusting behaviour to achieve the familiar equilibrium of the attachment relationship between carer and adolescent; therefore, in a secure relationship, arguments and transgressions will influence future actions so that equilibrium can be achieved again. An adolescent may decide to push the boundaries of curfews little by little and not see any serious consequence in the attachment dyad, but if they are caught and charged for vandalism or underage alcohol use, this may impact on immediate future behaviour so that feelings familiar with the secure relationship can be achieved again, before testing boundaries again.

Allen and Land (1999) believe that the quality of attachment directly impacts on the adolescent's need to attain autonomy, while at the same time maintaining the attachment style with the caregiver in order to re-negotiate the adult–adolescent relationship. With avoidant adolescents, this can present a challenge as these individuals are naturally withdrawn from the adult (or carer) relationship in the first place, so the re-negotiation process can take longer than those with a secure or anxious/ambivalent style. It is also important to note that carers of avoidant adolescents will also be less responsive to the needs of the individual – which will equally hamper the re-negotiation process. Conversely, the anxious/ambivalent adolescent risks becoming entrenched in running battles with the carer as the individual has an opportunity to use the argument to gain recognition and focus from the carer. Just like the anxious/ambivalent school child, even negative attention validates existence, and an argument can be a good way of ensuring that you have the carer's full attention. Behaviours in the adolescent may also be directed to gaining this attention from the main attachment figure, and externalising emotions is common. Rosenstein and Horowitz (in Allen and Land, 1999) suggest that adolescents with an avoidant attachment style are more likely to externalise behaviours which might result in antisocial behaviour and substance use, whereas those with an anxious/ambivalent attachment style were more likely to internalise behaviours which risks mental health issues like depression. Adolescents with a disorganised attachment style will continue to seek to control situations and relationships whenever possible in order to feel safe. There is also the risk that this control will be violent and, if violence and aggression are prevalent in the household, the adolescent may simply repeat behaviour from within the household – the fear and anxiety that they have always experienced will not go away, so there seems little point in employing strategies to foster positive relationships with adults.

Case Study

Part 2

James is now 16 and things at home have not improved. His father left home when he was 10 and now lives 250 miles away with his new wife and their 3-year-old daughter. James's Mum has been diagnosed with bipolar disorder and goes through periods where she is unable to work. James provides a lot of care for his mum when her mental health fluctuates. Because of this, his attendance at school is sporadic. He does not spend time with peers when he is at school and will usually go to the library to use the computers during break time and lunchtime and teachers describe him as 'a bit of a loner'.

James heard some of his peers talking about drugs and, in an effort to join their clique, he offered to supply them with some 'pills'. James stole some of his mother's medication and gave them to this new group of friends. One of them got caught by their parents in possession of the medication and this was reported to the school and the police. James was arrested for supplying drugs and became the subject of an adult protection investigation as police felt his mother was vulnerable and 'at risk'. When James returned to school, none of his new 'friends' paid him any attention. He tried to approach them but they told him to 'f**k off' so James attacked three of them. One of them, Helen, was injured so badly that she needed stitches to her face. James was arrested again.

   Discussion points:

- James is still demonstrating an avoidant attachment style – which factors from the case study suggests this pattern?
- If he continues on this path, what risks does he face/present?
- Given that avoidant attachment requires emotions to be suppressed, how do you think he might use substances to help with this?
- If James were referred to you as a social worker, what would you do next?

Taking these viewpoints into consideration, we are looking at a situation where there is reduced dependency in the relationship between the adolescent and the carer, rather than a loss of attachment:

- A securely attached adolescent should be able to transition in a straightforward manner but will test the boundaries, with the ability to use goal-corrected behaviours to find equilibrium in the relationship.
- An anxious/ambivalent attached adolescent may become embroiled in arguments with the main carers. This stems from a feeling of being out of control and requiring guidance, but at the same time being cautious about exposing need and facing rejection. There is also a risk of internalising emotions to the point of depression or other mental health issues.
- An avoidant attached adolescent will try to cope on their own, and an avoidant carer will let them. There is very little emotional connection between the two and externalised behaviours, such as aggression, may be used to express emotion.
- A disorganised attachment style is as unpredictable as in childhood. Triggers are deeply personal to the adolescent, but control must be achieved in order to protect themselves.

By adolescence, attachment styles become fairly set in stone and can predict the types of peer relationships, and romantic relationships, that may be entered into. While childhood peer relationships are a vital component for social learning when growing up, attachment does not tend to play a major role in these relationships and Ainsworth (1989) states that peer relationship attachment only begins to come into play in late adolescence when friendships serve the deeper functions of having a safe haven and a secure base within the relationship so an individual is free to explore, but also comforted when they return to the relationship. In this respect, the peer relationship attachment formed in late adolescence can aid the transition for the individual while they try to attain autonomy from the carer. Allen and Land (1999) suggest that this transitional period can be a clumsy one for most adolescents and can leave them vulnerable to peer group pressure as they 'aim to please' the new group of friends for acceptance; in the same way an infant tries to please the main attachment figure to enhance feelings of safety.

Howe and Campling (1995) highlight the dangers for those with insecure attachments in transferring anxieties from the carer relationships to the new peer relationships. They believe that anxious/ambivalent adolescents, in their need to feel close, can demand a lot of attention from their peers and they can try to ingratiate themselves in the new relationships by promising things to the group members. This can become overbearing for other members of the group. The anxious/ambivalent adolescent might also seek an exclusive relationship with popular group members who may not be forthcoming, and they constantly seek reassurance from the relationships that they are 'liked' and 'welcome'. This stems from their experience of relationships in which they could never rely on the carer to consistently meet their needs.

Similarly, avoidant adolescents have learned that relationships are hard work and that demanding behaviour is often the key to getting attention. Often, they have had no experience of gaining intimacy and recognition from relationships and, as previously explained, can manifest frustrations externally in aggressive manners, which will potentially lead to further isolation. Therefore, the avoidant adolescent becomes emotionally neutral and 'switches off' their emotions. This means that emotional responses are only elicited after a high degree of stimulation.

Critical Thinking

Take some time to consider your transition from adolescence into early adulthood.

- Were you brought into conflict with your carers?
- How did you deal with arguments/disagreements?
- How would you describe your attachment style based on your behaviour?
- How are your relationships with your peers now? Can you see similar patterns between the relationship you had with your carers and the relationship you have with your closest friends?

ROMANTIC ATTACHMENTS

Parkes et al. (2006) suggest three different factors in the selection of a lifelong partner, an adult attachment figure – or in plain English, a romantic partner:

1. The best-looking people will select equally good-looking people to pair off with, and then the next attractive will pair off with someone equally as attractive, right down to the ugliest pairing off with the ugliest – a Darwinian approach to dating which relies on image alone.

2. People are attracted to each other based on shared commonalities such as values, interests, religion, social background and upbringing. This is a very sociological perspective and would sit well on the outer fringes of Bronfenbrenner's socioecological model.

3. People are attracted to each other based on mutual benefits. If one person has a need to be complimented and another person has a need to be complimentary, then this suggests that they would be good for each other. Equally, if someone needs to be nurtured and someone else needs to be nurturing, then again, they could be suitably matched. This perspective suggests that if there is unmet need and someone else is prepared to meet this need, then a suitable match could be possible.

In truth, these are very simplistic approaches, but elements of all three of these perspectives may well be present in why we choose the partners we do. If we look at the third perspective and relate this to what we have learned so far about attachment styles we can deduce the following:

In a secure attachment, an individual has a high sense of trust in themselves, and a high sense of trust in others. They should be able to transition from adolescence into adulthood with a good sense of autonomy and should enter adult relationships that are interdependent on one another.

In an anxious/ambivalent attachment, an individual has a low sense of trust in themselves and a high sense of trust in others. The transition into adulthood will be fraught with arguments and they will enter adult relationships with a desire to know that they are loved, and will want to be reminded repeatedly. This can result in clingy behaviour and there will be a desire to have a dependable, strong partner. They may try to please in order to be accepted.

In an avoidant attachment style, an individual has learned that it can be risky to trust others, but they will have a high sense of trust in themselves. The transition into adulthood can be slow as there is very little emotional connection with the carer through the process, and adult relationships are either avoided or only entered into if the individual has a high degree of control, therefore a weak partner might be appealing.

It is not uncommon to see successful relationships comprised of one individual who has an anxious/ambivalent style with another who is avoidant in style. Remember, in Chapter 1, we stated that these are not 'bad' styles – they are coping strategies to help with relationships, and these two styles might be very compatible – both individuals get something from the relationship.

An individual with a disorganised attachment style will exit adolescence with a low sense of trust in themselves, and a low sense of trust in others. They can feel helpless in relationships, and that might appeal to someone with an avoidant style who wants a weak partner, or someone with an anxious/ambivalent style who wants to feel needed, but disorganised attachments are inconsistent and this can result in a volatile relationship.

Once an individual reaches adulthood, attachment styles also change name. The anxious/ambivalent, avoidant and disorganised styles are used with children and young adolescents, but when attachment becomes 'adult attachment' we refer to the following:

- A secure attachment remains the same.
- An anxious/ambivalent attachment style becomes known as 'preoccupied'.
- An avoidant attachment style becomes known as 'dismissive'.
- A disorganised attachment style becomes known as 'fearful-avoidant'.

These adult attachment styles will be explored in more detail in Chapter 7.

IMPLICATIONS FOR SOCIAL WORK

Of course, adult relationships are not reliant solely on psychoanalytic theories to flourish – psychological, sociological and biological forces all come into play, but attachment theory should not be ignored when considering why people are in the relationships they are in. For social workers, the important things to consider when working with young people and adolescents are:

- There are many factors of influence that impact on the behaviour of individuals, as demonstrated by Bronfenbrenner's model, but attachment theory helps us understand how relationships are formed, and why certain behaviours might manifest because of an individual's experience of previous relationships.
- The relationship between the carer and adolescent should be supportive, and, during transition into adulthood, there should be an understanding that it is not 'attachment' that is ending, it is 'dependency'.
- Behaviours throughout childhood and adolescence may well be explained by coping strategies that an individual has adopted to help them cope with relationships – sometimes clingy/needy behaviour or aggressive behaviour can be directly linked to anxious/ambivalent or avoidant attachment styles.

- Interventions to address attachment issues need to consider what is lacking from existing relationships and work towards repairing these deficiencies – examples might include trust, communication, boundaries or safety.
- The relationship offered by the social worker should be underpinned with the knowledge about the importance of a therapeutic alliance – this can underpin a relationship that exhibits 'earned secure' qualities so that the individual learns what a secure attachment is. This should also underpin any work with foster carers so that the importance of working towards a secure attachment is clear, no matter what the timescale is for intervention.

5 ERIKSON – FROM IDENTITY TO INTIMACY

Here, Erikson (1965) considers the teenage years and the years of young adulthood.

By the end of the chapter the reader should:

- Understand the importance of adolescence in the development of personality
- Understand how the concept of personal identity is complex
- Be aware that outward behaviour does not always reflect inner feelings
- Become clearer about the importance of relationships in human behaviour
- Have an appreciation of the concept of a life cycle as babies are born to adolescents and adults

---

Before we look at the nature of the life crises which form Erikson's fifth and sixth stages in more detail, it is worth making some specific points. There is some broad consensus in psychosocial theories that the pre-adult stage involves transition from the status of young, dependent child to becoming an adult with all the expectations and responsibilities implied by adulthood. While Erikson has been criticised for taking a Eurocentric approach in formulating his life crisis framework (Robinson, 1995), he has nonetheless identified a process which can apply to all cultural and ethnic groupings. Every culture has a set of expectations of what it means to be adult and a transitional stage which may also be termed a rite of passage. The specific processes and societal pressures will vary from culture to culture, but the broad life crisis is that of trying to establish a comfortable sense of identity, of who we are and what we value. The question of how fully we are able to do this as we reach adulthood is likely to affect our behaviour as adults, whatever our cultural base.

STAGE 5: IDENTITY VERSUS ROLE CONFUSION

There is also the difficult question of when these two stages begin and end; when does an adolescent become an adult? We stop being a teenager at the age of 20: does that make us an adult? Once again, we have to caution you about applying the age of an individual too rigidly to an Erikson stage, because the formation of a sense of identity is subject to a large number of variable factors.

Critical Thinking

Consider the factors which may impact on identity formation. These include:

- One's own individual, uniquely formed emotional development within the family setting
- The availability of role models
- The environment, culture and subcultures in which we have been raised
- Our successes or lack of success in activities
- Our involvement in networks of friends
- Employment opportunities
- Further or higher education opportunities
- Sexual activity
- Early parenthood

These are examples, but now that you have begun to identify them, think of others which combine to reveal a complex part of our emotional development.

The essential point which Erikson makes is that there is a difference in attitude and expectation between the two stages. The stage of 'identity versus role confusion' is very much about self: the word 'I' is the key, as in Who am *I*? What do *I* believe in? Who am *I* attracted to? What am *I* going to do with my life? and so on. This stage is, by its very nature, a stage of self-absorption, and to be selfish or self-centred is actually emotionally appropriate. The stage of intimacy versus isolation is, in contrast, about *us*, about being in adult relationships where people share aspects of themselves, and about being in adult–child relationships where the adult puts his or her own needs in a secondary position to a child's needs.

Erikson's Stage 5, 'identity versus role confusion', begins with the onset of puberty, the increasingly active hormonal activity in the body and the impact of societal expectations of a young person who is no longer a child, but not yet an adult. Erikson (1965: 235) suggests that young people 'faced with this physiological revolution within them, and with tangible adult tasks ahead of them are now primarily concerned with what they appear to be in the eyes of others as compared with what they feel they are'. To Erikson, the ideal of this stage is that young people develop as comfortable a sense of who they are as possible, and that the identity they work towards is their own doing, rather than one forced on them by others. This is an important point, because, if one is reasonably comfortable with one's sense of self, one is likely to move into more adult relationships with fewer emotional obstacles to a mature, sharing approach to relationships.

In the context of Erikson's overall framework of life crisis theory, this stage is possibly the most complex of all. Because of the significance and pace of the changes and events in the young person's life during these teenage years, Erikson argues that the earlier life crises are revisited in the quest to establish a sense of identity. To put it another way, any unresolved, uncomfortable or uncertain aspects from past experience can be acted out in adolescent behaviour in an unconscious attempt to achieve a more comfortable balance. The more positive the earlier balances, the less need there may be for acting out more childish needs, but it is difficult to imagine how anyone can go through adolescence without some degree of challenging behaviour unless they are compulsively following their parents'/carers' wishes or equally compulsively trying to please their parents/carers at all times.

Such an interpretation indicates that the life crisis of identity versus role confusion can affect everyone, regardless of social status, class or economic position. While Davis (2007: 30) notes that 'the majority of those who have contact with social workers come from the ranks of those who have least', we should also consider that those who may have most are not necessarily going to have a comfortable balance of identity. Deresiewicz (2014) notes how some members of the social elite in the USA who have been driven and steered by ambitious parents, led to believe that they are better than others and who absorb the elitist identity, are not entirely at ease with their identity or the process that they have been put through and lack the skills required for emotionally balanced adulthood. When assessing the impact of this stage on individuals, we have to avoid assumptions that only those from deprived backgrounds are likely to struggle and recognise that anyone who feels uncomfortable with the process of identity formation may experience consequential behavioural difficulty.

There is a lot of evidence from practice that young people are potentially deeply affected by the outcomes of earlier life crisis stages and have a need for therapeutic intervention (Millar, 2014). If the balance of basic mistrust from the first stage was strong, behaviour in adolescence might reflect a desire to test out others to see how reliable they might be. If the inner mistrust has not so far been offset by a more positive relationship with any significant other person, the testing behaviour is underpinned by a deep, unconscious belief that people are unreliable and so the positive response that you, the worker, make is treated with hostility. It can be very difficult for a worker to see through the outward veneer of an apparently aggressive adolescent to the vulnerable infant who may be desperately trying to trust others.

The adolescent who has had a poor sense of autonomy and a stronger balance of shame and/or doubt may be driven by an unconscious need to feel better about self by having some power or control over others, by creating a literal or metaphorical mess to upset adults or by pushing against the boundaries of acceptable behaviour. The example of pushing the boundaries may be more related to someone who, as a toddler, experienced more neglect and absence of controls on behaviour, but the behaviour of the other examples could stem from either too rigid a boundary-setting by carers or by an absence of boundary-setting. School bullies may, despite their adolescent swagger, be large toddlers who are angry and frustrated because of their experiences years ago. We do not, however, advocate that workers offer this assessment to a bullying adolescent! The challenge facing workers will be to help an adolescent feel a reasonable sense of self-esteem in the face of adolescent behaviour which is driven superficially by antisocial attitudes.

The earlier stage of initiative versus guilt, which formed the basis of relationship formation, confidence in social interactions and the beginnings of sexual identity, now also has a potentially major impact on young people who are actually wrestling with the emotions of identity formation. Now is the time to try to resolve unmet or frustrated emotions from the oedipal issues of the earlier stage: for example, the child who had a problem receiving affection from a desired carer may, as an adolescent, be driven to seek the unmet satisfaction in their relationships with peers or other adults. The child who came through the earlier stage with a greater balance of guilt arising from their unsuccessful attempts to engage in play or put-downs from others around them may lack confidence in their ability to deal with the life changes of adolescence and may over-identify with others. This may range from joining socially accepted youth groups to less accepted gang or cult groups.

Studies of causal factors of depression and suicidal feelings in adolescence have considered the importance of low self-esteem and negative sense of self which may increase vulnerability. Creemers (2014) identifies implicit low self-esteem, which links to the Erikson framework, as the result of negative early life experiences and poor experience of nurturing which has become part of one's inner self. He also identifies explicit self-esteem in adolescence, which is a consequence of more recent events and experiences, and which is less deep-rooted than implicit self-esteem. While there are, however, a variety of research conclusions in this field, he does suggest that the balance of implicit versus explicit self-esteem may be a significant factor in leading to adolescent depression, and that the internalising of feelings, particularly in relation to self, most probably is significant.

Erikson particularly refers to the need for adolescents to battle against well-intentioned adults in order to establish their own identity. It would be all too easy to extract from this that all adolescents should make life difficult for the significant adults in their life as a means to developing maturity, but we must be cautious in making such interpretations. The adolescent who sails through the teenage years without the need to engage in arguments with parents may genuinely feel comfortable with their identity. The adolescent who is constantly at odds with their parents may have a depth of frustration which remains unresolved throughout the teenage years and into adulthood. In the middle ground, those adolescents who experience the highs and lows of attraction and rejection in their attitudes towards their parents may indeed come through into adulthood with a more secure sense of identity, because they invested more emotional energy in the process and thus have fewer repressed feelings.

Crucially, at the stage of identity versus role confusion the adolescent is also dealing with sexual identity. How he or she develops sexual awareness depends on a number of factors from family attitudes and behaviours to cultural and societal norms and attitudes. Erikson's focus is, to remind you, psychosocial, and his primary concern is that people are able to relate to others in a positive and nurturing way. Everything is oriented towards the importance of successful reproduction: children must have their emotional needs met in order to move through childhood and adolescence in a reasonably balanced way in order to become adults who can provide for their children's needs and then move into adulthood and old age with a reasonable balance of satisfaction while their children move through their life cycle. Sexual identity in adolescence is all about trying to establish to whom we are attracted, trying to understand the mechanics and potential enjoyment of sex and, hopefully, developing a comfortable sexual self-identity.

Critical Thinking

What were your experiences of sex education and sexual activity as an adolescent? How did these experiences impact on your awareness of yourself as a whole person and how did they prepare you for your subsequent experience as an adult?

The critical difference between adolescent behaviour and adult behaviour, within Erikson's framework, is the difference between self-centredness and sharing. Adolescent sexual behaviour is self-centred, with the emphasis on one's own performance and one's own enjoyment. Sexual behaviour in adulthood needs to be mutual, according to Erikson, because the outcome of sexual behaviour produces children, and children, as we have seen, need adult carers to look after their needs. The adolescent personality is more concerned with his or her own needs and, therefore, according to Erikson's theory, less prepared for the demands of parenthood.

Identity can be further complicated by structural issues, such as economic and political factors, and an understanding of an individual's experience of adolescence must take this into account. Austerity measures which restrict the availability of work and money impact on an individual's employment identity as jobs become scarce. Political scapegoating of religious or ethnic groups may impact adversely on an individual's feelings of comfort with their cultural identity and belief systems. Sexual harassment or abhorrence of those who do not conform to a heterosexual identity from society or family sources can impact on the establishment of a comfortable sense of self. Even the individual who has come through the earlier stages with a positive balance of outcomes faces challenges in establishing a sense of identity, and it is possible to suggest that no one moves into adulthood with their identity fully formed. All one can hope for is a reasonably strong sense of self and a willingness to continue developing and maturing at an emotional level.

Critical Thinking

Note that we use words such as 'may' or 'can' rather than 'are' or 'must' when applying these theories. Because an individual's experiences are likely to be complex, and are certainly unique, it is important to proceed with caution when putting the jigsaw of a life together.

From what we have described above, you should by now question whether this adolescent stage in Erikson's life crisis framework applies only to the teenage years. While the extremes of adolescent behaviour may be most obvious during the teenage years, this does not imply that, on reaching 20, one suddenly becomes an adult. If we take a structural look at life again, we see those who go straight from school to higher education taking on the label 'student', which permits the continuation of self-centred behaviour. Those who leave school at 16 and go to employment or unemployment may be seen in an adult role capacity, and both groups may feel pressure to fulfil the role expectations. We cannot put a definite age range to this stage, and, indeed, for some adults the dominance of role confusion may impact on their adult life to the extent that their progress through subsequent stages is affected by a continuation of adolescent behaviour and attitudes.

Erikson (1959) himself went on to acknowledge that identity formation overlaps with the next stage of young adulthood: 'intimacy versus isolation'. He argued that the formation of identity was not complete until two adults formed a relationship in which their 'ego identity is complementary in some essential point and can be fused in marriage without the creation either of a discontinuity of tradition, or of an incestuous sameness – both of which are apt to prejudice the offspring's ego development' (Erikson, 1959: 40).

APPLICATION TO PRACTICE

Case Study 1

Terry is 15 and is a looked-after young person in a group home. He has been out of control, engaging in acts of vandalism, including setting fire to derelict properties, car theft and wilful damage to cars, alcohol abuse and suspected drug misuse. His father was a sergeant in the army when Terry was born and his mother, an army wife, was treated for post-natal depression. From his babyhood, Terry was substantially brought up in day-care facilities: his mother provided the most basic of physical care, his father expected him to do what he was told, as a baby, as a toddler and as a young child. Until he was about 9, Terry was a passive, rather withdrawn child who presented no behavioural problems at school, except that he was slow to learn and limited in communication. He was very much a follower and never instigated or suggested activities.

He began to hang around with a mixed group of young people who were looked down upon by the majority in the area because of their insolent, threatening behaviour to others. Terry's father was now out of the army, and with Terry's mother, was running a public house as a new business venture. As Terry's behaviour became more and more antisocial, the police became more involved with the family and Terry's parents became more and more frustrated with him. They attempted to restrict him, but their anger towards him made Terry more aggressive towards them. By the time Terry was 14, the situation within the family had broken down, both parents rejecting Terry to the point that he was received into the care of the local authority.

You, the reader, are now in the position of a member of the care staff in the group home. In order to try to understand Terry's behaviour and attitude, you can apply Erikson's framework in your assessment. He is currently going through the emotional life crisis of 'identity versus role confusion'. From the earlier life crisis stages, there are question marks about his capacity to trust, because it appears that his experiences as a baby may have been inconsistent; there are question marks about his autonomy, because it would appear that his father created a very controlling environment; there are question marks about his initiative, because relationships with his parents still seem to be based on their assumptions that he conform to their expectations and there is little evidence of a close attachment to either; and there are question marks about his industry because of low achievement and a low profile at primary school. These question marks should be considered in relation to Terry's behaviour in order to identify deep-rooted origins, and from his current behaviour there are significant connections.

Terry's potential balance of basic mistrust is making it difficult for him to relate to you or your colleagues, not to mention the primary adults in his life, his parents. His shame and doubt in himself is possibly driving his compulsiveness to vandalise and to take things, while his guilt leads him to alcohol and drugs because of his inability to relate to other people in a way that satisfies his emotional needs. His behaviour may be heavily influenced by these unconscious influences: they may be a major factor in shaping his behaviour now, but, crucially, he is not aware of this and is not making conscious connections with past events. Within the group care home, Terry's behaviour is continuously challenging: he can be aggressive towards other residents, he frequently tries to bring alcohol into the home and he is often brought home by the police following a disturbance in town.

Terry's sense of self, his identity, is weak, but his ongoing behaviour is causing problems for others, too. Intervention with Terry will undoubtedly require some behavioural controls and modification, but if Terry is, as we assess, deeply affected by earlier life experiences, he will struggle to accept any attempts to engage in a rational approach to modifying behaviour because he lacks the deeper emotional balance in his life which might help him do so. Terry really needs to *feel* the impact of a relationship, to experience someone as dependable and understanding, someone who will not reject him even when he is angry, aggressive and insulting towards them. For more detailed discussion of working within the life space in group care, read Millar (2014).

Critical Thinking

What if Terry was actually Tariq, born in this country to parents originally from Pakistan? Or what if Terry lived in an area which was predominantly home to people from Afro-Asian cultures? The problems in establishing a good balance of identity may be exacerbated if one's ethnic and cultural identity are further weakened by the absence of role models in everyday life.

Consider the implications of meeting the holistic needs of a young person in this situation.

STAGE 6: INTIMACY VERSUS ISOLATION

We move on now to Erikson's Stage 6, 'young adulthood', which he identified as 'intimacy versus isolation'. Here, in particular, we have to remember that Erikson first published his life crisis framework in 1951, and some of his theory reflects outdated societal attitudes. However, much of it has a clear message about relationships in adulthood which we shall now consider. For Erikson (1965), the psychological goal of young adulthood is the capacity to fuse our identities with others, to commit to a relationship and to remain in a relationship despite the ups and downs, 'even though they may call for significant sacrifices and compromises' (1965: 237).

Again, trying to give an exact age range for this stage is very difficult. Broadly, it encompasses the childbearing years, which can range from the teens to the forties, depending on individual circumstances. Emotionally, it is a point where we are actively engaged in all aspects of life with a sense of possibility and an awareness of life stretching out ahead of us.

According to Erikson (1965: 239), young adulthood seeks to achieve a 'Utopia of genitality' which 'should include:

1. Mutuality of orgasm
2. With a loved partner
3. Of the other sex
4. With whom one is able and willing to share a mutual trust
5. And with whom one is able to regulate the cycles of (a) work, (b) procreation, (c) recreation
6. So as to secure to the offspring, too, all the stages of a satisfactory development.'

This raises several issues which we need to consider. Bearing in mind that Erikson called this a 'utopia', suggesting that it is perfection, we have to question what exactly is good enough. Erikson himself indicated that while achieving mutual sexual orgasm was a desired outcome and is achievable, the ability to cope maturely with any frustration is an indication of adulthood and intimacy, different from the feelings one has as an adolescent. However, he is clearly, as a psychoanalytic thinker, putting good physical and emotional sexual relationships at a priority level for young adult relationships. His second level, the loved partner, implies the mutually affectionate relationship between adults, which is relatively unproblematic. However, the third level is definitely problematic, with its reference to heterosexuality as part of the utopia, and, although there remain individual and structural pockets of homophobia, we can argue now that heterosexuality and homosexuality/lesbianism are broadly accepted as the basis for long-term partnerships. The three remaining levels are probably more acceptable as they appear to describe a relationship based on healthy attachment behaviour, sound communication and role-sharing for the benefit of children born into that relationship.

A positive balance of intimacy, according to Erikson's framework, results in the ability to form a close mutual relationship with another adult which provides a structure for the successful nurturing of children. While Erikson's framework reflected an emphasis on heterosexual relationships, marriage and the nuclear family, consistent with the dominant values of the 1950s, we must consider its relevance to current patterns of behaviour. Marriage as an institution is statistically in decline, while co-habitation childbearing is more common than in the 1950s. In effect, marriage is one of several patterns of family life which has become normalised.

Helms (2013) suggests that the current pattern of marriage co-existing with other patterns of relationship and childbearing is without precedent, but notes that, given the large amount of scholarly interest, 'marriage continues to matter' (2013: 233).

Despite the changing values of society between the 1950s and present day, we can extract the essence of Erikson's message for current practice. That, in summary, would argue that a positive balance of intimacy in young adulthood equates to a mutual adult-to-adult relationship which provides shared sexual and emotional satisfaction in a context where the adults can reasonably work out their roles and meet the needs of any children in their care. Since the first publication of Erikson's framework, many other researchers have attempted to understand the factors which promote or inhibit positive adult relationships. Huston (2000) identified a three-level model of marriage which considered: the environment created by society's expectations; the traits of the individual spouse, including psychosocial, physical and personality, and interpersonal behaviour within the relationship. Donellan et al. (2004) identified neuroticism, that is, feelings such as anxiety, jealousy and moodiness, as well as the perceived agreeableness of the partner as factors which determine the success or otherwise of a relationship. While there are many conflicting research findings, there does seem to be a broad consensus in identifying personality as a key factor.

One can argue that adults who enjoy mutually satisfying sexual relationships are less likely to have an obsessive preoccupation with sex and are less likely to engage in displacement sexual activity (Gibson, 2007). One can also argue that there is a healthy hierarchy of attachment relationships in adulthood (Hazan and Zeifman, 1994), whereby adults may be less dependent on a primary attachment to one person. Close friendships, without a sexual component, may be realistically sufficiently satisfying to many adults, and Erikson's ideal of intimacy is perhaps best directed at those adults who do become parents by having children or becoming substitute carers. To suggest that adults who are childless or celibate are more likely to experience the negative balance of isolation is far too sweeping because of the hierarchy of friendships and attachments which may exist, and we need to be very careful in recognising what exactly the negative balance of isolation actually implies.

In a survey of 1052 adults in the United Kingdom conducted in 2014 (*The Observer*, 2014) 61 per cent thought that it is possible to be in a happy marriage or relationship without sex. Of these, women were more likely than men to believe that the relationship could be happy without sex. Interestingly, given Erikson's identification of mutuality as a key component of adult relationships, the survey identified trust as by far the most important factor in contributing to a successful marriage or relationship. However, the same survey revealed that over 50 per cent have accessed pornography on the Internet at some point, which may suggest that the absence of physical sexual relationships may require a displacement of sexual activity to other forms of sexual satisfaction.

Erikson identifies isolation as the inability to establish intimate relationships, but this does not necessarily apply only to those without one steady partner and without dependent children. It is possible to form a sexual relationship with another adult, to have children with that adult, to live together, and yet still to feel a sense of isolation at an emotional level (this will be discussed more fully in Chapter 6). It is possible to live in a group care setting, surrounded by people, and yet still to feel isolated. The ability to establish intimate relationships is more likely if one has had a reasonably positive balance of basic trust, autonomy, initiative, industry and identity from the previous stages, but this set of broadly positive earlier experiences need not routinely lead to marriage and parenthood. There can be intimacy between adults without the formal structure of marriage and without the daily care of children. By the same token, it should be possible to have no sexual relationship and no children, and yet still feel a sense of closeness to other people which requires trust and mutuality, and which can be described as intimacy.

There will be people who find it difficult or impossible to achieve intimacy with others, and many will be physically alone or unable to sustain peer friendships or engage in short-term relationships, or be resentful, frustrated or saddened by childlessness. Some of them may encounter problems because of that, problems of depression or behaviour which may bring them into contact with health or social services. Others may find a way of adjusting to the situation, which, although not bringing absolute happiness, brings a degree of acceptance. Once again, we stress the importance of gaining an understanding of the individual in making any assessment and the potential danger of applying Erikson's framework in a generalised, mechanistic way.

Critical Thinking

Personal and professional values

Consider how our personal values and professional values impact on our assessment of behaviour in relation to adult relationships and family development. Banks (2006) suggested that, in order to uphold professional values in practice, social workers should demonstrate respect for individuals' rights to self-determination, and promote these. They should also promote the welfare or well-being of service users and principles of equality. How do your personal values fit with the practice expectations implied by the professional values? What, for example, do you regard as acceptable sexual practice in society? What are your values with respect to marriage? Are children best looked after by two heterosexual carers? Can one carer or two same sex carers be as effective?

To what extent do you need to compromise your personal values in order to work within professional value expectations?

If we consider the factors which bring adults into contact with social workers or other care professionals, we can identify some that are not primarily based on quality of relationship. For example, extremes of poverty or deprivation may provoke theft as a means of basic survival, or extreme threat to safety may provoke aggressive reactions. However, Erikson's framework asks us to accept that the stronger or more comfortable one's sense of self (identity), the more able we are to form mutually satisfying relationships (intimacy) which help us cope with the demands of being an adult.

Case Study 2

It might be helpful to consider the case of Shirley, James and Michael, who were discussed in Chapter 3. We considered how their situation might be assessed by applying object relations theory, and, to demonstrate how the theories overlap and provide a slightly different focus to an assessment, we shall apply Erikson's framework now.

We begin with 'mutuality of orgasm', and this is a potentially difficult area of assessment. Our comfort or discomfort in discussing sex with others will vary, as will the relevance of the information obtained, and if a question is not pertinent, it is impertinent. Shirley and James were engaged in an active sexual relationship which was important to both of them, and which was, in actuality, probably the most important aspect of their relationship for each of them. So far, therefore, you might be inclined to assess that as a positive if you apply Erikson's approach in a rigid, mechanistic way. If we do not apply the next levels 'with a loved partner' and 'mutual trust', we are missing the whole point of Erikson's framework. While mutuality of orgasm may be the icing on the cake, as it were, the mutuality of loving, which requires shared awareness of each other, has to be included in the concept of a positive balance.

In this respect, Shirley and James were both obsessed with sexual satisfaction as a basic need for their individual sakes and were not seeking to enjoy a genuinely mutual sense of satisfaction. Their shared sense of trust was not exactly strong, because both felt in addition that they would only keep the other if they were sexually obliging or sexually competent. While you might argue that this implies some attempt to satisfy the other, and therefore could be describing a mutual relationship, the feelings are actually tied up with their own sense of trying to be competent, of feelings of inadequacy and of their struggle to achieve a sense of identity.

Again, you might also argue that they appear to have worked out the questions of work, procreation and recreation, because James is content to work while Shirley remains at home with her baby. However, the underlying question would be to what extent has this been satisfactorily agreed between the two adults, and to what extent does the arrangement suit their individual needs, both consciously and unconsciously. Does it, for example, suit James that Shirley takes the dominant role with Michael, and does it suit Shirley that she feels she has a husband who works to provide for her? In applying Erikson's framework, we must carefully examine the behaviour we are assessing to ensure that we are relating to the appropriate life crisis, and in the case of Shirley and James, it does appear that their behaviour suggests that they are still more engaged with the crisis of 'identity versus role confusion', while trying also to address the crisis of 'intimacy versus isolation'. The problem may possibly become one of isolation, because, although they are living together as a family unit, each member in his or her own way is feeling emotionally isolated.

The last of Erikson's levels in the utopia of genitality referred to the adults' capacity to meet the needs of children and secure their development. If we had any lingering doubts about how well James and Shirley are coping, we have some crucial evidence to support the assessment that they are really struggling to relate as mature adults and be mature parents from their care of Michael. Clearly, they are not tuned into his needs and are not securing his development.

In the same way that our adolescent case study highlighted the limitations of a behavioural intervention, Shirley and James's parenting may be improved by guidance, advice and modelling, but if they remain stuck in adolescent issues while trying to behave as adults, it is very possible that they will find it very hard to respond. They, too, may require some relationship-based approach, and for a more detailed discussion of this, we refer you to Phung (2014).

OUTCOMES OF ERIKSON'S STAGES 5 AND 6

Positive balance of identity: confidence in engaging with others: has opportunity to get things wrong: begins to understand the power and positivity of friendships: has opportunity to experiment with behaviours and beliefs: has clear plans for adult life: has safety net of genuinely nurturing carers.

Negative balance of role confusion: either obliged to conform or feels ongoing need to react against controls: superficial friendships: dependency on non-humans, e.g. substances: over-controlling or insensitive carers: no clear sense of what to do in the future.

Positive balance of intimacy: forms relationships with sensitivity: interested in partner: good balance of social, employment and family relationships.

Negative balance of isolation: difficulty in sustaining ongoing relationships: preoccupation with self.

6 OBJECT RELATIONS THEORY – LOOKING FOR THE PERFECT MATCH

Following the same pattern as we did in Part 1, we shall continue to consider the emotional development of individuals through adolescence and into young adulthood from an object relations theory perspective.

By the end of the chapter the reader should:

- Understand the impact of childhood splits on adolescent behaviour
- Develop an understanding of the need for therapeutic approaches to working with adolescents with behaviour problems
- Understand the difference between adolescent and adult behaviour
- Understand how we are attracted to people
- Understand how some relationships endure while some do not

We shall consider the implications of childhood splitting as early life experiences and emotions affect the developing sense of self, the widening of relationship opportunities and the growth of responsibility. We shall also consider how childhood splitting can affect the formation of one-to-one partnerships in young adulthood, how we choose our partners and what influences our ability to remain with partners in long-term relationships.

ADOLESCENCE

The adolescent is very much in the transitional stage of development within the object relations theory framework. The stage of infantile dependency is over, and the stage of mature dependency, with its expectations of emotional balance, personal responsibility and capacity to nurture others, lies ahead. There is quite an overlap in the theory of Erikson's life crisis framework and the application of object relations theory at this point, because both are placing a considerable emphasis on the ultimate importance of adults being able to nurture young children for healthy human development and the pressures that adolescents experience as they move from childhood and gradually begin to approach the adult part of their lives.

We considered how we split aspects of our selves and others in Chapter 3, and much depends on a young person's experiences through the later childhood and adolescent years in determining how the early splits formed in infantile dependency affect our development in the transitional period. Sutherland (1980) notes that a degree of splitting is universal, that is, we all engage in that dynamic without being aware of it. For a balanced and healthy interpersonal development, we hope that our central ego, our conscious, rational, problem-solving self, remains reasonably strong enough to adapt, to cope and to help us continue to develop. However, the extent to which any negative experiences in having one's needs met have continued throughout childhood is likely to create a structure within the individual's personality where the splits begin to dominate the way a person relates to others in day-to-day life.

Critical Thinking

In Chapter 4, you were introduced to Bronfenbrenner's (1992) ecological systems theory as it might relate to attachment theory. Object relations theory also recognises the importance of systems theory in the nature of relationships and the feedback which we get from our relationship experiences. A strong sense of self (central ego) relates with awareness and genuineness to real people (ideal objects) and receives responses from others which it can accurately recognise. Feelings engendered by these interactions are appropriate to the nature of the interaction, and subsequent behaviour is based on an honest, holistic interpretation of all these elements. This is the kind of open system which illustrates healthy personality development in object relations theory.

Compare the attachment theory and object relations theory information and try to identify the close relationship between the two approaches.

An adolescent is going to have a better chance of coping with the life events to which Erikson's framework in Chapter 5 refers if he or she has as strong a central ego as possible. Given that we all have experienced early childhood needs being punished or frustrated, we all, as Sutherland (1980) suggests, carry a mix of central ego, anti-libidinal ego (punitive child) and libidinal ego (needy child) within our personality. In the same way that Bronfenbrenner described the relationship of external systems, as outlined in Chapter 4, we can also describe the relationship of internal systems within ourselves and say that an open system potentially allows the splits to be less rigid, because the functioning central ego is able to experience the impact of the childish anti-libidinal and libidinal egos when they begin to affect behaviour and is able to regulate the impact. Systemically, the difficulties arise when our internal systems are closed, and the anti-libidinal/ punitive child and the libidinal/needy child operate without the balance provided by the central ego.

The language of object relations can be complicated, so we shall try to explain the above in what we hope is a reasonably straightforward way without losing the complexity of the theory. A child who comes through from childhood (infantile dependency) to adolescence (transitional stage) having experienced genuinely loving care from carers who have been actively engaged in his or her emotional, physical and cognitive development will be in a good position to deal with the highs and lows of adolescence. They will be able to relate to others and to come through any relationship difficulties with a good chance of success because they have experienced the successful balance of having loved their mother, father or primary carer and having felt loved by them in return. Such experiences are more likely to result in a strongly functioning central ego, enabling us to deal better with the realities of day-to-day living.

A child who has experienced the more frustrating aspects of care is more likely to have a greater balance of needy child (libidinal ego). This experience can take many forms. At one end of a spectrum, there are carers who set up too high expectations because they try to be 'perfect', meeting all the child's needs where possible. Such a carer is clearly loving, but if we look at the quality of the love, we see that it does not necessarily meet the child's developmental needs, because the child needs to begin separating from total (infantile) dependency at some point as he or she moves through the transitional stage. The carer, by being almost too caring, may be setting up the child's expectations: the child, having never had to doubt that someone will always be there to help, becomes dependent on this, and the carer becomes an 'exciting object', rather than a real person, while the child's libidinal ego is dominant. He or she just cannot get enough love. The loving care given to the child may actually make wider relationships more difficult, because the child has had very limited experience of having to deal with frustrations and thus finds it difficult to cope with people who are not always there to meet his or her needs. If we move along the spectrum, we come to the carer who does the best they can, but who is either busy in other aspects of life or who is chaotic in their approach to life. Here, a child experiences the pleasure of having needs met, but also the frequent frustration of not: the carer is not setting out to harm the child, but the child experiences the frustrations of wanting more of the affection they sometimes receive and a libidinal ego grows inside. Further down the spectrum, we find a less caring carer who makes their affection conditional on the child's behaviour: if the child behaves in a way which the carer dislikes, affection is withheld, and so the child becomes needy to get the desired affection.

> ### Critical Thinking
>
> Having read these examples, can you think about how a child might experience the pleasures of being loved in a way which leaves them wanting more? If you feel loved occasionally, and not regularly, try to imagine the anxiety of not being loved. It is this anxiety that produces the split libidinal ego in ourselves, which is split off from our conscious self (central ego) as a means of self-protection.

Now we will look at the child whose needs were hurt, punished, ignored or rejected, and who is more likely to have a strong punitive child (anti-libidinal ego). Again, we need to consider this on a spectrum of behaviours and experiences. Even a loving carer can become frustrated and speak harshly to a child. For example if the child has just scribbled on a clean wall, and the anger expressed by the carer, mild though it may be in the overall context of carer–child interaction, still gives a message that the child is not loved. Thus, even in what may normally be the happiest of relationships, the potential for an anti-libidinal/punitive child split exists. Moving along the spectrum as we have done above, some children will experience more criticism or physical punishment of their behaviours, some will experience wilful neglect, and, at the lower end of the spectrum, some will be constantly abused. The more the hurting aspect of carers' behaviour is experienced, the stronger the punitive split in oneself, and the internal structure of personality is more strongly based on an unconscious attitude that needs are bad, needs must be punished.

Erikson's (1965) outline of the adolescent stage indicated the potentially volatile nature of emotional development, and Zimmermann and Iwanski (2014) also acknowledge the emotional upheaval which can accompany the biological and social changes of adolescence. They refer to studies which confirm that emotional instability is a feature of adolescence, but, significantly, they note that this instability appears to continue into adulthood. This may add weight to Erikson's (1959) assessment that the stage of identity versus role confusion is not completed until an adult has established intimate mutual relationships with another adult.

Given that adolescence is widely viewed as a stage in our lifespan which is accompanied by physical, social, emotional and cognitive changes, we can see how the impact of our earlier experiences on our personality is significantly relevant to our capacity to move through this stage. The individual with a reasonably strong central ego, which can generally have a positive effect in regulating the libidinal and anti-libidinal egos, thus preventing them from becoming too dominant, is likely to come through this stage and into adulthood with a healthy emotional balance. Those who come through this stage with a more dominant libidinal or anti-libidinal ego may, because their internal system is more closed than open, retreat, as it were, further into these ego splits, which may dominate their personality even more as they enter adulthood.

Case Study 1

You are a social worker in a criminal justice/probation setting, working with Daniel, a 17-year-old who has been placed on a supervision order following his conviction for a series of petty thefts. Daniel moved to your area just over eighteen months ago, having lived previously several hundred miles away. His early life was spent in a variety of care settings, including both group and foster care, before eventually returning to his mother's care when he was 13. You understand that his mother had separated from his father when Daniel was 4, but she had an alcohol problem, and her care of Daniel had been deemed neglectful and damaging to his development.

Daniel and his mother had a very conflicted relationship after they were reunited, and Daniel's school attendance became erratic, his behaviour became aggressive and uncooperative, he began to go around with young people who were alcohol and/or drug abusers and he himself began to abuse both substances. His grandmother, who lived in your catchment area, offered him a room and a chance to get away from the undesirable influences on his life, and Daniel moved away, to try to give himself a new start, as he describes it. Months after moving there, his grandmother had a stroke and died. Daniel, having no residence history in the area, was not offered accommodation by the local council, and has since been 'sofa surfing', as he describes it. He is drinking, taking amphetamines and stealing to fund his substances.

Daniel is a really difficult service user and is frequently unresponsive or monosyllabic in his answers to you. He agrees to do the tasks you identify, but rarely follows through, and he says that he wants to change, but shows little active involvement in undertaking the change process. You have tried using a motivational interviewing approach (Marsden, 2014; Shirran, 2014) and a cognitive behavioural approach (Allan, 2014), but there is little evidence of progress. You are beginning to think that Daniel is a lost cause and that his re-offending risk is high, making the prospect of a future custodial sentence very likely.

If we apply object relations theory to an assessment of Daniel, we see an individual whose emotional development needs have not been met. He has grown up with a background of neglectful, possibly aggressive behaviour towards himself, a series of changes in his care patterns which suggests he was finding it difficult as a young child to engage with carers and a significant number of losses in his life (see Chapter 10 for more on loss). From this, he seems to have split off from his central ego a great deal of punitive feelings, resulting in a dominant anti-libidinal split, which may be so entrenched that it overrides both his central ego and the needy libidinal ego. As a social worker, you should not, therefore, be surprised that Daniel is making heavy weather of his stated desire to change. The central ego, his rational, aware self, does want to change, but his powerful anti-libidinal ego, his punitive self, also described by Fairbairn (1952 [1986]) as his 'internal saboteur', overwhelms his rational self.

The significance of the strong anti-libidinal ego affects behaviour in a number of ways:

- Daniel, having had his appropriate need-seeking behaviour punished as a child, feels his needs are bad, and, if he shows vulnerability, he feels he will be hurt again.
- Daniel may also feel *any* needs are bad, and may be intolerant of vulnerability in others.
- Daniel has to appear tough and hard to the outside world because his anti-libidinal ego is so strong.
- Daniel is not easy to like.

If you are going to make some impact on Daniel's behaviour, you are, theoretically, going to support him in building his libidinal ego, his needy child, in such a way that he allows himself to feel that it is safe to be vulnerable and to feel less punitive towards himself and others. As a result of this, the internal systems become more open and less closed, and you may be more able to help him engage his central ego, thus becoming more able to work in a more cognitive behavioural, task-centred approach. In other words, you have to encourage an appropriate amount of dependence on yourself and others in the helping professions. However, this is one of the trickiest methods, as many will see this approach as a 'soft option', and assessing what is an appropriate level of dependence is not going to be straightforward. If you are working in a statutory, criminal justice or probation setting, it may be difficult to undertake the kind of relationship-based approach that this method of intervention requires, and such work may have to be undertaken by other agencies which are better placed to do so.

Critical Thinking

To what extent do you believe that an adolescent who behaves as Daniel does is a victim of his past as well as an offender in the present? To what extent do we need to take his emotional development into account and try to address the childish elements of his personality as a priority? To what extent is this unwarranted, inasmuch as we should be actively challenging his offending behaviour and reinforcing his need to accept responsibility?

YOUNG ADULTHOOD

We now turn to young adulthood, the period in our lives when we are taking more and more responsibility for ourselves, forming relationships with others and becoming parents. As we discussed in Chapter 5 when considering Erikson's life crisis framework, people are put into adult roles at very different ages. Some will be holding jobs and bringing up children at 16, while others will be students with no fixed relationships at 22. However, we shall consider what object relations theory tells us about relationship formation and about the parents' responsibility for the care of children so that we may be in a position to assess individuals without making sweeping generalisations. Not all 16-year-olds will have difficulty meeting a child's needs, and not all 22-year-olds are necessarily better equipped to do so.

Dicks (1967) identified three main factors which bring people together in marital or meaningful adult partnerships. First, there are conscious factors, those of which we are fully aware, and these might include: overt physical attraction; recognition that the other person has personality traits which you like or which might enhance aspects of your own personality which you consciously feel are lacking; or the fact that you seem to share values or interests. Second, there are social factors, such as the expectations within your culture, class or environment. And, third, there are unconscious factors, of which neither partner is aware, which relate to our unconscious needs or anxieties, and which bring people together into a relationship. It is this third factor on which we shall focus, because it is the most influential in determining whether relationships can be sustained or not.

Critical Thinking

If you are currently in an intimate relationship with another person, try to explain what attracted you to that person initially, and, if you have been in the relationship for some time, what is the continuing attraction? How easy or difficult do you find this exercise?

Pincus and Dare (1978), recognising the unconscious reasons which lead people into marriage or long-term relationships, note from their clinical practice as therapists that couples do find it very difficult to provide clear and explicit reasons why they have stayed together. They point to a variety of unconscious reasons why adults form relationships, and all these reasons broadly relate to aspects of emotional development in childhood which have remained unresolved through childhood and adolescence. The principal reasons people come together are because they are trying to address unmet needs, to be with someone because he or she represents a familiar feeling from childhood or to be with someone because he or she might carry or express strong feelings which exist within us, but which we are afraid to express ourselves. The important thing to be aware of is that these are not conscious motivations, and we are normally, unless we choose to look closely at ourselves, not aware of them. In object relations terminology, we are looking at the splits, libidinal and anti-libidinal, needy and punitive, which impact on partner selection.

Skynner and Cleese (1983) reinforce this in their very entertaining book. Instead of using the terminology 'split', they talk about pulling 'a blind down inside our head to screen off the emotion that we don't want to look at' (1983: 27). From our understanding of object relations theory, it is impossible for anyone to come through childhood without splitting some libidinal and anti-libidinal feelings. Skynner and Cleese suggest that the most successful marriages involve partners who tolerate what each other has put behind their screen and who are able to look behind these screens, which can be uncomfortable and distressing, but which enables them to grow emotionally. To apply object relations terminology to this interpretation, we should describe this as two people with fairly strong central egos whose relationship and behaviour is occasionally affected by their needy/libidinal or punitive/anti-libidinal splits. Because of the strength of their central ego, they are able to reason, discuss and generally communicate with each other and thus become less and less influenced by their childish splits.

At this point, we can also demonstrate some of the overlap between object relations theory and attachment theory. Both describe the importance and significance of internal working models (see Chapters 1 and 4), which describes the basis of our capacity to relate to others. Our internal working models are formed in childhood, and, where attachment theory uses terminology such as avoidant and ambivalent, object relations theory uses terminology such as anti-libidinal and libidinal. Both theories suggest that we relate to others in adulthood using a template within our personality which is formed in childhood. Clulow (2001) demonstrates this close relationship between attachment theory and object relations theory, looking also at the notion of a secure base (Bowlby, 2008). A secure base can be seen in the definition of a successful marriage in the previous paragraph: both adult partners feel sufficiently secure with each other to be able to address unconscious fear, anger and anxiety. Such security originates from a mainly positive attachment experience in childhood, which is also the building of a strong central ego. However, everyone requires a secure base and adults who have more dominant libidinal or anti-libidinal egos are less likely to find this in partners and may be more attached to non-human objects, for example soft toys, pets, alcohol, tobacco or drugs. Object relations theory would describe these as transitional objects (Winnicott, 1964) which have an emotional importance because they are associated with comfort and security in the transition from infantile dependence to the challenges of mature dependence.

Case Study 2

You are providing a social background report for the local court on Gary, an 18-year-old living in a bed and breakfast, unemployed but seeking help from a community project in the area. Gary was stopped by police investigating a break-in on his way back to his lodgings. He protested his innocence, but the police asked him to turn out his pockets, and in his deep coat pocket they found a soft toy dog. One of the police ripped the dog apart to check whether anything was being concealed, and Gary exploded with anger, trying to grab it back. He was taken to the cells and appeared in court the next morning on an assault charge.

From your interview with Gary, you find a history of childhood neglect and abandonment. Gary has not seen his parents for several years, has been in and out of care, and he has been trying very hard to stay away from the drug scene. The soft toy has been with him since he was a toddler.

Can you explain to the court officials the emotional importance of this transitional object to Gary?

Looking at the types of splits people carry within themselves, we can describe how unconscious factors may bring people together. The individual who has a dominant anti-libidinal ego is unconsciously afraid of, and intolerant of, vulnerability and will find it incredibly difficult to form a mutual dependent relationship: to have even the slightest emotional dependence on another will be intolerable as indeed will any emotional demands made by the partner. However, this does not mean that they will not be able to form a relationship with another person or marry. If we consider Dicks's (1967) identification of reasons for marriage, such an individual may be physically attracted to someone, and/or he or she may be in a position where marriage would be socially or financially advantageous. Politicians, for example, may be in a better position to reach powerful positions if they are seen by the electorate as happily married. He or she therefore finds a partner who has a similarly dominant anti-libidinal ego. The two people enter a relationship which may be emotionally shallow, but neither will be showing vulnerability towards the other. In fact, they may be cool and indifferent towards each other, but, deep down inside their unconscious selves, these two punitive children have engaged with and are relating to the rejecting objects in each other, which derive from their experiences of significant adults in their earlier years, thus repeating the reassuringly familiar patterns of childhood. Skynner and Cleese (1983) describe how the angry child which lies within the personalities of such individuals can burst out in confrontation, which can lead to vicious arguments. While this can happen in any marriage or relationship, where couples have stronger central egos, they can recognise what is happening and try to resolve it. In marriages or relationships involving two deeply anti-libidinal personalities, the couple are not consciously aware of a problem and retreat from any attempt to understand each other. Despite the lack of empathy and mutual love, their relationship continues.

Alternatively, the individual with the dominant anti-libidinal ego forms a relationship with another who has a dominant libidinal ego. In this case, the adult's split punitive child may be attracted to the caregiving potential of the other adult's split needy child. The needy child is possibly desperate to form a relationship with another, and sees the vulnerability in the punitive child which excites the potential to be needed. This type of relationship illustrates the potential for individuals to employ the defence mechanism of projection (Freud, 1933) where we get rid of feelings which are anxiety-provoking or intolerable and, in effect, get someone else to carry or express them. Pincus and Dare (1978) and Skynner and Cleese (1983) provide examples of this behaviour, but, using object relations theory, we can say that the individual with a strong anti-libidinal ego has developed this because he or she has internalised that personal emotional needs are bad and are painfully punished. That does not stop the individual from being needy or vulnerable, but because of their anxieties, he or she cannot allow these to become part of their conscious behaviour. It suits that individual to find someone else to take these away and who better than someone who has a strong libidinal ego, and who is therefore very needy. The anti-libidinal person in the relationship now appears strong and capable because his or her partner plays the needy role. At the same time, the partner can project any angry or punitive feelings onto the other in return, while seeking to win over the rejecting parent (Gordon, 1982). Dicks (1967) used the term 'marital fit' or 'couple fit' to describe these patterns of relationship.

In both these examples of adult relationships, we are drawing on the extremes of libidinal and anti-libidinal splitting. There are a multitude of 'couple fit' patterns determined by the depth and strength of childhood splits, but recent research suggests that there are some patterns which are potentially more destructive than others. Whishman et al. (2004) found that relationships were less successful if the underlying psychological issue was a state of anxiety based on expectations of harm or failure, which corresponds to the infantile splits which we describe as anti-libidinal or schizoid (Brearley, 2007). Gottman (2014) acknowledges that conflict between partners does not necessarily imply that the relationship is dysfunctional and that the important factor is the balance between positive and negative feelings or attitudes. Gottman also found that the relationship was less successful the more the individuals were defensive about their emotions or withdrawn from any deeper emotional commitment to each other.

Our understanding of object relations theory as it applies to young adulthood also requires an awareness of the impact of splits on the babies born out of the adult relationships. Essentially, we hope that adults have a sufficiently strong central ego in order to relate to the baby as a whole person, which means understanding and accepting that the baby is totally dependent on the adult. We, as adults, are there to meet the baby's needs; the baby, in his or her responses to our love, gives us a good feeling, but the baby is not there primarily to meet our needs.

> ## Critical Thinking
>
> At this point, you may wish to revisit Chapters 1–3 to remind yourself of the developmental needs of the baby and the formation of positive carer–child relationships and attachments.

The risks to the baby lie principally in having as primary carers adults who see the baby as either a rejecting object or an exciting object. Such adults will have significant libidinal and anti-libidinal splits which dominate their personality in a dynamic way, or may have dominating libidinal or anti-libidinal splits in a more one-sided way. The very libidinal carer will indeed perceive the baby as being dependent, but by virtue of being very libidinal/needy, the carer will be unwilling or unable to permit the child to become more autonomous or outgoing in play and other relationships. A clingy carer will be actively seeking a clingy child. A carer who is dominated by both splits may want the baby to be cooperative and agreeable to meet the carer's needs, an exciting object, but when the baby behaves like a baby, crying for attention or because of discomfort, the libidinal split turns anti-libidinal, and the needy carer becomes punitive towards the baby, now a rejecting object. The anti-libidinal carer wants the baby to make as few demands as possible and will have little or no time for emotional demands for care or nurture. The baby will have to adapt to a regime which suits the adult, which make the baby very much at risk, because he or she is a rejecting object whenever they upset the narrow attitude of the punitive/anti-libidinal carer.

Case Study 3

Linda and James have been together for four years as a couple. They came together in their last year at school, which they left at 16, and James got a job with a local roofing company. Linda gave birth to Edward when she was 17. You are a social worker with the family care team who has worked with the family for the past two years, following a referral from the health clinic about Edward's failure to thrive. Both Linda and James were brought up in large families in very basic accommodation and with state benefits as the only legal source of family income. James's experiences, in particular, were of being physically punished frequently by his father and older siblings. James is a large man and has hit Linda on several occasions, but she has so far refused to complain formally and throughout she always calls him 'Jamesy'. She is superficially very anxious to look after Edward properly, but rarely complies with advice or guidance she is given by the health professionals.

Your assessment, informed by object relations theory, is this. James has a very strong anti-libidinal ego and a strong libidinal ego. He needs someone to meet his needs, but he would never see himself as anything other than a macho male, and

(Continued)

(Continued)

he is easily roused to aggression by anything that frustrates or inconveniences him. Although Linda has played down his aggression, you can see that she has been assaulted by James. So far, Edward has not been physically harmed, but you are concerned that he could be. Object relations theory advises us that someone who is so dominated by ego splits is going to find it very hard to relate to others as whole, real people, and that includes his own child. If Linda is treated aggressively as a rejecting object, there is a strong possibility that if Edward's behaviour in any away upsets James, Edward will not be seen as a child, but as a rejecting object, too.

Linda is very dominated by her libidinal ego and is particularly dependent on James, despite the clear indications that he physically hits her. James is her priority, but to make up for his rejecting behaviour she does occasionally lavish affection on Edward. However, this is inconsistent: Edward gets affection and love only occasionally, because when James is responsive, Linda concentrates her attention on him, to the detriment of Edward. The fact that she calls her partner 'Jamesy' suggests that she is relating to him as a child, which is further evidence of her very needy personality. The splits in Linda's ego seem to be aggressively needy/libidinal, with occasional punitive/anti-libidinal aspects.

You get a phone call from Linda saying that James has hit her because she did not have his tea on the table when he came home. She says that she has had enough of James's behaviour and wants out, but she has nowhere to go. You discuss with her where she might find a secure refuge and make arrangements to collect her, along with Edward, to go to the refuge. While you are concerned about Linda, you are also reassured that she has begun to see the reality, the whole person, of James. Her central ego is working, she has taken realistic stock of her situation and has made a considered first step to resolve it.

James is furious and makes abusive calls to you. His anti-libidinal ego is rampant and you are very definitely a rejecting object to him. He identifies you as the bad person who turned Linda against him. On day one of Linda and Edward's stay in the refuge, she is talking about finding alternative accommodation and possibly seeing the police. On day two, to your alarm, she is concerned about how 'Jamesy' will be coping without her and says he'll be missing her badly. On day three, she has returned to James. Her libidinal ego is too strong and, for the present, she is unable to sustain a realistic central ego. James is the exciting object to her because she can have her need to be needed satisfied by him. The safety of Edward is going to remain a major concern, and, without the opportunity to experience more positive patterns of relationship, Linda will not easily change this view of her partner. Unfortunately, neither will James.

The impact of childhood splits continues to affect behaviour and development in early adulthood, but, as we shall see in Chapter 9, the process can continue in the middle and later stages of our lives.

PART 3

ADULTHOOD AND OLDER AGE

In this section, all three chapters consider the life stages of adulthood and older age. Chapter 7 considers how adult attachments may reflect childhood patterns and how they may adapt as we age. Chapter 8 continues to discuss Erikson's life cycle theory and considers the crises or challenges facing adults and older people and the impact of previous life stages. Chapter 9 considers the Object Relations theory concept of mature dependency and discusses the potential effects of splits from childhood on adult behaviour.

7 ATTACHMENT – THE COMPLEXITY OF ADULT ATTACHMENTS

This chapter will focus on attachment in adulthood and consider how the adult attachment styles impact on significant relationships.

Already we have seen that insecure attachment causes disequilibrium to emotions, neurology and behaviour, so consideration will also be given as to how individuals with insecure attachments try to cope with increased anxiety as this might involve internalised and externalised behaviours.

Social work services deal with a vast number of adult service users, so focus will be given to some of these service user groups to look at how attachment theory helps us understand behaviour, as well as considering appropriate interventions to use when dealing with insecure attachments.

By the end of the chapter the reader should:

- Understand how attachment styles formed in childhood affect the formation of attachments in adulthood
- Understand the nature of affectional bonds in adult relationships
- Have an awareness of the adult attachment interview
- Understand the importance of attachment theory for parenting

---

INTRODUCTION

Chapter 4 looked at attachment through adolescence and into adulthood and suggests that attachment styles are determined by our experience of relationships. Within this chapter the focus will be on how we use our experiences to interpret and integrate with others, and the impact this has on relationships.

Allen and Land (1999) believe that attachment styles become predictable by late adolescence, but others believe that attachment is a bit more fluid and will continue to develop as we grow older – a child who has experienced disorganised attachment may return to a more predictable style, even if it is still an insecure attachment, that will allow it to function in relationships without being on constant alert to the threat of danger (Main and Morgan, 1996). Certainly, if we are looking at the links between neurological development and attachment theory, then brain development tends to mature at about age 15, but life goes on and human beings have to constantly adapt and learn from experiences, so there is no one point in time when we can say that we have a perfectly formed human being (Gerhardt, 2006). Therefore, we have to recognise that attachment relationships extend beyond childhood and adolescence and will affect interactions across the lifespan.

RELATIONSHIPS WITH PARTNERS

By adulthood, an individual is normally seeking relationships with a partner rather than the caregiver, and more often than not, with a sexual partner. The need for security and identity does not wain in adulthood and this can be a determining factor when seeking an appropriate partner to share life with – the attachment style developed in childhood and adolescence may define characteristics of personality which can be partially satisfied by the needs and desires of other attachment styles. This need for close relationships stems from what Bowlby (1979) termed 'affectional bonds'.

Bowlby (1979) believed that the affectional bond began in childhood with the infant demonstrating a desire to be close to the caregiver but remains with the individual throughout life and will continue to drive the individual to seek closeness and comfort from another individual – a need for proximity. Ainsworth (1989) went on to develop Bowlby's concept of affectional bonds and explained that the focus of the bond is always on a specific individual and tends not to be transitionary, hence the quality of the bond feels exclusive and unique to two individuals. The affectional bond also creates emotional significance between the two individuals and the consequence of this is a desire to be close to one another, spatially and mentally. Consequently, any imposed or unexpected separation from one another will create distress and emotional turmoil – Bowlby recognised the significance of attachment on coping strategies and wrote a trilogy of books exploring the issues, beginning with *Attachment* (1969), followed by *Separation: Anxiety and Anger* (1972) and *Loss: Sadness and Depression* (1980). These issues will be explored in later chapters within this book.

Bonds will impact on relationships with peers, workmates, and friends, but what set the affectional bonds apart from other bonds of friendship is the didactic benefits to the individuals sharing the affectional bond. With sexual partners, there will be a reproductive element to the relationship (this need not necessarily mean that reproduction is the aim), but this does not need to involve any emotional connection between the couple. When an affectional bond forms, there is a definite emotional connection between the couple, and, from this, if the relationship is truly formed from an affectional bond, will come a caring element to the relationship – both parties will desire good things for one another and seek to provide support for these opportunities to flourish. The quality of the relationship may change over time, but the affectional bond offers three prongs of support: physical, emotional and psychological.

The sexual element and the reciprocal nature of the relationship sets the adult style apart from attachment in children and adolescence, but Hazan and Shaver (1987) found many similarities between attachment in childhood and adulthood. Their studies in the late 1980s triggered a focus on adult attachment and how this manifests in choices of life partners. They identified that those early experiences which define attachment styles in children are carried into adulthood and affect the pattern of relationships when it comes to adult relationships. They suggested that the three dominant attachment styles of secure, anxious/ambivalent and avoidant are evident in attachment patterns within adult attachment styles and these findings have been backed up by other studies in the field (Fraley and Shaver, 2000; Shaver et al., 1988; Rholes and Simpson, 2006). What these studies revealed was that relationships across the lifespan are driven by a biological need to feel secure, but the quality of the relationship is determined by the experiences drawn from childhood, and this was directly linked to the 'internal working model'.

If you remember from Chapter 4, the internal working model is how we as humans interpret the world around us, our view of ourselves and our prediction as to how other people will act. If we have a good sense of self-worth then we will believe that other people should treat us well, and we would expect respect from people we engage with. Conversely, if we have a poor sense of self-worth, then we might feel that we do not deserve to be treated well and might expect the worst from people we engage with. When we apply this to choosing partners we can already see that the internal working model defines expectations. Bartholomew and Horowitz (1991) researched attachment styles in young adults and concluded that the internal working model could be categorised into two distinct areas – views of self and views of others – and that these two areas are split again into positive and negative domains. They found that attachment styles sat squarely in four domains:

Secure: good self-esteem + good views of others

Avoidant (dismissive): good self-esteem + poor views of others

Anxious Ambivalent (preoccupied): poor self-esteem + good view of others

Disorganised (fearful): poor self-esteem + poor view of others

Critical Thinking
What's my style?

Among their research questions, Hazan and Shaver (1987) came up with three descriptions which asked adults to 'classify' themselves into one of the three dominant attachment styles. Which one of these applies to you?

1. I find it relatively easy to get close to others and am comfortable depending on them and having them depend on me. I don't often worry about being abandoned or about someone getting too close to me.
2. I am somewhat uncomfortable being close to others; I find it difficult to trust them completely, and difficult to allow myself to depend on them. I am nervous when anyone gets too close, and, often, love partners want me to be more intimate than I feel comfortable being.
3. I find that others are reluctant to get as close as I would like. I often worry that my partner doesn't really love me or won't want to stay with me. I want to merge completely with another person, and this desire sometimes scares people away.

Source: From Hazan and Shaver (1987: 515).

1 = secure   2 = avoidant (dismissive)   3 = anxious/ambivalent (preoccupied)

Bartholomew and Horowitz (1991) later adapted the questions and added a fourth choice to capture disorganised (fearful) attachment:

4. I am somewhat uncomfortable getting close to others. I want emotionally close relationships, but I find it difficult to trust others completely or to depend on them. I sometimes worry that I will be hurt if I allow myself to become too close to others (from Bartholomew and Horowitz, 1991: 244).

Bartholomew and Horowitz (1991) offer the accepted four categorisations of adult attachment styles based on observations of trust in self and others, and opinions of relationships:

Secure: Generally, within secure adult attachments the individual demonstrates a good sense of self-image, self-worth, self-esteem, is autonomous, trusting, and feels comfortable with intimacy. This links with the secure child in early attachment styles.

Dismissing: A dismissive attachment style will see the individual having a strong sense of self-identity and self-esteem, but this will come at the expense of intimacy. There is often an emphasis on achievements but an avoidance of close relationships. These achievements may not always be positive, and notoriety might be just as attractive as success. This is simply a continuation of the avoidant attachment style from childhood where the child learns that they have to be self-sufficient as their emotional needs will not be met.

Preoccupied: Within this attachment style an individual can present as overly dependent, much like the clingy child from early attachment styles. They are suspicious of their partners and tend to question why their partner stays with them. They want to be intimate and crave relationships, but can often find they are rejected because of being overpowering and overbearing. They will often place their partner's needs before their own. Again, the link into childhood attachment styles sees preoccupied attachment aligned with anxious/ambivalent attachment wherein the child feels they need to rely on others more than themselves, and emotions are carried close to the surface in order to gain attention.

Fearful: Individuals with fearful attachment styles do want to be intimate, but are afraid that they will be hurt if they have to face rejection or loss. This can often drive them to isolation. Once in relationships, they can often keep partners at arm's length and reject them at the slightest provocation simply to keep them safe from becoming too emotionally involved, and face possible pain. The fearful attachment style is an extension of the disorganised style from childhood.

CO-DEPENDENCY

Howe and Campling (1995) suggest that insecure adult attachment styles can often lead to co-dependent relationships, wherein the co-dependent individual within the relationship is always giving care but rarely receiving love or care in return. They explain that this stems from feelings of being unloved, or experiencing erratic care when they were a child, and having an overwhelming desire for care and security within relationships. Accompanying these feelings is also the memory of anger, and this has the potential also to surface within adult relationships, but is often suppressed in favour of wanting to care and feel that they are needed.

Therefore, the co-dependent individual is often drawn towards people who have issues and need to be cared for – examples would include people with mental health issues, substance use issues, offending issues and those with a history of poor, broken relationships themselves. Cermak (in Howe and Campling, 1995) explains that there are five distinct characteristics that define an individual with co-dependent tendencies: they always want to please other people; they feel a responsibility to meet the needs of other people; they can be compulsive; they have low self-esteem; and they will engage defence mechanisms, particularly denial, when challenged about their situation.

Co-dependency applies to all of the insecure attachment styles. The five tendencies identified above are easily identifiable within a preoccupied attachment style, but individuals with a dismissive attachment style can become dependently attached to external sources, such as work, which will give a sense of identity that was absent when growing up – they will gain security in having an identity as a 'good worker' or 'successful employee' which may not be as secure as internal, emotionally driven relationships, but still gives a sense of purpose and drive within a world full of relationships.

Case Study 1

Jenny, who is 48, was referred to the hospital social worker as the nursing staff had concerns. She was admitted to hospital following a fall down stairs at home. She was married and had two teenage children but since her admission to hospital, none of her family had been to visit despite phone calls asking them to bring in nightclothes and toiletries.

Jenny was upset when the social worker visited her. She stated that she felt guilty for being in hospital and didn't want to create a fuss for her family. She was worried about how they would be coping without her and was keen to get home to cook their dinner, but realised that she could not until she was discharged. The social worker offered to go to the house to collect some essentials for her stay in hospital but Jenny refused and reiterated that she did not want to be a burden and would cope. Jenny got very angry with the social worker when he asked why her family hadn't been in to visit and the social worker had to leave as other patients on the ward were getting upset.

The social worker returned the next day and Jenny was calmer and pleased that he had returned. Over the next two sessions, the social worker was able to engage Jenny in conversation but found it very difficult to keep Jenny on a given subject as she liked to tell stories about the lives of other people she knew. However, she did explain that her husband had ongoing issues with alcohol and she was determined to make him stop drinking. She devoted a lot of time to her children, but they 'had their own friends now, and were not interested in Mum'. On the afternoon she fell down the stairs she had had an argument with her husband and had hit him several times. In her anger, she ran to the stairs but tripped as she got to the top. She stated that this was very out of character for her to resort to violence, but she thinks this might be because she was hit as a child.

The discharge team wanted Jenny to leave the hospital, so the social worker used the remaining time to look at support networks. He recognised that Jenny was demonstrating signs of a preoccupied attachment style and co-dependent tendencies and that an emotionally supportive relationship where Jenny could feel warmth, compassion and the ability to confide in another person would be beneficial.

- If you were the social worker, how would you explore these areas?
- What kind of 'support networks' would you consider?

As a profession, social work involves working with service users who need help and are vulnerable. The profession is a demanding and rewarding one wherein when change occurs you see the transition from helplessness to helped, and the satisfaction that you were an agent within the change process. For this reason, social workers need to be aware of their own co-dependent tendencies and ensure that their motivation is positive, that there is emotional support within the work structure and that there are opportunities to reflect on actions to avoid the risk of triggering internal or external anger. Having co-dependent tendencies is not a 'bad' thing, but research suggests that support can address issues that arise from this.

ADULT ATTACHMENT INTERVIEW

The 'Adult Attachment Interview' was developed by George et al., (1985) and consists of 20 questions which are designed to explore the upbringing of the individual being interviewed to determine their own experiences of being parented, and how these lived experiences may well be manifesting into skills they are using to parent their own children.

A lot of information can be gleaned from the answers given to the questions, and areas explored include experiences of early attachment, memories of loss and how this was dealt with, issues around stress and trauma and how this impacted on emotional regulation, and also issues around positive family memories and how these collective experiences have impacted on adult relationships. However, it is also important to consider *how* answers are given to each question as the style of communication can give an insight into adult attachment styles. The interview seeks to determine coherence in the narrative and the interviewer will be listening for signs of contradiction or illogical outcomes, enough information (but not too little or too much), logical answers in relation to the question being asked, and a good sense of identity. There is no specific question wording, but there are approximately 20 areas to explore and are roughly asked like so:

1. Can you begin by telling me a bit about your family, where were you born, and where you grew up?
2. Can you describe your relationship with your parents?
3. Can you choose five adjectives to describe your relationship with your mother?
4. Similarly, can you give me five adjectives to describe your relationship with your father?
5. Which parent were you closer to? And why?
6. Describe what you would do when you were upset as a child?
7. What are your earliest memories of being separated from your parents?
8. Do you have memories of feeling rejected as a child?
9. Did you ever feel threatened by your parents?
10. How do you think your relationships with your parents have affected you as an adult?
11. Why did your parents behave as they did when you were a child?

12. Were there any other adults in your life as a child?
13. Did you experience loss of a loved one when you were a child? And as an adult?
14. Have you experienced anything you would regard as traumatic in your life?
15. How were your teenage years in terms of your relationship with parents?
16. How is your relationship with them now?
17. How do you feel you cope with separation from your own children now?
18. Where do you see your own children in 20 years' time?
19. Have you learned anything from these questions?
20. How do you think your own children feel about your parenting skills? (Adapted from George et al., 2011)

The answers, and the answering styles, tend to align themselves with the four adult attachment styles as follows:

Secure: Coherent answers. Consistent narrative with a strong sense of value placed on attachment relationships. Answers will not be defensive in nature.

Dismissing: Answers might be short and lacking in detail. They may come across as unwilling to think about issues in depth. There may also be lapses in memory and recall, and a tendency to minimise past experiences. Tend to stress the normality of their experiences (often stating 'but that's just normal') and like to project a sense of independence.

Preoccupied: The narrative becomes long, rambling, and will go off-tangent to include irrelevant detail about other bit players in the story. Narrative also becomes emotionally entrenched in other people's problems. Can seem very angry about the past one moment, then ambivalent the next.

Fearful: The narrative appears to be very disjointed and reasoning can appear to be sporadic. Often, the interview can get disrupted by unexpected outbursts of anger relating to the unpredictability of triggers to the emotions which are always trying to protect themselves from the unpleasantness within the memory.

The Adult Attachment Interview is a useful tool when working with certain service users, but for others an interview might fill them with dread, particularly in relation to certain attachment styles where trust in others is low and talking to a social worker on a one-to-one basis might be intimidating. Other tools and techniques have been suggested to overcome this barrier and Halkola (in Loewenthal, 2013) suggests ways in which photographs can be used to initiate discussions about family relationships, thus the focus is on the image which can prove less intimidating than making eye contact in an interview setting. George and West (2001) have developed a tool to use set images which are shown to service users whereupon they are asked to narrate what is happening in the picture, again, using visual tools instead of solely relying on linguistic ones. When you consider problematic attachment styles and the effect this can have on neurological development, then adding an alternative visual method to enable communication is logical.

The advantages of exploring adult attachment styles with service users can enable informed choices about appropriate interventions to use, but can also help the social worker think about how the therapeutic alliance will develop. Ideally, one of the main aims would be to help the service user develop a coherent narrative to help make sense of the lived experience and the impact on current behaviour – the more coherent the story, the stronger the sense of identity, and the more secure the attachment. Research suggests that exploring the narrative and enabling learning about attachment styles can help re-educate the right side of the brain and become aware of emotions that may well have been locked away, or simply not named, and can lead to more empathetic, altruistic and compassionate behaviour (Mikulincer and Shaver, 2005).

EFFECT ON PARENTING

In Chapter 1, we looked at the effect on children when they encounter differing styles of care and how this can define their attachment styles, and this section completes that circle. We have looked at attachment from birth, through childhood, into adolescence and then onto adult attachment styles which considered the different characteristics and their impacts. If attachment issues are left unaddressed by professionals, then the characteristics of each style will impact on the child/children within the family.

Emotional attunement and clear communication will facilitate a secure attachment. If the child feels that the carer recognises needs, validates signals and responds appropriately, then the fertile grounds for a secure attachment are there. However, insecure attachments create problems which will impact on how emotionally attuned the carer can be. These issues can include anxiety (Manassis et. al., 1994), depression (Rosenstein and Horowitz, 1996), psychiatric disorders and even suicidal ideation (Kobak et. al., 1991). We also introduced you to Bronfenbrenner's socioecological model in Chapter 4, and social factors should also be considered within the context of pressures on parenting and the consequential impact on coping strategies. As we have seen in coping strategies with adult attachment styles, preoccupied attachment can lead to internalising problems, while dismissive attachment styles can result in externalising problems, therefore, with adult attachment problems professionals might actually have to begin by addressing issues caused by the resulting behaviours (such as mental health, substance use or criminal behaviour) before actually being able to address the attachment issues themselves.

Feeney and Noller (1996) point to the importance of communication within the parenting relationships. A secure attachment will involve responsive communication, and as the infant grows and learns more language skills they become more adept at expressing their needs and verbalising their internal states. A responsive carer will facilitate this communication by helping the infant to identify names for feelings and emotions. As the child grows, they will be able to project and imagine how their needs will be met when they are apart from the carer, because the continuity of care will be present when they are with the carer. The overarching result of this process will be that the child develops a positive internal working model, and a strong sense of self.

In a caring dynamic where the dismissive adult attachment style is present, the carer will be concerned with keeping themselves emotionally safe, and this may involve creating barriers within the relationship so that there is a reduced risk of getting hurt. Carers might appear distant, aloof, critical, intolerant and not empathetic in their responses to the child. In severe cases, a dismissive attachment style could lead to neglect if the needs of the child are constantly ignored. Crittenden and Ainsworth (1989) highlight the point that those carers experiencing dismissive attachment styles have raised levels of anxiety which is linked to the internal working model and memories of rejection. It may be that the carer initially felt loved and needed by their new baby but as the infant develops and begins to express need, then reacts negatively when needs are not, or cannot be, met, this can be interpreted by the carer as being rejected by the infant. If this is the case, then the carer engages familiar defence mechanisms, emotionally shuts down and protects themselves from possible hurt. The carer's emotions are prioritised over the infant's emotions, and the infant experiences an absence of attunement which can lead to the development of an avoidant attachment style. As dismissive attachment styles are also linked to externalising behaviours, professionals also need to consider how issues of control might be manifesting, and what strategies the carer is employing to help them cope with their stress and anxiety.

Similarly, preoccupied attachment styles create issues in the parenting relationship. Carers can often appear to be controlling and blaming and can be inconsistent in their responses to the child. Issues of control stem from the internal working model's experience of lacking control in childhood and craving the experience of continuity, regularity, and routine, yet with a developing infant the carer needs to be flexible and adapt to the growing, dynamic needs of the child which can prove challenging. Preoccupied attachment styles are linked to internalised behaviour which can include mental health issues such as depression. Low self-esteem and low self-efficacy are not uncommon, and emotions are carried close to the surface and engaged to attract help and attention from others. This can be frightening at times for the infant, to see the parent go from one extreme to another very quickly, and their internal working model tries to comprehend this behaviour by attuning their own emotional expressions to try to please those of the carer. Feeney et al. (1994) also highlight the point that preoccupied attachment can result in carers being overly compliant with others and supressing their own needs in order to satisfy the needs of others. This can only be maintained successfully for a short while before these unmet needs begin to have a knock on effect on their caring ability.

Not all children who experience disorganised attachments will go on to develop fearful adult attachment styles, but Kaufman and Zigler (1989) estimated that there is about a 30 per cent chance that if abuse has been experienced by the carer in their childhood, this will be perpetuated into their own parenting/caring experiences. As we have seen in previous sections in this book, the best way to describe reactions from within a fearful attachment style is 'unpredictable'. Feelings of anxiety fluctuate, experiences can trigger unpleasant memories, and defence mechanisms are engaged to try to protect emotions. Consequently, the carer experiencing fearful attachment will fail to recognise the child's needs, or simply ignore them. It is important to remember that these attachment styles are not conscious decisions: they happen deep within the unconscious and the behaviours experienced by each individual may well be frightening to themselves, as well as others. For social workers, a fearful attachment style is concerning as it can be a predictor of abuse within the caring experience. Control might be exercised through violent or sexual means, or psychological pressure might be exerted to demonstrate power. Not all abused individuals will become abusers themselves, but using observational skills and assessment tools such as the Adult Attachment Interview can give insight into coping strategies within relationships and give professionals the means to deal with potential issues before they become major catastrophes.

ATTACHMENT AND ADULT SERVICES

The impact of attachment styles, and the resulting behavioural issues, should be considered across all adult services within social work. We have already seen that insecure attachments can result in internalised and externalised behaviours to cope with anxiety, and underlying attachment issues can explain why some service users come into contact with professionals. One of the more common strategies for coping with anxiety issues is to use substances to help calm the mind and body, or to numb the emotions caused by feelings associated with insecure attachment.

Caspers et al. (2005) studied the implications of attachment styles and the correlation between substance use and found that preoccupied and dismissive attachment styles were equally as influential on an individual in terms of relying on substances to help cope with situations. They believe that this is caused by an inability to regulate emotions which results in psychological difficulties.

Their study suggested that although different insecure attachment styles were equally as likely to lead to substance use problems, there were implications in terms of considering the attachment style to help define treatment approaches. They report that those with preoccupied attachment styles would benefit from addressing negative thought patterns and breaking the cycle of focusing on unpleasant thoughts from the past which impact on self-esteem, while those with dismissive attachment styles should be encouraged to become more aware of their internal states and practice different ways of coping with stress and anxiety. Kassel et al. (2007) found that preoccupied attachment styles were more likely to impact on substance use because of poor self-esteem and cognitive distortions which supports the findings of Caspers et al. (2005), but both studies acknowledge that there are numerous complex reasons as to why individuals are drawn to substance use, and that an understanding of attachment theory can help to look at underlying psychological and psychoanalytical reasons.

Secure attachments foster positive self-esteem and good communication, factors which could be considered as protective factors when looking at the risk of using substances – if self-esteem is good then there is no psychological benefit to numbing emotional pain or distorting perceptions, and if communication within relationships is positive then healthy conversations can take place about using substances and the risks this might present. If these protective factors are removed, as with insecure attachment styles, then the perceived benefits of altering perception and temporarily numbing emotional feelings can be attractive. It might also be that the isolated individual experiencing a dismissive attachment style, or a fearful style, might find solace in a group of similarly isolated individuals engaging in substance use – a sense of identity is gained, even if it is a negative one.

Another reason for using substances might be to deal with the side effects of mental health issues. Preoccupied attachment can lead to internalising emotions which can result in anxiety disorders and depression; dismissive styles can lead to isolation, depression and sociopathic symptoms; while fearful styles can be similar to symptoms brought on by borderline personality disorders (Schore, 2003a, 2003b). George and West (1999) remind us that the purpose of attachment in adult relationships is to find protection and security and feel that the relationship provides strength and wisdom; when the equilibrium is upset, the attachment style experiences dysregulation, which can lead to continuing emotional turmoil. The consequence of this is that mental ill health can be triggered and this can manifest in the form of pathological levels of blame and anxiety, self-destructive behaviour, violence towards others and dissociated mental states. Tweed and Dutton (1998) found that preoccupied adult attachment styles positively correlated with borderline personality disorders, paranoia, passive aggressive tendencies, antisocial personality disorders and schizotypal personality disorders. Mikulincer and Florian (2001) found that dismissive adult attachment styles can underpin eating disorders, dissociative disorders and psychosomatic symptoms brought on by the fragmentation of the self. Fearful attachment styles can fluctuate between these extremes, but has also been associated with severe psychopathology (Main et al., 1985).

With modern society relying more and more on informal carers to provide care for vulnerable members of family and community, attachment should also be considered in the context of coping strategies. In Chapter 10, we will look at loss and change in more detail, but Merz and Consedine (2012) found that as people age and deal with consequential losses, be it loss of friends, loss of mobility or loss of independence, the attachment style will impact on how each individual deals with this transition. They found that dismissive and secure attachment styles actually dealt with these losses relatively well, whereas the preoccupied and fearful attachment styles tended to experience more stress and reduced well-being. If there is an added expectation that these individuals should provide care for partners or family members who are experiencing loss, then this can compound the emotional impact and increase stress. Preoccupied and fearful attachment styles are likely to experience an increase in anxiety levels, panic, depression, feelings of helplessness and being over sensitive, while symptoms of stress in dismissive attachment can manifest themselves through psychosomatic reactions. Reactions can also be extreme when dealing with grief: preoccupied and fearful attachment styles might experience chronic and complicated grief; while dismissive attachment styles might delay the emotional processing of the loss and try to avoid confronting grief, which may see the emotions surface when reminded of the loss years later (Bowlby, 1980).

CAN ATTACHMENT CHANGE?

Fortunately, evidence suggests that addressing attachment issues is beneficial, and change in relationships is possible if an individual who is experiencing problems can start to process previous relationship issues, and make sense of the narrative, connecting memories to current actions.

If someone has experienced insecure attachment throughout childhood, adolescence and into adulthood, yet manages to find a relationship which provides security, then this relationship is termed 'earned secure'. This earned security can come from any source (a teacher, relative, partner and so on) and gives the individual an opportunity to explore narrative, emotions, memories and feelings in a safe space. Basically, the components that make up a secure attachment (secure base, empathetic communication, understanding, non-judgemental, safety) are provided so that issues created by the insecure attachment can be explored and reordered. In effect, social work services should be providing the environment within the therapeutic alliance between worker and service user so that opportunities to find earned security are provided.

Earned security also fits into knowledge of resilience, which is explored in Chapter 12, and this acknowledges areas in an individual's life that are positive and negative, but helps to see where strengths and resources can be drawn from. Having a significant relationship which fosters positive attachment or earned security is one of those factors. As well as talking therapies, meditative practices such as yoga have been shown to provide psychological and neurological benefits as the body learns what an emotive state created by secure attachments should feel like (Shaver et al., 2007).

'Mindfulness' has also been shown to facilitate a shift in attachment. The practice involves a very basic form of meditation where the individual is encouraged to focus on breathing to begin with. As the breathing slows down, the individual is then encouraged to concentrate on the repetitive, calming nature of the lungs controlling the intake of air, and to avoid getting caught up in thoughts that enter the mind. The strategy behind mindfulness is to stop negative thoughts becoming dominant and affecting emotions. By slowing the breath down, this creates calming neurones from the parasympathetic system which helps control anxiety levels within the body. Over time, the body learns that anxiety can be dissipated by concentrating on the rhythmic pattern of breathing, and diverting the mind from pursuing negative thought patterns. Caldwell and Shaver (2014) investigated the effectiveness of mindfulness practice with a sample of women who reported that they had experienced maltreatment as children, and were classed as insecurely attached. They found that the intervention was easy to teach, tolerated by the participants, easy to learn and implement at home and had significant positive effects in the areas of emotional suppression, rumination, clarity and regulation.

Case Study 2

At 27 years old, Debbie had been through many ups and downs. Her father used heroin all through her childhood and died of an overdose when she was 9. Her mother also used heroin but stopped when Debbie's father died, but later developed problems with alcohol, which she still uses regularly. Debbie is the eldest of four children; the youngest two were taken into care when they were starting primary school.

Debbie experienced a lot of violence between her parents and states that she was relieved when her father died. She had a turbulent time at school and got involved in the 'recreational drug scene', sex and alcohol, which has continued into her 20s. When she was 26, she found out that she was pregnant and was very happy about this, stating that she would now have someone to truly love, and love her back. She gave birth to a son and called him Joel, but as soon as she left the hospital with him she states he became a problem baby. He would not breastfeed and Debbie thought that it was because he hated her. He would cry a lot of the time and she thought that it was because he did not want her near him, so she left him to cry in his cot for most of the time. The health visitor and GP eventually diagnosed Joel as having acid reflux and prescribed an antacid.

Although this helped with Joel's feeding and crying, Debbie still felt disgust when she looked at Joel. Debbie attempted suicide but was found by her younger brother. She was then referred to social work through mental health services. She found talking to the social worker beneficial and one of the first things she said was that when she looked at Joel she could see her father's eyes staring back at her. The social worker asked Debbie about her childhood and Debbie seemed unable to recall many specific details and described herself as being numb, taking on responsibility for looking after her siblings when things became violent in the house.

One of the first exercises the social worker asked Debbie to do was to draw out a lifeline – using a big piece of paper Debbie charted the high points and low points in her life so far and illustrated the rises and falls with little pictures. The social worker was able to identify gaps in Debbie's narrative and spent time asking Debbie about these periods so that she could begin to make sense of her life story. Debbie also went to parenting classes and spent time with Joel in the presence of the social worker and support workers. This provided a 'holding' environment, wherein she felt supported when dealing with Joel at times of distress. She was encouraged to make eye contact, give Joel feedback and talk to him about his emotions. She was also encouraged to concentrate on her breathing when she felt she was getting distressed and try to think about what Joel needed when he cried. At times when Joel was calm and settled, Debbie was encouraged to reflect on situations and think about what had worked well.

Over time, Debbie was able to make sense of her childhood and teenage years, giving clearer accounts of experiences she had been through and why this might be causing her to feel emotions she was currently experiencing. Her narrative was more consistent and she was able to identify times where she felt strong in the past, and relate this to her coping strategies now. Most importantly, she saw Joel as the baby he was, and was no longer seeing her father reflected in his eyes. She stated that although her life had been bad, Joel was the best thing that had happened to her.

This chapter has outlined how adult attachment styles can be considered in the context of relationship issues and social work service provision. In later chapters, we look at some specific areas that also impact on psychosocial skills and coping strategies, namely: loss and change, trauma, resilience, and family systems theory.

8 ERIKSON – FROM MIDLIFE TO CONTENTMENT OR DESPAIR

In our study of Erikson's life crisis framework, we have now arrived at middle adulthood.

By the end of the chapter the reader should:

- Understand the importance of previous stages of development on adulthood
- Understand some meanings of the term 'midlife crisis'
- Be aware of the importance of a sense of purpose in adulthood
- Understand the complexity of emotional development in older adulthood
- Have an awareness of implications for service delivery to older adults

---

As in previous stages, we are reluctant to put a definite age range to these stages as so much depends on an individual's personal and cultural circumstances (Gutmann, 1976). Some adults at the age of 30 will still be in the process of forming relationships that reflect Erikson's life crisis of intimacy versus isolation, while others may be in established relationships as parents of pre-teen or teenage children with much greater familial responsibility. Some may have established a behavioural pattern based on a balance of isolation from early adulthood, and you may wish to revisit the previous chapter for the discussion on avoidant attachment which has a strong connection to Erikson's isolation.

STAGE 7: GENERATIVITY

The nature of the adult life crisis is described by Erikson as 'generativity versus stagnation', but what exactly is 'generativity'? Dictionary definitions really do not convey the essence of what Erikson is trying to convey, and they link the word to 'generate' as in to 'produce'. Indeed, Erikson is suggesting that a positive balance in this stage of adulthood involves a satisfying sense of being useful, of being creative and of being productive. However, while he acknowledges the importance of these positive attributes, Erikson (1965: 240) argues that there is a more important aspect of generativity, which is 'primarily the concern in establishing and guiding the next generation'. In some aspects here, we have to look at generativity as a hierarchy of positive features, and, just as in Chapter 4 where we had to consider the importance of mutual orgasm in his ideal of intimacy, we have to consider at this stage whether Erikson is correct to suggest that greater satisfaction can be obtained by being in a position where we can help those younger than ourselves, the next generation.

Erikson himself acknowledges that a positive balance of generativity does not depend on having children of our own, and that people may have abilities and aptitudes to satisfy the drive for generativity in activities which do not involve their own children, if, indeed, they have any. But, to understand this adult stage in life crisis, life cycle theory, we have to consider the cumulative impact of earlier stages and, in addition, be aware that after adulthood comes older age. Not just the past, but also the implications of the future, affect an adult's progress through this stage. Time becomes a factor in determining life choices, and at this stage the awareness that life is finite and will come to an end can influence how adults behave and react to events.

We considered in Chapter 5 how earlier stages of childhood and adolescence impacted on young adulthood, and now we have to repeat this exercise but with the addition of the outcome from the intimacy versus isolation stage. Adults who have acquired a positive balance of intimacy are more likely to have developed good enough relationships with adults and children, whereas those with a negative balance of isolation make less good use of relationships in all aspects of their adult life. Erikson (1965) argues that maturity in adulthood involves a need to be needed, which suggests that those who find relationships difficult may struggle to achieve a positive balance of generativity, which Erikson equates with maturity.

Critical Thinking

Erikson's assertion (1965: 240) that 'mature man needs to be needed' shows that he is closely connected to the thinking behind object relations theory. In Chapter 6, we considered scenarios where adults had a need to be needed in an immature way, and, because he is definitely not talking about immaturity, it may be worth clarifying Erikson's statement. In identifying maturity, Erikson is effectively identifying the concept of 'mature dependency', which, as we have seen, is the ideal psychological position of an adult according to object relations theory. Erikson is linking the need to be needed to the dependency aspect of mature dependency, but he is also arguing that adults have a need to guide and influence the younger generation by giving of themselves, and this is the mature part of mature dependency. Thus, there is a significant difference from the very needy person whose libidinal ego draws them to exciting objects: they need to be needed, but in a very selfish way which is more concerned with their own feeling rather than those of others.

At the root of Erikson's identification of generativity as the positive balance of the adulthood life crisis lies the implication that adults need to feel satisfied, fulfilled and valued in their activities, and the more they can recognise a positive impact of their efforts on others, particularly younger people, the more they achieve a sense of generativity. Our capacity to have a sense of security in our relations with others (basic trust), a feeling of confidence and self-belief (autonomy), a sense of optimism (initiative), comfort in our abilities (industry), a feeling of satisfaction about who we are (identity) and satisfying, rewarding relationships with others (intimacy) would enable us to be in a strong position to achieve a positive balance of generativity. For some people, this may well describe their positive experience of adulthood, but the reality for most people is that they experience a number of challenges posed by this potentially lengthy stage of the life cycle.

During the span of adulthood, an individual is likely to encounter events which require an adaptation of behaviour and a response to situations which change aspects of their life. Children growing up and moving out of the family home, changes in employment and place of residence, the loss of family members and feelings of bereavement are expectable in the vast majority of people's lives. However, such expectable transitions can also be overlaid with more critical features: children's behaviour becoming so challenging that they are expelled from the family home, redundancy, inability to pay rent or mortgage, the sudden death or departure of a very close relation or friend, the need to seek refuge or asylum from extreme danger. The variables in an individual's experience of adulthood are numerous, and this leads us to a consideration of what we commonly call the 'mid-life crisis'. Individuals may experience a state of crisis at any time in their lives, so what exactly is a 'midlife crisis'?

If we consider definitions of the term 'crisis', we find a consensus among several commentators that it describes an upset or unbalanced state which may result from changes to or loss of a previous balance in life (Rapaport, 1970; James and Gililand, 2001; Parker and Bradley, 2007). However, we have to incorporate Erikson's developmental stage into this definition and insert the factor of emotional satisfaction with the state of adult life experience. The midlife crisis is not a fixed event which takes place at a certain age, but a reaction to feelings which provoke a re-appraisal of life, and which may lead to a questioning of values, beliefs and behaviours which have become a steady pattern. Brim (1976) reinforces the view of the midlife crisis as an upset which is determined by transitions from one steady state to another. Upsets to the steady state may be caused by external factors or may come from within the individual. External factors might include major disasters such as war, violent attack, sudden death and sudden loss of job, home or physical health and ability, and our capacity to deal with or cope with these will vary according to the balance of positive outcomes we have experienced in the previous life crises of our life so far. Personal qualities and attributes are likely to be crucial, but, as a coping mechanism, the ability to engage with other people as realistic sources of support and assistance is a major factor in any personal attribute.

The upsets which come from within may be less easy to assess in a straightforward cause and effect way. Because of the nature of the unconscious parts of ourselves, we are generally likely to be unaware of the frustrations or anxieties which remain unresolved from earlier stages. In Chapter 5, we suggested that the stage of identity versus role confusion offered the adolescent the opportunity to revisit or act out unresolved aspects of early childhood stages. In this chapter, we are suggesting that adults with unresolved aspects from the identity versus role confusion and intimacy versus isolation stages may well be driven to actions which reflect these stages in the life crisis of generativity versus stagnation.

Critical Thinking

Unresolved aspects from adolescence or early adulthood are very common. We assume that most of the readership is adult, either younger or older, and, as such, can you try to identify any behavioural traits which you have which could be related to either of the stages? Do you have, for example, a significant concern about how you look, what you wear, a strong desire to be the same as or different from your peers, a tendency to mock authority or to be intimidated by authority, or any other traits which might be described as adolescent? Do you stress about whether people like you, or avoid social gatherings or have any other trait which may signify an issue with intimacy?

We are trying to convey, as in all previous stages, that the successful outcome is a positive balance. The fact that we all have unresolved issues from adolescence and young adulthood does not imply that we all have significant problems in our lives. The examples in the box above describe behaviours which may apply to any of us but they do not necessarily prevent us from leading satisfying lives. Erikson (1965) uses the term 'pseudo-intimacy' to describe the more negative balance at this stage, and it is feasible to assume that, just as adolescence offered the chance to resolve some childhood issues, adulthood may offer the chance to resolve some adolescent or young adult issues. An adult who becomes uncomfortable with pseudo-intimacy may not consciously realise that this is the basis of their discomfort, but may be suddenly inclined to engage in behaviour which shows a definite upset in a steady state. A couple may have been married for years, leading outwardly very comfortable lives with social status, well-paying employment and a circle of friends from similar upper-middle-class backgrounds. The apparently sudden decision by one or both to have an affair may shock those who know them, may create upset in the nuclear family and may jeopardise their social standing.

If we apply Erikson's concept of 'generativity versus stagnation', what part of this life crisis does such behaviour describe? On the face of it, it is a negative event for the family and perhaps, therefore, you might be inclined to label it 'stagnation'. In doing so, however, we may be taking too simplistic an assessment, and we need to consider the behaviour in a wider way. While discomfort of the pseudo-intimacy of isolation and stagnation may have provoked the behaviour, the behaviour itself may be either generative or stagnant depending on the outcome. If the affair leads to a new relationship with a partner who assists in the development of a more mutual and fulfilling approach to relationships, then the affair, upsetting though it has been, leads to a more positive balance of generativity. If, however, it simply permits the existing relationship to continue with recriminations and possibly occasional brief sexual affairs, the outcome is a more negative balance of stagnation. The possibility that one person's actions can be seen as ultimately generative does not mean that this is true for the partner left behind, and if they cannot make any emotional development themselves, they remain stuck in the stagnation side of this life crisis.

Up until now, we have concentrated on the relationship aspect of generativity, which Erikson identified as critically important, but he also drew parallels with Marxist theory and thus identified productivity and employment as another major factor in establishing one's position in society (Marron et al., 2011). For emotional health in adulthood, the satisfaction of employment is very important, and we can also relate the transitions caused by loss of valued jobs to the behaviours associated with a midlife crisis. Again, the capacity to cope with this kind of crisis depends significantly on the balance of positive outcomes from previous stages as well as the more structural situation of employment availability. Beckett and Taylor (2010: 127) suggest that the struggle for a positive balance of generativity depends on 'the nature of the challenges that we face, the legacy of the past, the opportunities available'.

Case Study 1

Frank is 52, and for the past ten years he has been the financial director of a manufacturing company. As the country's economy shrank, the company's profits were badly hit and the owners decided to make redundancies. Frank was one of those made redundant. His job had rewarded him to the extent that he had a large

(Continued)

(Continued)

house, a wife who worked part-time, two children currently at university and two expensive cars. Both he and his wife enjoyed socialising, were members of clubs in the area and had a status in their community. Financially, he received a generous redundancy settlement, which could help the family sustain their existing lifestyle for a few years, and Frank began the search for a new job, but did not tell his children of his altered circumstances. He was invited to a number of interviews, but was unsuccessful in all his attempts. His initial feelings that he had a reputation in his work field which would be recognised by others began to erode, and, after a year, his self-esteem was eroded as he began to feel angry and bitter towards those who were still employed and towards those who were rejecting him after interviews. He began to spend longer periods of the day in front of his computer, to withdraw from the numerous social events he might have attended with his wife and to have regular vindictive arguments with his wife over his inability to occupy himself productively.

Around this time, Frank's routine social drinking became more and more frequent until he had become dependent on alcohol on a daily basis, drinking both spirits and beer, to the extent that he was often incontinent and aggressive. His wife moved out and sought legal help to begin divorce proceedings. Ultimately, the house was sold, Frank had to downgrade to a single bedroomed flat in a depressed part of town, and he finally accepted a referral to an alcohol counselling agency.

A knowledge of Erikson's life cycle theory can guide the agency support worker's intervention with Frank. Indications are that any positive balance of generativity was built on his successful work role identity. Other aspects of his self-esteem are more fragile, because Frank has not been able to make effective or positive use of his relationships within the family or within his social network. He and his wife had great difficulty working together to resolve the problems, and they did not include their children in the situation, which illustrates the pseudo-intimacy of the relationship. Despite the fact that outwardly they had appeared to be a very successful family, the reality was more of a stagnating relationship, which might have continued at a low level of intimacy had it not been for the crisis of unemployment. Frank's personality is perhaps not as strong as it may have appeared to the outside world when he was working; his inability to make positive use of relationships with others suggests a lack of basic trust, his quickly eroding self-esteem suggests a lack of a positive balance of autonomy and initiative, his fragile identity is based almost entirely on his capacity to earn a lot of money and have social status, and his intimacy is fragile. Although he has been in a relationship, it seems to have been more isolation than intimacy, where each person has been connected within the family in a very superficial way.

The alcohol has been a substitute for relationships in Frank's life. Work with him will have to focus on helping him rebuild the capacity to form purposeful relationships with others, and, given his acceptance that he is in a critical state, he may now be motivated to accept help from the agency and, through a mix of individual and group support, his willingness to trust others and his self-esteem may be strengthened, to the point where he becomes able to take more responsibility for his life.

STAGE 8: OLDER AGE

We now arrive at Erikson's final stage in the life cycle, the life crisis of older age, which he describes as 'ego integrity versus despair'. This stage is influenced by the clear awareness that life is finite and that the expectation of life's end is in the foreseeable future.

Critical Thinking

As you read further in this section, consider how the need to review one's life may also apply to those diagnosed with terminal illness, but who may be much younger. Might it, therefore, be possible that this stage applies to anyone whose relatively imminent ending of life is part of their ongoing reality?

Before looking at how this stage of life unfolds, we should deconstruct Erikson's terminology. Ego relates to our self, and by that we mean how we see ourselves and how we feel about ourselves. Integrity has more complex meanings: on the one hand it implies wholeness, and on the other it implies honesty. To put these together, ego integrity means being able to see ourselves and look back on our life with realism and accepting the wholeness of our past experiences, the good and the bad. Erikson (1965: 242) also uses the term 'ego integration', which Beckett and Taylor (2010) describe as acceptance of our life as we have lived it and acceptance that we made our own choices. At this point, you may wish to reinforce this view by playing the songs 'No Regrets' by Edith Piaf and 'My Way' by Frank Sinatra! You will find that the lyrics express these views of ego integrity or ego integration.

Erikson (1965: 242) links the negative balance of this stage, despair, to a 'feeling that time is now short, too short for the attempt to start another life and to try out alternate roads to integrity'. While he suggests that despair also amounts to a fear of death, it would not be unusual to hear those in a state of despair claim they cannot wait to die. In terms of linking this life crisis to direct practice, it is more likely that as workers in a caring profession we shall meet more older people who may be struggling to reach a positive balance of ego integrity and whose behaviour is more inclined to despair. The implications for practice are that we must beware that our interventions do not enhance the balance of despair.

There have been many attempts to define when this stage might begin (Beckett and Taylor, 2010; Walker and Crawford, 2014), but in applying Erikson to practice, and in making an assessment of an individual, it is important to consider the individual's emotional state within a wider context. Some, for example, may have the opportunity to – or given future predictions of having to work longer, may have to – continue working until they are in their seventies. For them, the stage of generativity versus stagnation may continue till then. For others, illness or disability may prevent working in their late fifties, and, for them, the stage of ego integrity versus despair arrives sooner. One of the key issues for practice is that too often we class older people as a homogenous service-user group. Baltes (1987, 1993) found that there was no evidence for significant general cognitive deterioration in older people: results were very varied and it was not possible to generalise. In understanding an individual's experience of this stage of life, we have to consider other factors such as physical and mental health as they force change and transitions and as they influence the attitudes of others towards the individual.

Studies have found that ageist attitudes are driven substantially because of perceived frailty and illness (Roth et al., 2012). While older people can become physically frail or acquire mental health problems such as dementia, not everyone does, and yet attitudes towards older people become shaped towards a belief that they are a dependent group. Orth et al. (2010) found in research among older people from both black and white ethnic origins that there was a common decline in self-esteem in the over-sixties which was linked to changes in social and economic circumstances and a decline in physical health. Wu et al. (2012) found a link between depression in old age and medical factors, but concluded that the relationship between old age and late-life depression is extremely complex.

Erikson and others have deliberately used the term 'older adulthood' rather than 'older age', and this provides a further useful message for practitioners. Perhaps by concentrating our minds on the concept of adulthood we may remove some of the ageist attitudes which see older people as an age group in need. For an individual to achieve a positive balance of ego integrity at this stage almost requires an amazing combination of factors: positive balances from each of the preceding life crises which permit an honest and reasonably comfortable reflection on past life; satisfying current relationships; as well as sufficiently good health to be able to continue making personal choices. The problem is that when people do have health or social problems which brings them into direct contact with caring services, the potential to sustain a positive level of ego integrity becomes threatened.

Critical Thinking

Different cultures and ethnic groups have different attitudes towards older people. In some, age is associated with wisdom, in others it is not. What are your experiences? Is old age seen as older adulthood with implications of maturity and life experience or is it seen as a time of life when people become more of a drain and a problem? If you can, compare your experiences with others.

If we look at a spectrum of personalities, we shall begin with someone who is quite positive and optimistic, quite outgoing, someone who is generally likeable. In Erikson's framework, this is someone with an apparently positive balance of ego integrity. What might this person's experiences be if he or she had to come into a residential care setting? This would be a major transition presenting challenges, and the responses of carers in the establishment will be critically important. Do the staff encourage, or permit, choice? Where can one sit, can one choose when to have a meal and when not to, can one get up in the morning when one chooses, can one maintain relationships with who one chooses and can that include sexual relationships? Can that include hetero- and homosexual relationships? Unless the establishment is run on very person-centred lines, it is unlikely that all of these very basic day-to-day choices will be offered, or indeed tolerated in some settings. Napoli et al. (2013) found evidence of a need for care staff working with older people to develop more awareness and understanding of sexuality in late-life, in addition to an understanding of how to cope with sexual behaviour. Thus, the risk of enhancing the despair side grows, but someone with positive balances from earlier stages may still have the resilience to cope and adjust and maintain a balance of ego integrity. Someone, on the other hand, who has had a more mixed experience with some fragile positive balances from earlier stages, may become oppressed by the experience and move towards a balance of despair, not having the inner emotional strength to be as resilient.

Moving to the other end of the spectrum, what about the individual who has had predominantly negative balances from the early stages? Given that this implies a lack of self-esteem, difficulty in engaging in mature and mutual relationships, such an individual is likely to be bringing an inner balance of negativity into this stage and a predisposition to behaviour associated with despair. Such a person may come across as unhappy, bitter, ungrateful and, significantly, unlikeable. As we have discussed in previous chapters, mature relationships are based on giving and receiving, and social convention expects a degree of reciprocity. What do you do if faced with an 80-year-old service user who receives ungratefully and gives apparently nothing in return?

Carers may feel personally frustrated and angry by such behaviour, which brings us to the risks faced by older people in dependent situations. If a carer's feelings become so frustrated, there is a risk of aggressive or abusive behaviour towards the older person. There may have been unresolved issues between parents and children over the years, children feeling let down or angry about their early life care. As these children become adults, and as the parents become older, the balance shifts, and those who were cared for now find themselves in a more powerful position in relation to their ageing parents. Consciously or unconsciously, there may now be an opportunity to get back at the parents, either through neglectful behaviour or abusive use of power.

Here, we can see the importance of understanding human development and behaviour for effective professional practice. If we can understand how a person's personality has evolved, we can begin to understand that behaviour is not simply a response to immediate events but has been shaped by emotions and experiences from throughout the lifespan. The ungiving, unhappy 80-year-old has had negative experiences which have resulted in his or her present behaviour: as professionals, we have to see beyond our immediate feelings of frustration and personal dislike and try to reach out to foster even a slight shift from despair to ego integrity. Historically, we can see potentially ageist attitudes in the structural approach to service delivery. Staff working with older people have traditionally had low-level or no qualifications; staff ratios in care settings do not, in most cases, permit time for the development of talking and listening therapeutic relationships. Yet, as older adults, people in the later stages of life require professionals who have a knowledge base which encompasses the whole of life and who have communication skills which can be applied with purpose in very difficult conditions. An understanding of emotional development, of attachment behaviours and family dynamics may be needed to work with the apparently 'simple' problem of arranging social care for a frail older person. We must, as professionals, not fall into the trap of identifying work with older people as a matter of care provision: the emotional development towards a balance of ego integrity is vital.

Case Study 2

Jane is 89 and has come into a nursing home because she has great difficulty with mobility and is unable to care for herself, needing assistance to dress, toilet and bath herself. In addition, her eyesight has deteriorated in the past ten years, and she can now see only shades of light or dark. Since her husband died twenty-five years ago, she has lived in the same house as her son and daughter-in-law, in a one-room self-contained flat with same-level access to a toilet, but relationships, while superficially cordial, were not close, and, indeed, rather strained. As Jane's son, now 71, is himself becoming less mobile, the family has agreed that Jane would be better cared for in a nursing home, and Jane, who has been complaining about her present circumstances where no one appears to want her, is committed to the move.

She moves into the nursing home but, after a few days, is unhappy, complaining about the other people in the home who she describes as 'mad', rejecting attempts by some of her peers to make conversation and moaning constantly to staff about how others get more attention than her and how unhappy she is. The staff initially try to make light of things and try to jolly her into participation with no success. Gradually, they give up, and while they meet Jane's physical needs without much enthusiasm, they give up trying to make her happy.

Someone taking time to get to know Jane would observe a woman with low self-esteem and an almost obsessive need to compare her own situation with the apparently better situation of others. If we took time to find out about Jane's life, we would discover that she grew up in a large family with just enough money to live simply and basically. She left school at 14, was married at 17 to a man who worked as a grocer's delivery assistant and who fought in and survived the First World War. They had two children, both of whom left school at 16 and both married. Talking about her life, Jane has a lot of regrets about what she could not do and seems to have had conflicted relationships with siblings, although she was quite dependent on their company. She lost her daughter five years ago. She speaks warmly of her grandchildren, but sees them very infrequently.

Within Erikson's framework, Jane appears to have a significant balance of doubt in her very low self-esteem. There are suggestions of unmet issues of identity, as she regrets lack of, or missed, opportunities. There are issues around intimacy, which now extend to her life in a nursing home: although she is in a setting with people all around her, she feels isolated and cannot bring herself to accept opportunities to get to know others. Although she has brought up children, she is not bringing any positivity to her life which a balance of generativity might have provided. She lost her husband and more recently her daughter, she has lost the ability to care for herself and she has substantially lost her sight. Now she is also coping with the transition to a new residence and her behaviour is heavily marked by the sense of despair which Erikson describes as the negative balance of this life stage. Staff avoid Jane, because she depresses them, and it seems that Jane will give up the will to live and die in a state of despair.

Ethically, it may be argued that Jane has the right to self-determination, and, if she chooses to behave in this way, she is, after all, an older adult with the right to live her life as she pleases. This is true, but our knowledge of psychodynamic and psychosocial theory tells us that there are aspects of Jane's life which lead to her behaviour in ways that she does not consciously recognise. While we do not suggest that Jane should be made to reflect on her life, we do suggest that, despite her negativity, Jane may be craving a relationship which will value her as an individual. Someone who can provide this, talking and listening, but most of all accepting Jane as someone of worth, will do more for her balance of ego integrity. The emotional aspect of Jane's situation is as important as, if not more important than, her physical needs.

OUTCOMES OF ERIKSON'S STAGES 7 AND 8

- *Positive balance of generativity*: sense of purpose and general contentment: satisfying interactions with other adults and young people: feeling of being valued
- *Negative balance of generativity*: bored and unmotivated: not much satisfaction from interactions: stuck in routine: no feeling of purpose in life
- *Positive balance of ego integrity*: content with memories: able to interact with others to mutual satisfaction: likeable
- *Negative balance of ego integrity*: unhappy, complaining, bitter: not likeable

9 OBJECT RELATIONS THEORY – MATURITY OR IMMATURITY

In this chapter, we shall consider the implications of object relations theory on the development of personality and behaviour in adulthood and older age.

By the end of the chapter the reader should:

- Understand what is meant by mature dependency
- Be aware of the impact of unconscious splits on adult relationships
- Understand how extremes of aggressive behaviour may have their origins in childhood
- Understand how older adults may be drawn to childhood issues of dependency
- Have considered if change in attitude and behaviour is possible in older adulthood

As this is the final chapter focusing on object relations theory, it may be helpful to recap the main themes of the theory before we continue. Remember that our personalities are shaped by three aspects of splits: our central ego (the rational, aware, realistic part of our self); our libidinal ego (the needy, frustrated, 'I want more' part of our self); and our anti-libidinal ego (our angry, punitive, avoidant, self-sufficient part of our self). This influences our relationship with others, who can be subject to the following splits: the ideal object (relating to the whole person, based on honest and realistic awareness of the other person's positive and negative traits); the exciting object (seeing someone as all good, someone who will meet your needs); and the rejecting object (seeing someone as all bad, useless, a waste of space). Although these splits formed substantially in early childhood, it does not follow that, now we are adults in mid- and later life, we are fixed personalities, and, indeed, we may continue to develop or change aspects of personality and behaviour. Crucially, all still depends on our relationships at this stage in our lives.

Veroff (1978) sees adulthood as an opportunity for individuals to become aware of opportunities to build interdependent relationships. In such relationships, adults can negotiate or work out roles and be part of social networks, built around tasks associated with parenting, family and career. His use of the term 'interdependent' is significant: the motivation in adulthood is not 'independence' but ***interdependence***, which links to Fairbairn's (1952) description of the goal of adulthood as 'mature dependence'. It is important to note that the concept of mature dependency, which denotes maturity, includes the element of dependency, and this acknowledges that our central ego is probably never going to be the whole of our self, because some part our mature adult self is content to have our dependency needs met. Finkelstein (1988) notes that Fairbairn himself suggested that a healthy and intimate adult relationship might include the gratification of childhood parts of behaviour, which was echoed by Winnicott (1964) who suggested that the pleasure of a marriage was built in part on the couple's ability to play together. Dicks (1967) suggested that a sign of intimacy and close adult attachment was each adult's ability to tolerate the needy, dependent, libidinal child in the other.

The ideal of mature adulthood does therefore appear to be a question of balance. Provided we are generally realistic and, for a large part, accepting of each other, we can successfully incorporate some childhood splits within our personality without compromising our adult maturity. This view sits comfortably alongside Erikson's idea of a positive balance at each of his stages, with positive factors outweighing negative but co-existing. Bennett (2014), writing in *The Times*, cites a study of 400 families in a piece of research jointly undertaken by the University of Zurich and the State University of New York which also confirms the conclusion that adulthood is about achieving a positive balance. Disagreements between parents witnessed by children, or criticism of children's behaviour were tolerated by children without apparent negative effect provided that there was a significant balance of affection shown by parents towards each other and of positive feedback and praise towards the children.

Critical Thinking

A behavioural approach to the development of a psychologically healthy personality might concentrate more on the power of reinforcing desirable behaviour and modelling good behaviour. How important do you think this is in terms of mature adult behaviour towards children? How far do you agree with the object relations view that some arguments and some criticism can be tolerated without long-term harm provided the adults are generally affectionate and supportive?

Using an object relations perspective, we can see that mature dependency is achievable in a relationship where an individual with a strong central ego, and some libidinal and/or anti-libidinal splits, sees his or her partner as an ideal object, but occasionally relates to the exciting or rejecting object splits. However, as workers in caring professions, we may meet such personalities only when they encounter a significant problem which is beyond their customary coping skills. These are the service users who can be helped in a pretty straightforward way, because their strength of personality, their strong central ego, can take advice and act on it. With temporary support they are able to work alongside you, the professional, and resolve the problem. The more difficult, less straightforward, individuals are those whose splits are more dominated by libidinal or anti-libidinal ego.

Skynner and Cleese (1983) suggest that healthy relationships as described above may apply to a minority of couples. Similarly, extreme splits of anti-libidinal ego, punitive child behaviour between partners may also apply to a minority. They use the term 'middle range' to apply to a majority of relationships where the central ego may be slightly stronger, but where there are nonetheless significant aspects of libidinal/needy splits and/or anti-libidinal/punitive splits within the personality. Such individuals may remain in continuing relationships, unconsciously colluding with each other not to think about or go anywhere near understanding the origins of these splits. This might be similar to Erikson's terminology of 'pseudo-intimacy'. If we bear in mind that libidinal and anti-libidinal splits were formed because as babies, infants and young children we were frightened by feelings we had in our relationships with parents and carers, we can begin to understand the reluctance to expose ourselves to a primitive, gut fear, to the anxiety it may create which may become a conscious anxiety, and the preference to avoid looking closely at the past. However, within this middle range, some individuals may confront and challenge their own, or their partner's, splits, which may result in confrontation or upset, but which, if both partners are reasonably motivated to do so, may actually strengthen the relationship. As our dependence on childhood splits lessens, even slightly, so our central ego becomes stronger. Alternatively, one partner confronts his or her splits, becomes less needy or punitive as he or she becomes more aware and more comfortable with an understanding of the childhood fears and anxieties. If the other partner is not ready or motivated to do so, the relationship which had been built on collusion is now unbalanced and the partners separate.

The problem with keeping our splits out of sight may also affect the dynamics of a relationship. As occasionally some part of our libidinal or anti-libidinal ego may slip into our consciousness, we have the opportunity to address it in our central ego, or avoid it by ignoring it and returning it to our unconscious. Continued protection of ourselves from childhood anxieties inevitably leads to presenting only a part of our whole, real self to partners and the wider outside world. Hawkins et al. (2012) in a study of individuals going through divorce found that 55 per cent cited 'growing apart' as their reason for divorcing and 53 per cent cited 'not able to talk together'.

While other reasons were also given, these two were the most common. Finkenauer et al. (2009), in a study on perceived concealment in relationships, found a high correlation between individuals' perceptions of their partner's concealment of information and the growth of dissatisfaction within the relationship. While the nature of information concealed varied, it is possible to extrapolate that those who may be perceived as concealing important childhood information, even if they are consciously unaware, may be placing their relationship at risk.

Case Study 1

Bertin (1993) describes a couple who came to Relate, the counselling agency, for help with their relationship. The couple, identified as John and Mary, were in their 30s and had been married for a few years. Both came from families that could be described as closed systems (Minuchin, 1974), with John having been especially close to his mother. Mary had been expected to conform to her mother's expectations of being a good girl, and, as a child, had a poor self-image. They were consciously attracted to each other for these reasons: John liked Mary's self-discipline and self-containment, while Mary liked John's strength, warmth and ability to show affection. After they got married, Mary put on weight. John was unhappy with this and became sexually uninterested. He insisted she lose weight, and, to please him, she did so. Mary succeeded, became attractive to John again and they conceived a child. John was horrified as he did not want children, Mary was delighted as she did. There were financial pressures, and Mary coped with a very difficult pregnancy by working until the latest possible day and by being fiercely independent. It was a very difficult childbirth, which altered Mary's attitude and values. John concentrated on his business and on making money for the family and expressed surprise at the depth of his love for the child. Mary managed baby, home and work commitments, but the relationship deteriorated as John made more demands that Mary be self-sufficient, and sex came to an end between them. They were considering separation when they came to Relate.

Although the couple were drawn to each other for reasons which were clear to them and although, coming from similar backgrounds, they believed that they had shared attitudes, there are clear signs that both personalities are influenced quite strongly by libidinal and anti-libidinal splits. Mary has a libidinal split, which makes her needy for John's affection and approval (just as she needed her father's affection and approval); but she has a strong anti-libidinal split, which punishes that need and results in her being competent and able to manage herself without making emotional demands on John. John has a significant libidinal split, but he seems to be seeking the perfect mother. Mary is, for him, more of an exciting object than a real person or ideal object. He wants her to look fabulous, to be able to care for their child and to manage her work/play balance, but he does not want her to make emotional demands on him. In that respect, when she behaves too needily, his anti-libidinal, punitive child becomes stronger and he relates to her as a rejecting object. Mary's experiences of childbirth have resulted in her being less controlled by her libidinal and anti-libidinal ego: she is now more accepting of the need for an interdependent relationship, rather than the independent relationship which John needed.

Counselling now needs to explore whether they can grow emotionally together. Feilberg (2014) provides examples of psychodynamic counselling which would potentially help the couple explore the transference defence mechanism whereby they relate to each other as if each were a much desired parent, rather than the real persons they actually are. This might result in the need to confront feelings of anger which have created the anti-libidinal ego in each of them and which may lie underneath the surface behaviour and feelings. It may also expose them to the sadness of unmet needs which have created their libidinal ego.

THE NEEDY ADULT

We shall now consider the adult who has a dominant libidinal ego. This implies an individual who has a very fragile central ego, and who is so deeply unhappy about the unmet needs of childhood that he or she will have a strong aversion to any insightful scrutiny of the basic sadness and frustration. There is a very conscious need to be needed, coupled with a reluctance to upset or challenge others in case they break off a relationship and a reluctance to problem-solve, in the hope that someone else will remove the problem for you. Sutherland (1980) observed that severe splitting arising from frustrated needs in childhood can lead to pathological patterns of relationship, including obsession, and noted Fairbairn's (1952) theory that, for such a rigid split of either a dominant libidinal or anti-libidinal ego in adulthood, the unsatisfying relationships of early years would have had to continue well into childhood.

Critical Thinking

You have or plan to become a worker in a carer profession. Think about your motivation for this and try to identify the reasons. Once you have consciously carried out this exercise, try to reflect more deeply. How much personal satisfaction do you get from the feeling that you are needed?

The obsessively needy person may be described as aggressively needy, and this can be illustrated from fiction by the character played by Glenn Close in the film *Fatal Attraction*. While this may represent an extreme example of behaviour, it illustrates that extremely needy people, if frustrated in adult life, can move from aggressively needy to aggressively punitive. A dominant split effectively means that we cannot relate to people as they really are, and someone who is dominated by their libidinal ego is destined to relate to people as exciting objects, that is, people who exist primarily to satisfy the needs of the other. This may be unproblematic if need can be satisfied in a socially acceptable way, such as, caring for animals, but can become problematic in so many other ways. The libidinal parent may direct their neediness towards a child, lavishing affection on the exciting object which the child represents, but, in doing so, binds the child to the parent and restricts the opportunity for the child to broaden social relationships. The libidinal adult may find satisfaction in caring for others, but, if aggressively needy, will have a strong, unconscious desire to keep others in a dependent state. In any such example, the outward presentation of self to others is of a caring, loving individual, but the underlying motivation is not genuine interdependency but a deep-rooted self-centred need to be satisfied by relationships based on the complete dependency of others on one's self.

THE PUNITIVE ADULT

The other ego split is the anti-libidinal or punitive child, built during childhood as a result of needs being punished. In earlier chapters we have considered how all of us may have a balance of libidinal and anti-libidinal parts within our personality, but now we consider the personality dominated by the anti-libidinal split ego. At this point, we can recommend another piece of music to help you. Play Paul Simon's song 'I am a Rock', as sung by Simon and Garfunkel, and listen carefully to the words: they express very clearly the personality of someone with a dominant anti-libidinal ego.

At the extreme end of the spectrum, psychopathic behaviour is associated with cruel and callous crimes against others. Brody and Rosenfeld (2002) cite a study by Meloy (1988), which identified significant characteristics in the personalities of individuals imprisoned and diagnosed as psychopaths. In relation to their alienation, they reported histories of physical abuse in childhood, parental drug use, depressive disorders and substance abuse and unemployment. They displayed a lack of trust, intimacy difficulties, instability in relationships, a limited capacity for empathy and no real sense of belonging. They were egocentric in their self-centred behaviour and mistrust of others, and insecurely attached in their sensitivity to rejection. Providing a link between Erikson's theory and object relations theory, Meloy noted that a lack of basic trust makes the satisfying internalising of parental or primary carer images very problematic, and the good feelings which build a strong central ego cannot be internalised. Brody and Rosenfeld make the point, which is so relevant for workers investigating or assessing adult behaviour in suspected child cruelty cases, that people who are psychopaths can present themselves as calm and charismatic to the outside world, but this can hide the underlying emotional pain from experiences of rejection in the early and mid-childhood and the loss of love from significant others. A knowledge of the potential impact of splitting can make us more aware of the powerful way in which those with a dominant anti-libidinal ego can present a false persona to others, and, where there are grounds for suspicion about an adult's behaviour, it is vitally important to obtain not just a detailed early history of an adult's life but to be able to recognise warning signals from theoretical knowledge. If someone has had a significantly poor experience in childhood and there are no subsequent events or experiences which may have offset the negatives, then there has to be concern that a dominant anti-libidinal ego continues to influence behaviour in adulthood.

Staying with extreme examples of behaviour, there have been a number of cases of nurses or doctors, people very much in 'caring' professions, who have killed patients in their care. One particularly horrifying situation occurred at the Lainzer Hospital in Vienna in the late 1980s, when a small group of nurses was discovered to have killed a very large number of patients in their care (Heidkamp, 1994). Their childhood histories are not particularly detailed but show indications of unmet need, and to confirm any meaningful application of object relations theory would need to be expanded. However, to summarise one of several possible reasons to explain their behaviour, one might say that they came together through some unconscious recognition of similar personalities, weak central ego and dominant libidinal and anti-libidinal ego, the anti-libidinal being particularly strong. The ward in which they worked was a high-dependency ward for older people, many of whom were terminally ill, and it was extremely pressured because it had to admit anyone referred to it. The potentially dangerous combination of split personalities working under extreme pressure may have resulted in the needy splits of the nurses' personalities becoming overwhelmed by the punitive splits. As they have difficulty in relating to people as they really are, the nurses may firstly have seen the patients as exciting objects, meeting their needs, but as the pressure of work grew, the patients became rejecting objects. Here, the word 'object' is fully justified: the nurses had never related to them as 'people', and when their anti-libidinal, punitive splits became so dominant, it was not so difficult to end the lives of objects with whom they had no meaningful relationship.

These are examples of really disturbed behaviour, and there are other explanations which can be sought to explain the behaviour. However, object relations theory does provide one significant perspective which identifies the strength of those feelings split off from consciousness in childhood as a source of violent behaviour in adulthood which some might prefer to dismiss as 'evil'.

Critical Thinking

The term 'evil' is employed, not infrequently, to describe actions which are horrifying and apparently inexplicable. Two such examples were the murder in 1968 of young children by Mary Bell, herself an older child, and the murder in 1993 of James Bulger

(Continued)

(Continued)

by two older children. At the time of the trial of the boys accused of killing James Bulger, sections of the UK press, and at least one of the detectives who interviewed the accused, expressed the opinion that the boys were basically evil (Morrison, 1997). While object relations theory cannot in itself provide an explanation for such behaviour, it can begin to explain some of the factors. An experience of childhood which has led to emotional splits resulting in an inability to relate to people can lead to an inability to see a younger child as he or she really is. What begins as an unplanned adventure, two needy/libidinal children taking a younger child, the exciting object (and here the term 'object' is correct: they do not see an actual real person in the child), to have control over, gets out of their control. The younger child is not happy, does not want to be with them, and their coping mechanisms are in no way adequate. Their punitive/anti-libidinal personalities become dominant as James becomes more and more a rejecting object.

This is not an excuse: it is one way of trying to explain behaviour. In order to reach a more comprehensive understanding, one needs to be aware of other influences including the sociological aspects of environment, including the levels of background aggression and violence, and the social learning, including the influence of violence portrayed in media outlets.

Think about such attitudes: why might we find it easier to label people as evil rather than try to understand the possible reasons for behaviour? How plausible do you find object relations theory as one explanation for an individual's capacity to be violently aggressive?

The impact of an anti-libidinal ego can be demonstrated in other less violent examples, and, indeed, may not necessarily be a drawback to an apparently successful lifestyle. The individual who can live his or her life avoiding close, emotional interdependent relationships may become very successful in business or politics. A strong anti-libidinal ego, which derives from a deeply split fear of dependency, can allow one to think only of oneself without any conscious guilt or anxiety. Other people's emotional needs are discounted and avoided, and one can be single-minded in pursuing tasks with little or no feeling for how others might be affected. As long as such an individual remains in control of situations throughout adult life, the deeply feared childhood splits that needs are punished can be safely kept out of sight as a successful career continues.

INTO OLDER AGE

This is an appropriate point to consider the implications of object relations theory in the older adult years. Given that older adulthood inevitably involves transitions (Walker and Crawford, 2014), it is a period in our lives when we are faced with challenges of adaptation. We have considered the theoretical material provided by attachment theory and Erikson's life cycle theory in previous chapters, and now object relations theory provides another overlapping theoretical perspective. Beckett and Taylor (2010) identify the importance of feeling that we are in control of our lives, and, in older adulthood, it is at this stage that our feeling of being in control is most likely to be threatened for physical, cognitive and emotional reasons. As we discussed in the previous chapter, our care services have to be aware of the potential impact of taking responsibility away from older people and of ageist attitudes which treat older adults as inadequate. The more we remove a sense of having control over how we live, the more we force an emotional regression to the dependency needs of childhood.

We left the section on the punitive child in adulthood by considering the successful careerist, and it is this personality that could be most challenged in older adulthood. An individual who has spent the greater part of a lifetime avoiding need and dependency will be hugely threatened by any situation which requires his or her acceptance of any form of care, particularly any care which requires relinquishing control over daily decisions about all aspects of life. An individual who has been needy for the greater part of life may become over-dependent on carers because the dependency needs are being met: carers may collude with a 'good patient' and willingly limit any control that the older adult might have been encouraged to use.

Critical Thinking

Cumming and Henry (1961) wrote about disengagement in older adulthood as a justification for people's withdrawal from activities and interactions, putting a positive emphasis on more contemplative, reflective use of energy. Atchley (1989) and other theorists have placed more emphasis on a continuation of activities and interactions from adulthood into older age.

Given your knowledge of the individual development explained by object relations theory, how would you critically evaluate disengagement and activity theory?

In any adult-to-adult interaction it is vital that we are as aware of ourselves and our own possible splits: we need to be engaging our central ego as far as possible. If we can do so, we are likely to engage with other people as ideal objects and less as exciting or rejecting objects. The more we engage our central ego, the more we encourage the other person to use or to strengthen their central ego. While those individuals who have more dominant libidinal or anti-libidinal ego in older age may have invested so much of their personality in these splits that they will be unable to change the way they consciously feel, there are many others in the middle range who will be able to respond to a mature adult approach to their situation.

Case Study 2

Sandy is an 87-year-old former farm worker who lives in a small house in the countryside about ten miles from the nearest town and services. The house has been a family home for three generations, and Sandy has been, like his father and grandfather, an active worker throughout his life. He has never been physically ill-treated or abused, but he certainly grew up without affection: the emphasis in the family was on productivity, and the family myth (see Chapter 11) was probably 'men have to be strong'. As a result, in object relations terms, Sandy grew up with a huge unconscious fear of being dependent, and so he had to split off and punish any feelings of need which would sit painfully with his self-image. While he had the occasional girlfriend in his teens and early adult years, he could never sustain a relationship and he remains single and childless. He is, however, well-liked in the area, because he has been a handyman helper to lots of farming neighbours, and, despite his age, his physical strength was considerable.

Sandy has recently had a stroke, which has left him with weakness down one side of his body. You are a member of a care management team and have been asked to assess Sandy by his GP. Sandy is very definite about several things: he will never leave his home, he will not accept anyone coming into his home to do housework or cooking and he will not travel to be part of any group activity. He gets by with difficulty, and his house becomes less clean. There is a small network of farming neighbours who have begun calling in and delivering meals to Sandy, so he is regularly fed, but he refuses any further offers of help. You have discussed options with him, but he politely and firmly tells you not to bother. You can see that what some people might call 'pride', but which in personality terms is a dominant anti-libidinal ego, prevents Sandy from accepting help. Physically, he is frail, there is a growing health risk in the house and Sandy would be safer in a more sheltered or residential setting. Emotionally, however, Sandy would be most unhappy, unsettled and stressed in such settings, even if some feel he would be 'better off'.

Ultimately, an electric heater in Sandy's cottage develops a fault and a small fire breaks out while he is asleep. It extinguishes itself eventually, but Sandy is found dead next day by one of the neighbouring farm workers, having died from smoke inhalation. The local press runs a feature criticising the care services for leaving Sandy alone in a fairly remote area.

Some guilt would be a human reaction, but careful reflection would hopefully convince you that there was nothing else you could have done without grossly interfering with Sandy's rights. You could have oppressed him with other professionals into accepting a safer course of action against his clearly expressed wishes. His dominant anti-libidinal ego which directed his feelings and behaviour was not a mental illness, but a way of relating to the world and was built up since childhood. He had been able to accept some assistance from others, but only those he knew well enough to be comfortable with, and even here there were limits. His right to self-determination had been ethically upheld, and any risk he presented was to himself and not to others.

CONCLUSION

This chapter concludes the chronological section of the book. We hope that you will now be able to identify common areas of thinking within attachment theory, life cycle theory and object relations theory. We also hope that you now have more options available to you in order to explain and understand aspects of behaviour which stem from infancy but affect life at any time.

PART 4
SURVIVING LIFE'S CHALLENGES

We have spent time looking at chronological development in relation to three key psychoanalytic theories, but in the next section we will look at other factors which need to be considered alongside attachment, life stage development and object relations. As we have stated throughout this book, when working with service users we need to consider a multitude of theories to inform practice, and psychoanalytic theories are just a small part of the whole toolbox. A good understanding of psychoanalytic approaches will help understand coping strategies as life events pose challenges.

In this section, we begin by looking at loss and change, an area of study which initiated many of the psychoanalytic theories used in social work today – Freud wrote about loss, Bowlby was influenced by the effect of loss on children to inform his writings on attachment, and it is an area that will touch every human life. These can be anxiety-provoking times, therefore we look at coping strategies and how these can be determined based on theoretical exploration.

Not all change is unexpected, and some changes occur naturally, so in this section we look at the psychological impact of transition. Reference will be made to Bronfenbrenner's model again, and the areas of influence he defined will be considered within the context of families, trauma and resilience.

10 LOSS, CHANGE AND TRANSITIONS

One thing we can say with certainty is that life is uncertain. As we grow, we change physically, mentally and emotionally. We learn about love, life and loss, and we have to adapt to ever-changing situations. For most people these changes are dealt with in their stride, but for others change can become overwhelming and coping strategies become challenged.

In social work, we deal with people who are trying to come to terms with some kind of change – a change of circumstance, a change in liberty, a change brought on by ageing, even a change of caregiver – and these changes inevitably accompany loss. In this section, we look at some of the dominant theorists who have attempted to define the essence of loss and change to explain what is happening to us when faced with new situations. For some, these models might perfectly define a passage through loss and change, but for others grief can become problematic.

Focus will also be given to change and the psychological aspects associated with the process, known as 'transitions'.

By the end of the chapter the reader should:

- Understand what loss means
- Have considered different approaches to understanding stages of mourning and grieving
- Understand the impact of change, and resistance to change
- Be familiar with the psychological process of transitions

LOSS

It is seen that many of the troubles we are called upon to treat in our patients are to be traced, a least in part, to a separation or a loss that occurred either recently or at some earlier period in life. (Bowlby, 1979: 81)

The role of a social worker involves helping service users deal with change, and change usually happens because of a loss. This loss can take many forms – it might be loss of a loved one due to bereavement; it might be loss of independence due to an accident or the ageing process; or it might be loss of a role due to redundancy or financial ruin – the reasons that service users come into contact with social work are varied, but each will involve a loss and a consequential change. Experiencing the death of a loved one is the ultimate loss we will ever know, and the emotions felt will be greater than any other loss, but in social work we have to deal with these emotional outpourings from service users experiencing loss on many different levels. It is therefore important to understand the processes of loss and change, the theoretical stages we go through, and the impact of problematic grief. It is also important to understand that loss and change are situational experiences, the readjustment process which we move through on a psychological level is known as 'transition', and some examination will be given to this process, too.

FREUD

Most of the theorists who have written about loss and change approach the subject from the perspective of bereavement. In 1917, Freud [1957] wrote about 'Mourning and Melancholia' and termed the process of mourning as a 'normal' one. He recognised that the emotions felt when mourning, and when melancholic, were very similar in that they involved experiencing painful dejection, lack of interest in surroundings, an inability to express love and a lack of motivation. Freud went on to write that the two states can only be differentiated by the addition of a sense of worthlessness and an expectation of punishment which accompanies feelings of melancholy. Freud believed that the ego became entrenched in working through the experienced loss. He recognised that individuals invested emotional energy into relationships, which he termed 'cathexis', and that bereavement involved a withdrawal of this energy, which was followed by detachment, or 'decathexis', and then reflecting on thoughts, beliefs and memories of the deceased, which he termed 'hypercathexis'. The result of this process, Freud believed, was a detachment from the relationship. As Freud had identified the libidinal energies involved in cathexis, his writings became influential in psychodynamic literature and impacted on the work of object relations theorists, as well as attachment theorists who were informed by his writings on attaching and detaching from loved ones.

The grieving process should culminate in the ego accepting the loss, emotionally relocating the deceased person and allowing the ego to look for new attachments. Freud recognised that these new attachments may never 'replace' the lost relationship and that, once emotionally relocated, a continuing connection can still be had with what was lost (Mallon, 2008). Problematic grief occurs when the cathexis continues to fixate on the lost person and cannot accept the fact that they are no longer available. When this occurs, Freud believed that mourning tips into melancholia.

This proved a useful starting point for many of the theorists who currently inform social work practice as Freud had identified the importance of attachment, acknowledged that grief was a natural process which had to be worked through, and that problematic grief happens when there have been unresolved issues within the relationship. It demonstrates the importance of attachment within relationships, the loss of which results in detachment and searching for the lost relationship. When the loss of the relationship is greater, there will be a number of associated losses. To put this into perspective, it is worth considering Maslow's hierarchy of needs.

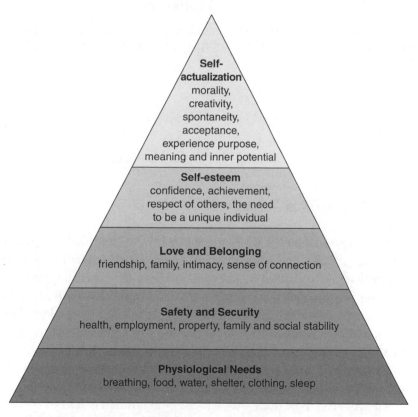

Figure 10.1 Maslow's (1943) hierarchy of needs

Maslow (1943) studied the psychology of human motivation and proposed that we all have needs that require satisfying. If needs are not met, then anxiousness and other negative emotions tend to dominate and motivation to address more advanced needs is non-existent. This basic model (Figure 10.1) can help to understand losses when grieving. When a significant relationship ends, the associated losses usually include love, financial security, routine, friendship and warmth and there will be an impact on identity. Loss of identity may impact on confidence and self-esteem and lead to isolation from networks of friends and other support structures, therefore a sense of connection is lost. If the financial loss is significant, then security could be jeopardised and there may be consequential impacts on health and well-being due to stress and mental ill health. Over the course of a few weeks, the losses experienced could see a person move from the top of Maslow's hierarchy (self-actualisation) to the bottom (physiological needs).

Critical Thinking

Try to think about some of the losses you have experienced in life that have *not* involved bereavement. How have they affected your journey on Maslow's model in Figure 10.1?
   Examples might include:

- loss of a job
- the breakup of a relationship
- loss of a valuable possession

MOURNING AS A TASK?

Worden (2008) expanded on the work of Freud when he identified the grief process as being a series of tasks that someone needs to move through. The first task he identified was that the loss had to be accepted and the comprehension that a reunion was never going to be possible had to be achieved. Once this has been accomplished, the next task involves experiencing the pain and grief caused by the loss. The third task entails adjustment wherein environmental and psychological factors need to be reassessed and reordered in order to cope in a world where the deceased is absent. This can be a lengthy process because the number of readjustments can be sizeable. There can be issues around identity, security, finances and accommodation, and each and every one will need to be dealt with which could ultimately lead to the adoption of a completely new lifestyle – and not necessarily in a positive way. After the process of dealing with acceptance, grief and adjustment, the fourth task involves emotional relocation where the deceased still has a presence in the life of the bereaved, but in an altered manner, allowing the bereaved to proceed with life.

Worden offers a simplistic view of the process, reducing the process to tasks, but at the core of Freud's work, and Worden's tasks, lay issues of attachment and dealing with a significant change within the established norms of the relationship. For some, the process of grieving will happen in a linear manner as described by these theorists, but for others grief becomes problematic and 'stages' become impossible to progress through. Wortman and Silver (2001) identified four distinct patterns of grief – normal, chronic, delayed and avoided – and in order to understand what impacts on differing coping strategies, we need to turn to the work of Bowlby and consider attachment in further detail.

BOWLBY AND PARKES

In Chapters 1, 4 and 7, we looked at Bowlby's attachment theory, in which he described the ways in which children form relationships so that their needs can be met. These needs have to be met in order to stave off danger, and to a child, one of the main dangers that they experience is separation from the caregiver. This separation can indicate abandonment, and for a helpless child who cannot meet their own needs, this is a life-threatening situation. Bowlby recognised a pattern within children who experienced separation, both short-term and permanent – a child experiences sadness to begin with, but soon moves on to anxiousness and protests against the separation; this is followed by grief, and if the separation is permanent there will also be a period of mourning (Bowlby, 1980).

Parkes and Prigerson (2010) viewed the process of grieving as a psychosocial transition, wherein the bereaved person has to deal with the loss, but within the confines of what is deemed socially acceptable. The bereaved person should not cry non-stop and wander round the neighbourhood shouting for the deceased person night after night, nor should they continue their daily routine as if nothing has happened – society dictates that a balance must be found, and every society has socially acceptable ways of dealing with loss from the outset, but at the same time, not many societies have guidance on how to deal with the long-term grieving process. Parkes (1988) believes that this is an emotional balancing act, in which the bereaved person has to find the acceptable point between avoidance and confrontation. The psychosocial transition is a process of re-learning about the world in which a loved one is now absent.

Both Bowlby and Parkes identified a change that occurred when a loss was experienced. Parkes (1988) states that the change occurs in the assumptive world, in that all of our assumptions about the person who is absent are now challenged – we assume that they will return home at a given time, we assume an identity because of the relationships we are in, and we assume that there is order and reliability in our world – all this is overturned and the assumptive world is challenged when confronted with loss. Bowlby (1979, 1980, 2008) talked of a secure base and safe haven which can also be threatened when loss occurs. He believed that an affectional bond was broken when loss is experienced and that the natural process of grieving begins, but will be very much shaped by environmental factors as well as psychological ones. This led Bowlby and Parkes (1970) to propose four stages of grief through which people move:

- The first stage is defined as *shock and numbness*. This usually proceeds after the immediate news of the loss but can go on for several days when the reality of the situation is not comprehended and denial is often witnessed. This stage usually involves physical distress and emotional outpouring, but is viewed as a cathartic process in that the bereaved person can work through these emotions and understand why they are being experienced, and then arrive at a more effective way to communicate inner feelings. The danger at this stage involves an inability to move onto the next stage because of complex feelings associated with the deceased, such as anxious/ambivalent attachment (or disorganised attachment), or suppression of emotions because of an avoidant attachment style to the deceased.

- *Yearning, separation and pain* follow, where the void becomes a reality and the bereaved person tries to find reminders of the deceased wherever possible. This stage will see grief coming in waves and an increase in anxiety, which can compound existing issues already causing feelings of anxiousness. There may well be a sense of guilt that the bereaved person did not do enough to keep the deceased alive and 'what if …' thinking dominates. Bowlby and Parkes (1970) state that there is a risk of becoming entrenched in searching for reminders and becoming preoccupied with the deceased, thus preventing natural progression through stages. Looking at the theorists covered so far, we can see that service users who already live with guilt complexes, or preoccupied attachment styles, might face particular difficulties progressing through this stage.

- *Despair* follows when acceptance dawns on the bereaved. Things are never going to be the same again and that knowledge has become a reality. This stage will be accompanied by many emotional responses, which include hopelessness, anger and questioning. Moods are low and depression is not uncommon, and the danger here is that the bereaved person remains angry and depressed. There is a general sense of being disorganised, which, on top of an insecure attachment style, can add additional stress to coping strategies. It is not uncommon to become withdrawn from other people at this stage, which can isolate individuals from support networks.

- The last stage should involve *acceptance and reorganisation*. Hope and faith return and the recovery process begins in earnest. The bereaved can start to think about future plans and goals and the attachment with the deceased has been readjusted, and in some cases, let go. Bowlby (1980, 2008) described this stage as loss receding in the mind to be replaced by returning trust and positivity, but the loss never disappears, part of it remains with us forever and will play a role in influencing future actions. A common expression one might use at this stage is 'moving on with life'.

Parkes and Prigerson (2010) further developed theory on the stages of grief. In the process of yearning, separation, pain and despair, the impulse to search for the lost person or object was highlighted, reflecting our inner need to bring back or find whoever or whatever we have lost, a need which becomes stronger in relation to the depth of attachment we had. This stage may be complicated if, for example, someone is lost at sea and no body is recovered, or goes missing with no further contact. The stage of anger and guilt was also more clearly identified, and the stage of mitigation was introduced. As part of our adjustment to a loss, it is important that we can come to terms with the reason for it. For example, the loss of an aged grandparent may be distressing, but it is possible to understand death as a part of ageing. The loss of a child may be harder to accept and comprehend. These stages may be short-lived or long-lived, depending on the complicating factors surrounding the loss, and it is so important to consider the unique circumstances of each individual based on the pattern of attachment which has been lost, the nature of the loss, the manner of the loss and the extent to which the loss is expected or unexpected.

Critical Thinking

To an extent, the stages of grief described by Bowlby and Parkes (1970) underpin all stages of loss. Imagine you went to unlock your car door and accidently dropped your keys down a drain. Not only were your car keys on the ring, but your office keys and your house keys were, too – and all of your belongings are locked in the car!

Describing the process using the four stages of grief might go something like this:

Shock and numbness: Panic and distress take over as you realise that your keys are now at the bottom of a drain. You cannot believe that this has just happened and you try to get them back by pulling at the immovable grate and poking the water with a twig, and you search your pockets for a big magnet that you might have left in there, knowing full well that you are carrying no such object.

Yearning, separation and pain: The reality of the situation dawns on you. You realise that all of your belongings are in the car, and you have no house keys or office keys anymore. You know that this is going to be complicated (and expensive) to fix and you might even cry, but you then pull yourself together to think about the situation again, before another wave of realisation hits you that your phone is also in the car and you cry again. You want to call for someone to come and help, to fix the situation, to make things better, but there is no one around and no phone to call from. You think that everything would be easier if you had your phone and tell yourself 'what if I kept it in my pocket all the time, instead of in my bag!' and 'what if I had just held onto the keys!'

(Continued)

(Continued)

Despair: The situation appears hopeless and there is no one to blame but yourself. You are angry and disappointed and just want to be home. Because you are so angry, it is difficult to think straight and there is a temptation to simply wallow in the despair of the situation.

Acceptance and reorganisation: You realise that the only way to fix the situation is if you take charge. You begin to consider your options and become aware that the solution is going to involve a long walk to find someone to help. Twenty minutes down the road is a newsagents, so you go in there and explain your situation, and the manager lets you use the phone. You call your partner, who takes a note of your phone number and calls you back with a number for a locksmith who specialises in car locks.

Once the situation is rectified you might even change the way you carry possessions in case of future emergencies, so some reflection might be beneficial to the way you continue to live.

Clearly, this is a low-level example of a loss to illustrate the use of Bowlby and Parkes's stages, but can you think of other losses that you might have experienced that you can relate to these stages? It is important to consider this process when dealing with service users experiencing loss as their emotional reactions might well be influenced by these stages.

KUBLER-ROSS

Not all loss is unexpected, and Elisabeth Kubler-Ross (1970) worked with terminally ill patients for a number of years, recognising the stages of loss experienced by people who knew that loss was coming. She felt that Parkes and Bowlby's stages of grief were important, but identified that terminally ill patients also moved through similar stages when preparing to die. She wrote about five stages:

1. *Denial*: When the initial diagnosis is given there is a period where belief is suspended and there is an inability, or unwillingness, to accept the news. If we relate this to Freud's defence mechanisms, this is a basic way for the ego to protect the id.
2. *Anger*: Eventually the news sinks in and denial gives way to anger. The anger can be directed at anyone – family members for being overly sympathetic, medical staff for not being quick enough to recognise the symptoms – and the service user will ask themselves 'why me?' Anger is a natural response when norms are challenged and social workers may often be at the receiving end of this as they engage with service users to facilitate processes through loss and change.

3. *Bargaining*: Kubler-Ross recognised that there is often a spiritual element involved in the process and she identified that God (or another force) is called upon and asked to give a cure, or at least some extra time.
4. *Depression*: Reality dictates that there is only one direction that the prognosis is going in and this is the lowest point in the process.
5. *Acceptance*: If there is an adequate amount of time for the service user to move through the grieving process, Kubler-Ross believed that they will arrive at a point where they accept their fate and allow for a period of reflection and contemplation where life is assessed.

Kubler-Ross stated that the stages were not linear, and that a person moving through the process could move from one to another in a random fashion, missing out some, and maybe becoming entrenched in one of the stages throughout the whole process.

In social work, there is an increasing emphasis on carers from within the family taking on a larger share of the provision of care and it becomes increasingly important to consider the ability of these family members. It is not only physical abilities that need to be taken into account, but emotional and psychosocial aspects, too, and Kubler-Ross's stages should also be considered when looking at the coping strategies of family members as they will also be moving through the stages as well. If a carer is in denial, will they be able to cope as the condition deteriorates? If the carer is in acceptance and the service user is at the stage of anger, how will that affect the dynamic? These theoretical approaches should force the profession to move beyond tick-box assessment of practical issues and actually look at the psychological impactors on the situation, too.

LE POIDEVIN'S CATEGORIES OF CHANGE

Linear models of grief may not explain the process of grief for a large majority of the population, and Payne et al. (1999) introduce Le Poidevin's multidimensional model as a means of understanding grief as it occurs across a number of dimensions. Susan Le Poidevin worked with Parkes and identified seven specific areas in which loss impacted which, she felt, should be considered by any professional working with a bereaved person to help understand areas that might be affected, provide insight into circumstances and help understand grief reactions. The seven areas are:

1. *Emotional response*: Professionals need to be aware that strong emotional responses are normal. Attachment patterns can impact on these responses, with avoidant/dismissive styles seeking to supress or deny emotional outpourings, whereas anxious/ambivalent (preoccupied) styles, as well as disorganised styles,

can become overwhelmed by extreme emotional reactions. Le Poidevin sought to discover how comfortable the bereaved person was with their own reactions, and how controlled they were in their responses.

2. *Social impact*: Loss affects social networks and this might result in a loss of status and a loss of role. Changes within the wider social network should also be considered and professionals should be asking who else will be affected by changes to the bereaved, too.

3. *Physical symptoms*: Stress and anxiety are damaging to physical health and it is not uncommon to see physical side effects when bereavement is faced. Professionals should always be on the lookout for physical ailments related to these emotions.

4. *Lifestyle*: The loss of a loved one might have significant financial implications for the bereaved and may result in the loss of security, and loss of the family home. Social workers will need to ask difficult questions at this time to ensure the bereaved is getting all of the benefits they are entitled to if the situation dictates.

5. *Practical issues*: Consideration will need to be given as to what the deceased provided in the relationship. As society becomes more reliant on informal carers, it becomes increasingly likely that the bereaved may have had a level of reliance on the departed and may have been receiving meals, bathing and medicine if the deceased was in a caring role. Other practical issues that might be affected include the ability to go to the shops for food and access to mobility services.

6. *Spiritual*: Kubler-Ross identified a spiritual element within her stages when preparing for loss, and Le Poidevin recognises that a significant loss can affect an existing belief system and may result in the loss of faith. Professionals should not be afraid to broach this subject and consider the impacts that a loss of faith may bring with it, while also considering if any 'meaning' has been attributed to the loss.

7. *Identity*: Any change in the previous six factors will impact on identity, and professionals need to consider how self-esteem, self-efficacy and self-worth are affected. There are no clinical tools that social workers can use to ascertain these concepts, so professionals need to be subjective in their assessment, but always on the lookout for ways in which these concepts can be enhanced.

These seven concepts provide a framework for professionals to consider when working with someone who has been bereaved. Negative changes in all seven areas would suggest an extreme reaction to grief, but consideration of all the areas can also help to identify support structures that may already exist within the lives of the bereaved.

We have looked at a number of theories that propose how we cope with loss, but losses come in all shapes and sizes, and ultimately it comes down to the human ability of dealing with change that underpins the process.

CHANGE

Peter Marris (1986) writes that all change involves aspects of loss, but the intensity of the loss experienced will depend on how the change occurs. He viewed change as a concept that fell into one of three categories: first, change might involve *substitution* wherein the old is replaced by the new, which is normally viewed as a positive change; second, change might involve *evolution* where the natural course of events see change happen over a period of time which may involve the re-evaluation of attachments within relationships; and, third, change might involve *deep loss* where something that has been loved disappears suddenly. Marris recognised that humans generally struggle with change because we have a need to try to retain familiarity – we like predictability and routine because it provides reassurance in a chaotic world. Bowlby talks of the importance of the secure base which allows exploration, but with a knowledge that we can return to a place for safety and security – Marris would reiterate this viewpoint by arguing that we retain this need for safety and security throughout life and we psychologically obtain this through predictability – if this is taken away from us then we feel threatened and we try to hold onto the familiar in an attempt to avoid change.

Marris (in Parkes et al., 2006) explains that there are a number of factors that can affect ability to cope with change. To begin with, anything that disrupts our ordered, patterned, view of the world may trigger feelings of bewilderment and futility, particularly when they threaten existing attachments. Sudden changes in relationship status can cause disruptions, and Marris points out that loss of self-esteem and self-identity can be just as disruptive.

He goes on to explain that all inexplicable events are disturbing, but when they threaten attachments the effect is compounded. Events become inexplicable when they do not fit into the norms of everyday life, or when they challenge our cultural values. The crashing of planes into the Twin Towers in September 2001 was one such event that remains completely inexplicable to most human beings, and that event has caused changes across the planet, but also for anyone living through the event, it has caused changes in our perceptions of what human beings are capable of. Similar feelings are caused when young children get a diagnosis of serious illnesses and we struggle to comprehend why someone so young, healthy and innocent should become ill.

The timing of events can also cause significant disturbance. If change is both sudden and unexpected there is no preparation time, and we are plunged into an immediate juxtaposition. However, Marris also identifies protective factors and states that supportive relationships can cushion feelings associated with change, especially if relationships are based on mutuality. Open communication allows the free flow of emotions which can help through the change process.

Finally, Marris points towards the importance of attachment and believes that a loss experienced in childhood might lead to a mistrust of attachment and, instead of basing future interactions on quality of attachment, they are based on ambivalence:

> The motives for living are confused by anxious impulses to test, conciliate, or defend oneself against attachment figures…this underlying mistrust is likely to inhibit the relationships which could provide support in misfortune. (Parkes et al., 1991: 83)

In 1967, two psychiatrists named Thomas Holmes and Richard Rahe devised a social readjustment rating scale to measure stressful responses to 43 life events and rated each event so that an individual could total up the cumulative stress factors and ascertain how this stress may impact on health:

1.	Death of spouse	100	20. A large mortgage/loan	31
2.	Divorce	73	21. Foreclosure of mortgage/loan	30
3.	Marital separation	65	22. Change in work responsibilities	29
4.	Prison sentence	63	23. Child leaving home	29
5.	Death of a close family member	63	24. Trouble with in-laws	29
6.	Personal injury or illness	53	25. Outstanding personal achievement	28
7.	Getting married	50	26. Partner begins or stops work	26
8.	Losing job	47	27. Starting/ending education	26
9.	Marital reconciliation	45	28. Change in living conditions	25
10.	Retirement	45	29. Revision of personal habits	24
11.	Change in health of family member	44	30. Problems with boss	23
12.	Pregnancy	40	31. Change in work hours/conditions	20
13.	Sex difficulties	39	32. Change in residence	20
14.	Gaining a new family member	39	33. Change in education	20
15.	Business readjustment	39	34. Change in recreation	19
16.	Change in finances	38	35. Change in church activities	19
17.	Death of a close friend	37		
18.	New job	36		
19.	Increased arguments with partner	35		

36.	Change in social activities	18	40.	Change in eating habits	15
37.	A moderate loan/ mortgage	17	41.	Holiday	13
38.	Change in sleeping habits	16	42.	Christmas	12
39.	Change in family get-togethers	15	43.	Minor trouble with the law	11

If you score 300+, then you are at high risk of illness in the near future due to stress.

If you score 150–299, then the chance of becoming ill is moderate to high.

If you score less than 150, then the chance is only low to moderate. (Holmes and Rahe, 1967)

Every single factor identified by Holmes and Rahe involves change, and they established a clear link between change and stress – even positive change will produce a certain amount of stress. Our internal working model is challenged when faced with change and the familiarity and security requires reassessment.

Within social work, change is at the heart of the profession. The job of the social worker is to help someone through the change process and to do that effectively we have to be aware of the stress that change can cause, but also underlying psychosocial factors that might impact on stress levels. When considering the impact of attachment theory, for example, we can assume that someone with a secure attachment will be resilient when faced with change; a preoccupied attachment may become entrenched in the process of change and be prone to anxiety attacks, or become overly needy and resort to exhibiting learned helplessness tendencies which the worker needs to be wary of as this can work against empowerment and enablement; dismissive attachment might result in either avoiding the situation or becoming overly controlling of the situation, but there are increased health risks in terms of psychosomatic reactions because of an inability to externalise emotions; and disorganised attachments can result in significant bouts of depression. It is also important to remember that social workers are not immune from change processes themselves and need to be aware of how change in their own lives is impacting on their practice.

Case Study

Albert and Wilma had been married for 65 years until Wilma's death from cancer. Wilma had been caring for Albert for the past seven years since his ailing health began to impact on his physical abilities. Now, with Wilma gone, Albert has been struggling to cope on his own at home.

(Continued)

(Continued)

A care management assessment was arranged through the GP and there were a number of risks identified that indicated that Albert might be better supported in nursing home care, primarily around personal care issues. A place was found in an establishment thirty miles away from his house and he was transported there by ambulance with a boxful of his possessions. His lawyer began proceedings to sell his house to contribute towards the cost of care. It took three weeks between the time of the death of his wife and moving into the nursing home.

Albert moved into a room in the nursing home which had a view of the neighbouring factory. He spent most of the day propped up in bed. A care assistant came through to take him for lunch and swung his legs out of bed, at which point Albert struck him with his stick and told him to 'show some respect!' The care assistant filed a complaint, the care manager was contacted and a meeting was convened.

At the meeting, it transpired that the staff had other concerns about Albert. He was agitated, cried a lot, kept shouting for Wilma and had been verbally aggressive on occasions. The staff felt that he might require an Elderly Mentally Infirm (EMI) unit to manage his behaviour.

Task

- Given what you have read about loss and change in this chapter, consider how much of Albert's behaviour can be attributed to this process.
- List the losses and changes that he has had to face.
- How could you work with Albert to help him address the losses and changes that he has been through?

TRANSITIONS – THE PSYCHOLOGICAL ASPECT OF CHANGE

Change will always occur and is something that we as humans have to deal with. Some changes are sudden, like the loss of a loved one, while others are gradual, like puberty and the ageing process. Bridges (2004, 2009) viewed change as being situational – such as a new job, a broken down car, lost keys, or starting university – and he believes that it is not necessarily the change that we have issues with, but, rather, *adapting* to the change. He explains that it is the psychological aspect of change that can cause problems for people, and he termed this process 'transition'.

When faced with change, Bridges explains that everyone has three options on which to focus their energies: to begin with, a person might choose to focus on the past as there is familiarity, routine and comfort in certainty, but this brings with it a danger in that it inhibits forward progression and growth. He recognises that this is a comfortable position for many. Second, a person might focus on the future, but this does require a leap of faith into the unknown. Bridges explains that focusing on the future can bring hope, development and growth and can bring excitement, but in social work we have to recognise that optimism is required to reach this point in the transition process and might not be immediately available to many service users we come into contact with. The third area in which energies can be focused is the neutral zone, which is an area where the psychological impacts of change are tested as we explore the ambiguity of new situations. Bridges warns that there can be a tendency to slip back into the past when in the neutral zone because the ambiguity might prove too much for a person forcing them to retreat to the familiarity of the past, so people who are in the neutral zone should be encouraged to consider future possibilities, and this is where social work can provide a safe space for service users to explore emotions and express negative emotions in a non-judgemental environment.

BRIDGES – THE THREE SEASONS

Seasonal elements are often equated with the process of transition. Autumn is linked to endings, when things naturally draw to a close; winter represents the emotional void left by what used to be, but provides time to ponder opportunities; while spring brings about rebirth and new opportunities.

Autumn

Every change begins with an ending of some kind. Take, for example, the process of losing a job – the process of change begins when you get notification that your job will be terminated. The familiar processes outlined earlier in this chapter begin and you move into denial, then shock and pain. The psychological process is uncomfortable and you have to face up to the fact that things are ending and will never be the same again – your internal working model is challenged and this is not a nice feeling – uncertainty is unsettling. You also have to contend with associated losses which might result in loss of financial security, loss of purpose, loss of self-esteem and a loss of identity. It might even impact on your social network. The emotional turmoil experienced at this stage can produce overwhelming feelings of anxiety.

Even positive changes bring on anxiety – if we consider the feelings associated with a job ending because of a new job offer, there are losses to be dealt with in that scenario, too – loss of routine, loss of familiarity, loss of workmates. Many endings are marked by an occasion to formalise the process: moving jobs often results in a social gathering, a card and a present for the worker who is leaving; a family meal might mark a child moving onto university and out of the family home; and even the most significant of endings, the death of a loved one, is marked by the formal occasion of a funeral. These occasions are helpful in the process as it definitively marks a turning point, but not all changes can be marked by these events.

Winter

The neutral zone is represented by winter.

At this point, the change has been made and there is time to contemplate what was, but also consider what will be. Using the analogy of losing a job there will still be a high degree of uncertainty, and the consequences of the associated losses will need to be addressed, but within this there are also opportunities for creativity. More often than not, negative emotions will dominate at this stage because of the fear and uncertainty brought on by the change – there may be anger and confusion, and certainly stress. As the process progresses there should be signs of positive emotions beginning to dominate, particularly if hope is viewed as an outcome of the change.

This stage has been compared to being on a trapeze, where the person going through change is between two safety zones – the one they left in the past, and the one they are heading for in the future, and this brings on feelings of both danger and opportunity. It has also been referred to as 'being in limbo' and if you have spent any time waiting for something to happen which will affect your life, this feeling should be familiar to you.

This is an important point to consider in social work service delivery as the majority of service users we work with are 'in limbo' and between two safety zones. Children and Families social work might see a child placed in temporary foster care while a permanent option is investigated; Substance Use services might see someone being placed in residential detox for a set period of time; Care Management services might be assessing a person for long–term nursing home care but have to wait for an appropriate setting to become available – as social workers, we need to be aware of how this elongated process can impact on the psychological coping strategies of already vulnerable service users.

Spring

Spring represents new beginnings and this should grow from the previous two stages. There may well be a formal announcement of the new way that has been chosen, and this might bring with it further issues of loss and change, after all, what might be a new way for one person may result in a change for someone else and force them to readjust to the new situation. This might present resistance and resentment from other people which will reignite feelings of anxiety. For some, this might be too much to cope with and may well tip someone back into the now familiar territory of the neutral zone to think again.

However, if hope prevails then the change should be embraced by the person who has gone through the process and there should be enthusiasm. This is not the time for social work to abandon the service user if they have successfully transitioned this far as support is required to maintain the change. Useful techniques at this stage would include goal-setting and the consideration of objectives that the service user would like to consider working towards to enhance the change.

Bridges (2004, 2009) advocates the use of the four Ps to assist in the final stages of transition. He explains that the process can be supported by using the following technique:

Purpose: The reason for making the change must be clear. Understanding why change has to be made can reinforce the positive emotions around enthusiasm, creativity and hope.

Picture: Visualise where the process will end. If the service user is artistic then use creative techniques to support the process of visualisation, but certainly conversations clearly expressing an end goal will enhance the purpose of change.

Plan: Think carefully about what needs to be done to achieve the end goal. Using the SMART analogy to ensure that the plan is Specific, Measurable, Achievable, Realistic and Time-bound can be useful in defining steps in the process.

Part: Consideration finally needs to be given to who will also be involved in the process. Are there significant people in the service user's life who need to know about the steps being taken? Where might animosity come from once the change has been achieved, and can it be minimised from the outset? Supportive roles also need to be considered within the process, too.

Critical Thinking

Consider the process of transition outlined above and think about significant changes that you have experienced. They may be changes brought on by rites of passage, or they might be sudden, unexpected events that meant that you had to re-evaluate your life quickly. Can you chart the process by drawing out a timeline of events to represent your emotions throughout the process?

11 FAMILY SYSTEMS AND PSYCHODYNAMICS – IS THERE SUCH A THING AS A 'NORMAL' FAMILY?

When exploring interactions in their socioecological model, Bronfenbrenner and Bronfenbrenner (2009) recognised that the first course of influence on an individual was the relationship with their immediate family. We are nurtured by them, we observe them, we communicate with them and we learn from them, and these interactions will all impact on how we behave as we form relationships with other people.

This chapter focuses on the family as a unit and looks at how professionals can consider issues in the context of the family system. We will begin by looking at the life cycle of a family before focusing in on how families function as a 'system'. This can help define rules and beliefs within the family, which, in turn, can impact the structure of a family which will also be explored.

Psychoanalytic theories will also be considered throughout to illustrate family attitudes which underpin behaviours, and this will be linked back to attachment theory, object relations and Erikson's writings.

By the end of the chapter the reader should:

- Be able to identify and apply the family life cycle
- Understand the importance of differentiation of the self
- Recognise and use family systems theory
- Consider family structures and psychosocial consequences
- Realise the potential for creatively working with families to identify issues

FAMILY LIFE CYCLE

A useful starting point when working with an individual where you envisage the family may well impact on the issue at hand is to plot the family life cycle. The family life cycle incorporates a number of elements that we have covered in previous chapters: Erikson's recognition that there are stages in life where conflicts need to be resolved before healthy progression can continue; Freud's analysis of anxieties and how we adapt to try to reduce this; theories around loss and change in acknowledging that there is a psychological process which must be gone through; and transitions that naturally occur throughout life and place us in states of uncertainty and fear. Carter and McGoldrick (1988) developed the family life cycle from the work of a sociologist named Duvall (1977) and set the transitions that families progress through against the backdrop of a socioecological model similar to Bronfenbrenner's. They acknowledged that as families go through a life cycle, they will be impacted upon by external forces such as employment, education, mass media, local government, culture and values as well as national laws and policies.

Carter and McGoldrick (1988, 1999), as well as Carr (2003), recognised that there were generalisable steps that families transitioned through and defined these in eight stages:

Stage 1 – The origin family

The family is viewed as a base for exploring and learning. Bonds and attachments are built between parents and siblings, as well as the extended family unit. An individual learns what it means to be a member of that family and what is expected of them. There might be family history that impacts on all of the members of the family – for example, their surname might be synonymous with success and achievement, or trouble and crime. A child enters the world of education, but returns each day to the hub of the family and assimilates learning with experience. This is their family of origin.

Stage 2 – Leaving home

A strong sense of self has been established, but now the child who is leaving home has to work out a new identity for themselves while retaining elements of their familial identity. To do this they have to test out relationships and behaviours with their peers. Autonomy is enhanced and an individual moves towards independence by moving away from parents, getting a job and generating an income for themselves. It is also a time for experimenting with sexual relationships and forming appropriate adult-to-adult relationships, while adjusting relationships with parents accordingly to reflect these mature responsibilities.

Stage 3 – Pre-marriage

By now, the individual will have established the kind of romantic relationship that they wish to pursue and will have a clear idea about who they want to choose as their life partner. There may well be periods of trial and error within this but ultimately a decision should be formed at this stage, and then further decisions about where to live are required. Identity is usually enhanced at this stage by the involvement with another person and there can be a sense of achievement, and relief, once in a long-term relationship.

Stage 4 – Married (pre-children)

Decisions have been made, ceremonies performed and now married life begins in earnest. Traditionally, this was seen as a period of adjustment as the newlyweds got used to life together and incorporated each other's foibles and habits to enable harmonious living, but this will depend on whether the couple lived together in the pre-marriage stage or not. There will certainly be adjustment in relationships with parents and peers as a larger network of family and friends are incorporated into the lives of each person.

Stage 5 – Family with young children

Roles are reassessed and realigned. Individuals have now become parents themselves and have to adjust to the new responsibility. Lifestyles change, finances change and new networks develop, usually around other parents with young children. The education system is re-entered, but this time as an interested observer rather than a direct participant. A balance in parenting styles must also be negotiated, as well as adjustment in the roles of other family members who gain status changes when becoming grandparents.

Stage 6 – Family with adolescents

Adolescent children begin to become more autonomous and there is a shift towards independence, and this requires adjustment within the parenting relationship. This may also be a time to take on a caring role for older family members, particularly parents from the origin family. It is also a time to assess achievements in life and to think about the direction that careers will take.

Stage 7 – Family with children leaving/just left home

Now the time has come for children to leave home and the loss of the presence of the family within the home must be dealt with. Back at Stage 2, the relationship between children and parents had to be considered and adapted to reflect the adult roles, and the situation is now reversed and the individual is on the receiving end of this adjustment and must reflect on the transition they faced themselves. The family may grow in size as children pair off, marry and more in-laws enter the family circle. This may also be the time to confront the ailing health and death of family members from the origin family in Stage 1.

Stage 8 – Later life

Physical decline becomes a reality and this has to be processed. The carer becomes the cared for and children become the primary focus for meeting the needs in old age. This is a time of loss – loss of independence, loss of spouse, loss of friends, and eventually, loss of life. But it is also a time to reflect and benefit from the wisdom built up over a lifetime.

The family life cycle model is based on cultural norms and assumptions and aims to suggest a framework which recognises family norms and identifies where 'normal' periods of stress and anxieties can occur. However, the model has come under heavy criticism and has been accused of being applicable only to middle-class, nuclear families from a bygone era (Carr, 2003). The model does not consider homosexuality, arranged marriages, childless relationships, divorce, career changes, education at a later life stage, long-term unemployment or criminality, to name but a few. However, what it aims to do is to help families recognise that there will be periods within the life course of a family where problems naturally occur, and this does not mean that the family is 'bad'; it means that the problems need to be identified and processed so that the family can progress onwards.

> ### Critical Thinking
>
> Consider your family life cycle. Where are you at on the 8 stage journey? How about other members of your family? Is there anyone within your family who does not fit into any of the 8 stages neatly?
> Does the family life cycle model represent your view of what a family should be?

For many, this model might be too simplistic, stigmatising, or too far from the picture as to how their own family is presenting. Therefore, instead of viewing the family as a cohesive unit moving through a process, it might be better to view them as a system. In taking this approach, we need to look at the behaviours and beliefs of each member of the system to see where the problem may lie.

FAMILY SYSTEMS THEORY

We have already looked at Bronfenbrenner's socioecological model in relation to factors that impact on the functioning of an individual in everyday life, and Murray Bowen (1993) proposed that we need to recognise this approach when working with families. Families are not a solid unit – they are made up of a number of individuals who are all interconnected and interdependent and will be impacted on by one another's emotions and behaviours. He explains that we cannot work with an individual without recognising that they are part of a family system, and that family systems will impact on them. In turn, the family system will be affected by wider social, cultural and economic factors dictated by society

The basic premise of family systems theory is that every member of the family has a role to play. These roles are defined by birth, marriage, age and social status and are unwritten roles. Society will influence how these roles should be played out and the most common roles are 'father', 'mother', 'brother', 'sister', 'son' and 'daughter'. The traditional role of 'father' in UK society was of the family bread-winner, providing financially for the other members of the family and being an authority figure for the children; 'mother's' traditional role was to provide care for the children and to tend house while her husband was at work. Clearly, these are outdated definitions and it is important that role assumptions are not made by social workers who might have different familial experiences than those of their service users.

A useful starting point is to explore roles with members of the family to determine what their understanding and expectation of their individual roles might be. When these roles change because of events within (and out with) the family, the family tries to adapt their own roles to meet the challenge in an attempt to find equilibrium, but sometimes this can be difficult to achieve and problems arise. When these problems arise, anxiety levels increase and the emotional functioning of individuals within the family unit becomes jeopardised. Bowen identified eight interlocking concepts that impact on functioning within the family.

Differentiation of self

Bowen (1993) identified the impact that the formation of a sense of 'self' has on the ability to have an individual identity which is separate from the family. His standpoint recognises the work of Erikson, Fairbairn, Maslow and the attachment theorists in the importance of developing autonomy in an appropriate manner, and striving for self-actualisation, so that independence of intellect and emotion can be achieved. If a person has a poor sense of self then they are more prone to conformity, be it with peers or family. Bowen termed this 'low differentiation' and explained that, in the absence of a strong sense of self, the temptation is to view your identity as part of a group or collective who will accept the person, and approve that person, as a member of their group – this will involve conforming to group norms and group attitudes. The more entrenched and interdependent the group become, the more individual changes and stressors affect everyone, and the impact of the anxiety that is created becomes greater.

Nuclear family emotional system

The term 'nuclear family' might seem outdated, but Bowen was looking at relationships within the family unit, and, in particular, what happens when stress increases within the unit, and where signs of stress and anxiety might show. He believed that there were four main relationship patterns which could be affected by the stress:

- Conflict becomes apparent between the marital spouses and each one externalises their anxieties onto the other one and finds faults, criticises and tries to control the other.
- One spouse becomes dysfunctional due to the added pressure exerted on them by the other spouse. The dysfunctional member is simply yielding to issues of control from the other and trying to maintain family equilibrium, but at a cost to their own emotional coping strategies, mental health and physical well-being.
- Impairments within a child might become the focus of the stress and anxiety and the marital spouses become entrenched in their concerns for the child, which can be negative or overly idealised. The child becomes aware of the focus and tries to please the parents by adjusting their behaviour which risks affecting their own emotions, as well as performance at school.
- Similar to the adult attachment style of avoidant attachment, each family member withdraws and becomes emotionally isolated to protect themselves from potential hurt. The risk that each member faces is in becoming too isolated.

Triangles

Triangles are an important concept within family systems for professionals to understand because there is a risk that they can become an element of the triangle themselves. Bowen viewed a single relationship as a dyad, but explained that at times of tension a triad was often created to diffuse the stress. This triad often involved another person, or entity, and allowed energy to be refocused.

In theory, this should provide some stability, but problems occur when collusion between two of the elements within the triad excludes the third member. If a husband and wife are arguing, and the wife confides in their daughter and she sides with her mother, this can exclude the father from the relationship and risks isolating him. Similarly, if the husband views his work as a diffuser, he might spend more time there and exclude his wife from the relationship, thus isolating her. Instead of triangulation providing homeostasis, the relationship risks becoming perverse and pathological (Haley, 1967).

When working with families, professionals need to recognise that they risk becoming the third member of a triad. Members of the family may try to get the professional 'on their side' and present evidence as to why another family member is 'bad' and should be punished.

Family projection

It is important to remember that these eight concepts interlock, and family projection follows on from the 'Nuclear Family Emotional System', wherein the problems within the family manifested through concerns for a child. A parent may believe that the child has problems and focus more attention on that child; the child becomes aware of the increased focus on them and begins to adjust behaviour because of this; the change in behaviour confirms the parents' suspicions and they believe the problem is manifesting through this change. The child feels a responsibility to alleviate the parental concerns and becomes anxious and might develop heightened need for approval and attention. In essence, the whole process becomes a self-fulfilling prophesy and where there was no original problem with the child, one develops.

Multigenerational transmission process

Bowen proposed that many issues within families have been implanted by previous generations through conscious and unconscious processes. He explains that this stems from differentiation of the self and the impact this has on self-identity, as well as choosing life partners – the more differentiated an individual is, the better the chance of picking a life partner who is similarly comfortable with their self-identity, and the better the chance of developing a family who are equally as able to differentiate appropriately. Conversely, the lower the differentiation, the higher the chances are of seeking out a partner who also has low differentiation, and the greater are the chances of developing a family who are entrenched and unable to differentiate. Thus, the problems increase, generation after generation.

Emotional cutoff

Within the Nuclear Family Emotional System, the strategy of emotional isolation was identified and here Bowen recognises the impact of that strategy. He explained that everyone has a degree of emotional cutoff within family relationships and may choose not to talk about specific issues that are known to cause friction, but occasionally this can become extreme and topics for conversation can become very limited. When this happens, the temptation to withdraw completely from the family is increased and this may result in an individual totally removing themselves from the unit, breaking contact and never going back home.

The risk in this strategy is that the fleeing individual looks towards new relationships to fill the emotional gap left by the family void and this puts pressure on new partners, and new children. Bowen warns that patterns of behaviour which have been fled from will eventually re-emerge in new relationships and cause problems again. He suggests that contact with extended family members should be encouraged wherever possible as this still bonds an individual to the family, though at a distance.

Sibling position

In the 1960s, Walter Toman (1993) wrote about the effect of birth order on relationships within the family. Bowen built on this and explained that personalities and life partners are all influenced by the position within the family in relation to sibling relationships. The overarching propositions that Bowen and Toman suggested were that common characteristics were noticeable in individuals depending on their sibling positioning – generally, the oldest child tended to take on the role of leader (which often impacted on employment choices in later life), whereas younger siblings have a tendency to be followers. They also stated that problems within adult relationships could possibly be traced to sibling positioning and explained that if the oldest sibling marries someone who is a younger/youngest sibling, then this suggests that the relationship will last because both individuals will be familiar with their 'roles' from positioning as siblings. Conversely, if an oldest sibling marries someone who is also an older sibling then this might lead to problems in the relationship as they both vie for leadership.

This also affects the relationship between parents and children as it can be common for the oldest child to have experienced parental expectations which are higher than those for his/her siblings. This might result in the oldest child taking on more of a 'parenting' role themselves towards their brothers and sisters (Winek, 2009). The oldest child also goes through life first and is a pioneer for the sibling group in terms of being exposed to experiential learning which means the younger family members can learn from his/her mistakes, and the brunt of the parental frustration and anger is often directed at the eldest. Middle children will also have different experiences and may feel slightly 'forgotten' if the focus of attention is on the eldest and youngest child, whereas an only child may have constant parental attention while growing up and may bring this expectation into future relationships. Memories of sibling relationships are therefore a useful area for professionals to explore as these expectations may indicate relational problems in adult relationships.

Societal emotional process

The final concept that Bowen identified was the role of society on the family system. He believed society goes through periods of regression and progression, and the actions of large institutions such as the courts and education and attitudes of the mass media will filter down and impact on parenting styles within the family unit (which mirrors Bronfenbrenner's observations of relationships within society). He linked this back to differentiation and believed that society could be emotionally reactive in times of regression, but long-term strategies were generally utilised during periods of progression.

Societies are forever changing and adapting which can see populations living through uncertain times and competing ideologies. Here, we can see the impact of societal emotional processes when we look at the strategies of governments in dealing with threats from abroad – reactions are often in direct response to threats without any long-term planning and strategies, and Bowen may argue that this illustrates that we are in a period of societal regression. Individuals within society learn from what goes on around them, and if the message is short-term strategies for short-term goals, then this message may well filter down into family strategies, too.

The eight concepts that Bowen identified recognised the psychosocial impact on the development of a family and underpin current therapeutic family practice. From a social work perspective, this is a useful outline to consider when looking at problems arising from within the family and can help open up discussions with service users to minimise anxiety, exclusion and rejection, and to facilitate understanding and acceptance of the family unit (Schweitzer et al., 2007). Walker (in Lishman, 2007) explains that taking a family systems approach requires the professional to look for the problematic rules and beliefs within the family and work to change these, and to do this the worker needs to be impartial and neutral and also to investigate points of views from all members of the family by using techniques such as 'circular questioning' to illicit opinions on relationships between other family members. This approach can be used to ask each family member to define their perspective of the problem at hand, thus building up a picture of the relationship between individuals and the problem, as well as how they relate to each other. Often, the same questions are asked to each and every family member so that the practitioner can look at patterns of familial interactions. This differs from lineal questioning which can see the practitioner following a line of questioning to ascertain the cause and effect of a problem.

Critical Thinking

Genograms

A useful method for using family systems theory in social work practice is to ask the service user to pictorially represent their family by using a genogram (Figure 11.1). A genogram is a family map made up of symbols to represent each family member and lines between each symbol to represent relationships between family members. These lines might assign roles and societal norms such as 'married to' or 'children of', but they can also include colour and shape to indicate emotional relationships between each person, so a red line might indicate 'hostility', green might indicate 'harmony' and a broken line might indicate an estranged relationship. Below is a simple representation of the Simpsons family using shapes to illustrate gender, and different lines to represent relationships.

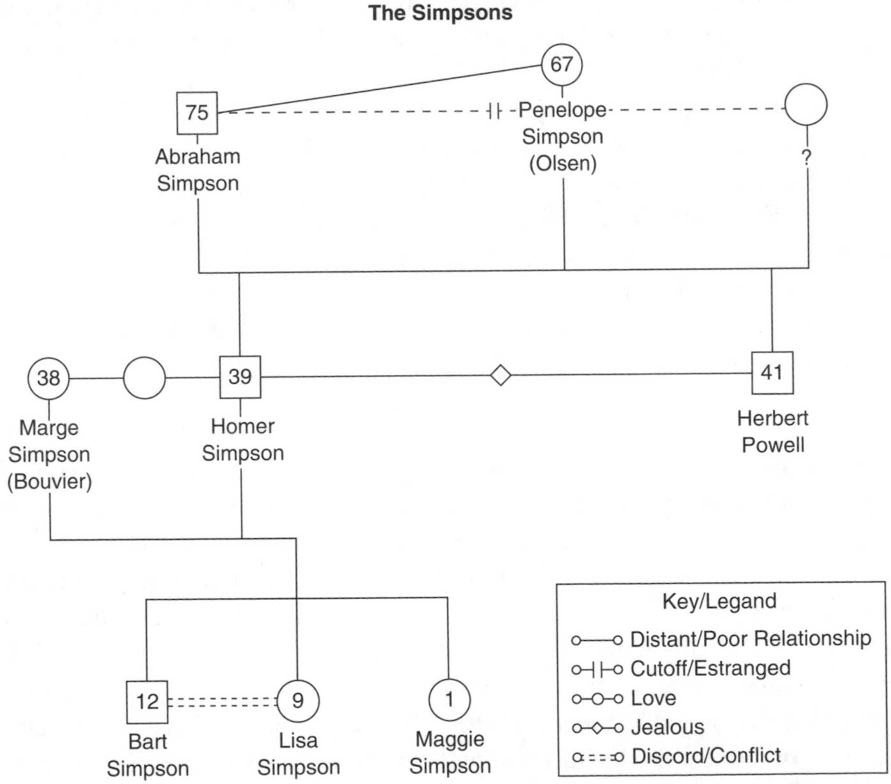

Figure 11.1 'The Simpsons' – An example of a genogram

Source: Pomerantz, 2014

Using genograms is an easy technique and helps to create a visual tool to understand relationships. There are established symbols which can be used for each family role, but asking the service user to come up with their own is also a good technique as the kind of symbol they draw can give insight into how they feel about the person they are representing.

Task

Using your own creative abilities, illustrate your family through the use of a genogram.

FAMILY STRUCTURE

Where family systems theory looks to change the established rules and beliefs, a family structure approach aims to change the roles and positions of individuals within the unit, the assumption being that the past has resulted in individuals within the family becoming entrenched in roles that they find conflicting, anxiety inducing, and stressful. Minuchin (1974) also recognised the importance of psychosocial development within the family and focused on the structure of the family to identify solutions to problematic behaviours and patterns. Many of the concepts he identified reinforce observations by Bowen and he viewed transactions within families as being the key to establishing family norms and structure – the more transactions are repeated, the more norms and structures are reinforced. In Minuchin's work, there is recognition that in order to change the structure, role and positioning of family members, you also need to consider rules, norms and beliefs within the family. Burnham (1968) explains that family structure is maintained by two different systems. The first is a generic system which governs family organisation, structure and lines of power; and the second is an idiosyncratic system which underpins expectations of the family members within the unit. Both should be adaptable, and both should provide family members with clearly defined roles and boundaries.

A family structure approach begins by looking at relationships within the family and trying to ascertain the overall structure of the unit. Minuchin identified that problematic families can be *enmeshed* or *disengaged*: an 'enmeshed' family becomes preoccupied in each other's lives and the actions of one family member is scrutinised and agonised over to the point where it dominates the actions of other family members (which echoes the preoccupied adult attachment style); while the 'disengaged' family have become so individually isolated from each other that there is virtually no emotional connection between each family member and they all exist in relative isolation from each other (which echoes the dismissive adult attachment style). These two extremes also mirror Bowen's Nuclear Family Emotional System and Differentiation concepts.

Minuchin also recognised the importance of Triangulation within relationships, but he focused more on relational 'subsets' within the family unit. These subsets might be natural in structure such as a spousal subset, a sibling subset, a parent–child subset, a grandparent–child subset, and should function appropriately depending on the individual roles within each subset. However, Minuchin highlighted that subsets can also be dysfunctional and actually harm the overall functioning of the family. Perhaps, a father–child subset might be used to discuss marital problems, thus challenging the mother–child subset and the spousal subset, and Minuchin would state that the problematic subset must be addressed and roles clarified so that the father–child subset could function appropriately wherein the child was not being used as a relationship counsellor for their parents. He also believed that the clarity of boundaries within each subsystem was more important than individual membership.

No matter how dysfunctional the family system appears, the chances are the family will be working towards maintaining an existing *homeostasis* because the rules and norms that have been established are firmly embedded and underpin behaviours. 'Homeostasis' can hold families together and there may well be a powerful matriarch or patriarch who exerts a positive influence on the rest of the family; but, equally, the control can be negative and prevent the healthy development of individuals, thus leading to dysfunction within the system. If one family member breaks the rules or goes against the norm, then other family members may well gang up against them to put pressure on them to change back their behaviour. In a way, it is like poking a jelly – you can push it and prod it, but eventually it wobbles back to the original position – Chapter 10 recognised the resistance that individuals can put up when faced with change, and a bigger system, such as a family, can be very influential in the behavioural change of individual members of the unit. This fact should emphasise to professionals the importance of working with all of the members of the family when looking at problematic behaviour and thinking about change. All members must be aware of the potential implications of change, preferably being able to recognise the benefits rather than the costs.

Another challenge the practitioner must face when working with family structure is to decipher the cause of the problems. Often this can be quite straightforward and we can see that there is a clear 'cause and effect' which is impacting on behaviour with the relationship. To give an example, a husband might be going out regularly after work with workmates, drinking too much, coming home, arguing with his wife, and causing unrest and discontent within the relationship. The cause is his alcohol consumption and the effect is upset within the martial home – this is an example of *linear causality*, where one problem leads to dysfunction. For professionals, linear causality is relatively easy to address; the problem is identified and everyone works to address the root cause.

Another form of dysfunction stems from *circular causality* and this makes the root problem difficult to identify, but the effects on individuals within the family is apparent. For example, a husband and wife argue at home, the children get upset, the oldest child slips out late at night to hang out with friends, the oldest child gets into trouble with the police for sniffing glue, parents argue, youngest child truants from school, parents argue … In this scenario, there is an ever-increasing circle where behaviour impacts on emotions, which impacts on coping strategies. When dealing with circular causality, there is often very little point in identifying a core issue: a more appropriate technique is to get the family to realise that there is a problem and to communicate with each other about how they are feeling and identify ways to deal with problems appropriately as they arise.

PSYCHODYNAMIC APPROACHES

As well as the family systems approach and the family structural approach, theorists have also identified the importance of psychodynamic approaches which incorporate considerations from all of the previous areas, but also focus in on specific issues which may lead to isolation of individual family members or the continuation of problematic behaviours (Burnham, 1968; Minuchin, 1974; Janzen and Harris, 1986). Some of the more common issues are outlined below, and these should always be considered in the context of theories which help to inform *why* certain beliefs and behaviours might be prevalent.

- *Family Myths*: Erikson recognised the attraction of homogeneity within relationships within his writings on intimacy versus isolation and speculated that we are drawn to partners with similar beliefs, values, attitudes, social class and cultural backgrounds as ourselves. This can underpin a family belief system wherein attitudes are adopted as general rules to ensure conformity and unity. As generations pass, these become almost like a family motto and can influence the behaviour of all members. Family myths are extreme versions of these, and are generally wholly without truth and are used to project an idealised image of unity, rather than reality. Family myths generally incorporate the collective 'we' and examples might include statements like 'we all love one another and look out for each other', which might hide turbulent relationships on the interior; 'we all believe in choice and freedom', yet the boyfriends and girlfriends of the children are closely scrutinised and criticised if they do not live up to expectations; and 'we are a tough family, we take no nonsense and stick together', projecting a hard exterior that not every member will be able to live up to. Family myths, because of their idealised status, are difficult to live up to, but when family members fall out with the boundaries of the myth, they can be ostracised and punished by other members who attempt to abide by the myth.
- *Family Secrets*: inevitably, keeping a secret involves holding power over others, but depending on the nature of the secret it can also involve shame, anxiety, stress, and a mix of other detrimental emotions. Family secrets might extend over generations and be linked to the true parentage of a child, the criminal activity of a grandparent or extramarital affairs from the past, or secrets might be kept about recent events and activities such as a sexual assault, addiction or mental health issues. Generally, the secret remains hidden because the person holding onto it is afraid of the reaction they might get from other family members. As a social worker, there may be opportunities to help to create an environment where family secrets can be aired and dealt with in a therapeutic environment.
- *Transference and Counter-Transference*: Skynner (1976, in Barker and Chang, 2013) warns against the dangers of transference and counter-transference within the therapeutic relationship. He explains that, through interventions, emotions are exposed where defence mechanisms may well have kept them hidden and 'under control', and the feelings created may well be directed at the professional. This is also due to the fact that the professional is sometimes

viewed as being a 'parental' figure within the therapeutic relationship and may remind the service users of past experiences of being parented, which may well have been unpleasant. Skynner also highlights that professionals might have to deal with emotions that are stirred up within them because of what they are hearing, and they have to be wary of counter-transference, projecting inappropriate feelings and emotions onto the service user because of these memories. If service users are encouraged to communicate these awoken emotions to each other, rather than to the professional, this should help avoid transference. In Chapter 1, we highlighted a number of other defence mechanisms which professionals should have a good knowledge of when engaging with various family members. It is not uncommon for one family member to project their own emotions onto another as a means of externalising unconscious feelings such as anger, shame or sadness. This is often known as 'scapegoating', where one family member becomes the focus of blame for other family members, and, if reinforced, the individual who is being scapegoated begins to believe their assigned role.

- *Splitting*: Throughout this book, we have looked at object relations theory and how it can impact on development across the lifespan and this is where we get the term 'splitting' from. 'Splitting' is a term which is often misused as a word for the conscious act of dividing and conquering, where one person plays two others off against each other to their own benefit. Splitting is actually the unconscious act of being unable to see yourself, or another person, as an emotional 'whole'. Because of this, their good qualities, or their bad qualities, dominate and there is an inability to view the self or others as a mature, functioning adult capable of a multitude of qualities, good and bad. Thinking becomes very black and white and people are viewed as *all good* if needs are being met, or *all bad* if they do not meet your needs. This can also apply to the therapeutic relationship with professionals – when things go well, then the professional is all good, but if thinking is challenged and uncomfortable realities surface then the risk is that the professional is viewed as all bad.

- *Interlocking Pathology*: Freud believed that if we have unconscious memories of pain, hurt and sadness, then our unconscious will try to remind us of these feelings by influencing our behaviour as a means to create situations where the emotions can be re-experienced, a term he called 'repetition compulsion'. Within families, this manifests by creating tension, stress, anxiety and arguments between members, particularly the marital partners. This results in one partner behaving in a manner which hurts the other, and then the other partner returning this action by inducing hurt through their behaviour. This ends up hurting both individuals and they repeat the process in a cycle of hurt. The challenge for the professional is to break this cycle, but also to create an environment where the unconscious desire to feel hurt can be explored.

Critical Thinking
Sculpting

Family sculpting is another practice approach that social workers can use to get an insight into the structure of a family. A good way to do this is to start off with a variety of objects of your choosing. It might be a tray full of random items, or it might be a bag of coloured marbles, but whatever you choose to use the service user needs to have a degree of choice when picking items.

Begin by asking the service user to identify who the main members of their family are, and once they have done this ask them to select an object to represent each family member. As they begin to select objects, ask them to place the objects/ person in positions to illustrate relationships within the family – if they are close to certain other family members then ask the service user to position them together. Conversely, if they never speak to certain members then place the items to represent this split.

Once all the items/people have been arranged, you can explore relationships – is there a powerful figure who heads up the family? Are they enmeshed or disengaged? Are there key subsets of family members? There is also opportunity to explore the choice of object to represent each person – explore object choice and colour choice as well as positioning. You can end the session by asking the service user to rearrange the objects to represent how they would like to see the family relationship when considering a positive outcome.

Case Study

The following is an example of a narrative with Brian. The social worker noted their thoughts and these are included here in parentheses next to some of Brian's statements. Read through and refer back to the chapter to familiarise yourself with some of the concepts included here:

'I've got two kids, and I'm married ... have been for 14 years now. I work for an oil company in town, driving forklifts in the warehouse and I like the work – it's a good social scene and I regularly go to the pub with the boys after work for a few drinks. (In terms of Family Life Cycle, the social worker assumes that he is Stage 5–6.)

My wife is a nag. Every night I get it in the ear for coming home late. She doesn't realise how hard I have to work during the day and I just need my time with the boys in the pub to unwind. I talk about my family a lot though. We are a unit! We look out for each other. (The social worker begins to consider Differentiation, but also gets an insight into Family Myths.)

Our youngest, Sam, is not doing well at school. He's not good at writing and the teachers think he might be dyslexic, or autistic, or something like that. He doesn't have any friends and spends time looking at magazines instead of talking to other kids. We think he just needs to learn how to behave. He can be shy but he play-fights at home with his brother a lot. I blame my wife a bit, she mollycoddled him

(Continued)

(Continued)

when he was younger, him being the baby of the family. He is just being a wimp really and needs to grow up and face the real world. (The social worker considers Nuclear Family Emotional System and wonders if the youngest child is becoming the focus of family problems – danger of Scapegoating.)

Sam and her, my wife, they talk a lot together and then go quiet when I come into the room. I am getting sick of it and just want them to stop the whispering. He's driving a wedge between us and we haven't, you know, haven't had sex for months. (Social worker now considers Triangulation and Family Sub systems.) I guess that's why I like spending time away from home. The boys in the pub don't give me grief (and here the social worker considers Emotional Cutoff).

I guess I just have to get on with it. I've made my bed, so might as well lie in it. (The social worker notes that Brian is looking for Homeostasis.) Sam just needs to get a grip as he is going to destroy this marriage. He's always been different from his brother, Dave. Dave's the good one.' (Here, Brian ends on a statement that indicates thought patterns stemming from Splitting.)

ADVANTAGES OF SYSTEMIC PRACTICE/EXPERIENTIAL APPROACHES

Working with individuals is often the starting point for any family based intervention as the behaviour of the individual can be symptomatic of problems within the family unit. Trying to address the problems in that one individual, and then expecting them to go back into an environment where the causes of the problems continue to be perpetuated, is not going to be a recipe for success. Therefore, it is better to look at the whole family as a system to see if environmental factors can be addressed for the benefit of every individual who exists within it, in this case the environment is the family.

However, family work should not just focus on problems – strengths must also be identified as these can be built on and areas of resilience developed (Sharry, 2004). In previous chapters, we have also looked at the impact of family care on the development of the brain and how this might impede emotional and intellectual development, and Deacon and Piercy (2001) highlight the benefits of using creative approaches to assess issues within families. In this chapter, we have mentioned sculpting and genograms but research suggests that artwork, photographs and re-enactment through psychodramas can also illicit an enormous amount of information about the history and coping skills of family members.

12 TRAUMA AND RESILIENCE

Trauma can be one of the most emotionally damaging experiences a human being can face. The enormity of the situation can overwhelm any coping mechanism we have established, and everything that we have learned becomes meaningless and useless. Often, social workers come into contact with service users who are currently dealing with trauma, or are still trying to process events from the past which have been traumatic.

This chapter will look at trauma in more detail and discuss how this impacts on emotions, behaviours and the physiology of our bodies (including brain development). This will be considered against the backdrop of social work involvement and we will look at appropriate ways of working with service users experiencing this overpowering emotion.

We also need to recognise that many people can deal with significant life challenges and will draw on strengths from internal and environmental sources to help them through. This is termed 'resilience' and we will look at what this is, where it comes from and how it can be built up in order to help service users through challenging times.

By the end of the chapter the reader should:

- Understand what is meant by 'trauma'
- Consider the effects of trauma on individuals
- Understand what is meant by 'resilience'
- Recognise factors which present a risk or protect
- Comprehend how to support resilience in others

TRAUMA

What is trauma?

Historically, trauma was viewed as a form of hysteria, and Ringel and Brandell (2011) explain that because hysteria was a phenomenon that occurred largely in female populations, the common treatment was to remove the uterus by means of a hysterectomy. At the end of the 1800s, a French physician, Jean Martin Charcot, studied these hysterical phenomena and determined that the symptoms (which included memory loss, sensory impairment, convulsions and sudden paralysis) were actually psychologically rather than physiologically induced.

Freud was also interested in the symptoms of hysteria and published *Studies on Hysteria* with Josef Breuer in 1895 in which they concluded that significantly disturbing incidents from the past could render these experiences into the subconscious, but that these could resurface and impact on behaviour to bring about an altered state which they termed 'dissociation' (Breuer and Freud, 1957). There was also recognition that verbalising these emotions could be beneficial in reducing the symptoms of hysteria. A common treatment for the condition was hypnosis, and, during the First and Second World Wars, soldiers suffering from shell shock and extreme reactions to warfare were often hypnotised and then encouraged to return to the front.

In the 1960s Gerald Caplan (1961) developed crisis intervention and identified that, at periods of extreme crisis, the normal responses of human coping strategies can be lost in some people and they can enter into a state of complete disorganisation, which impacts on emotions and mental well-being. In his work with Parad, they identified five factors that contributed to the coping strategies:

1. The stress caused by the event is overwhelming to the point that there appears to be no solution.
2. Previously relied upon problem-solving mechanisms offer no guidance, so learning from previous experience appears redundant.
3. The event makes the individual feel vulnerable and threatens well-being.
4. Stress caused by the situation builds up to a point which causes extreme tension.
5. Issues from the past are re-awoken and add to the stress experienced. (Parad and Caplan, 1960)

These approaches recognised the spectrum of factors affected when experiencing trauma – physical, psychological, and environmental – and have informed current thinking about trauma and linking it to issues such as brain development, as well as the forming and disruption of attachments:

> Trauma is essentially a confrontation with damage to body or mind. It may be the body which is disabled or killed, or the psychological self which is hurt or destroyed. In either case, one person's subjectivity is denied by another person. (Gerhardt, 2006: 134)

The word 'trauma' conjures up a sudden incident which has life altering impacts, such as a road accident, a plane crash or fleeing from a war zone, but trauma is also caused by events that take place in our cities streets, and houses. Domestic abuse, physical violence and sexual perversion are traumatic events for those who experience them, and also for those who witness them. Human beings are social animals and learn from each other, and also have empathy for one another, so witnessing traumatic activities will impact on the psyche – the events do not need to be directly experienced to have an effect on emotions. In its basic form, trauma is about experiencing pure fear without any way out. Everything that has been learned about the world becomes meaningless as it cannot explain what is happening, or how to escape from it.

This puts the professional practice of social work into the front line of trauma-based practice. All across services, the profession comes into contact with those who have experienced, or are experiencing, trauma. Trauma affects service users from across the lifespan, from young children experiencing significant issues of violence and neglect within households, to asylum seekers arriving in the UK who have fled unimaginable horrors in their home towns, and an understanding of the psychological mechanisms that are at work to deal with what has been experienced can give the profession an insight into accounting for the emotions and behaviours that are often witnessed.

TRAUMA THEORY

Attempts to define trauma theory have been made by a select few (Caruth, 1995; Bloom, 2013) but an overarching definition is difficult to pinpoint. Instead, it is better to think of trauma theory as an approach to working with trauma. Viewing trauma as an 'injury' rather than a 'sickness' can help to normalise symptoms, as opposed to pathologising them (www.nonviolenceandsocialjustice.org), and Bloom (1999) suggests that instead of professionals approaching the situation with the question 'What is wrong with you?' they should be asking 'What has happened to you?' By adopting this approach, we can begin to approach trauma in three steps:

- Understand the impact of trauma

The impact of trauma is varied. Often an individual who has experienced trauma can be withdrawn, isolated, disorientated, and unable to follow conversations in a logical manner. Emotions will often be fragile and outbursts can be directed at people completely unrelated to the traumatic incident which can make things challenging for friends and family who are supporting someone through trauma. Trauma also has physical impacts and these can manifest through somatic conditions, stress and anxiety, and affect the general equilibrium of the body. Unfortunately, the memories of the traumatic incident can lie dormant for months/years, so the impact can be short- and long-term, though professionals suggest that the earlier the trauma is dealt with (after the traumatic incident), the better the chances of recovery.

- Understand where the cause is coming from

There are a number of ecological models to help understand where the source of trauma has stemmed from, but in Chapter 4 we introduced you to Bronfenbrenner's socioecological model (Figure 12.1).

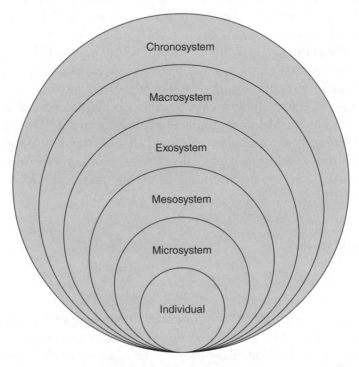

Figure 12.1 Bronfenbrenner's socioecological model

The model explores relationships across several domains and can be a useful tool for exploring traumatic events. The individual is nested in a microsystem and this consists of family, friends, peers and other members of the community who have direct contact with them. Trauma caused by domestic violence, neglect, verbal abuse or exposure to problematic behaviour may well be occurring in this domain. The mesosystem and exosystems look at the wider interactions within the environment and the influence of behaviours and attitudes. Mass media plays a role in shaping views and it might be that trauma is caused by discrimination, oppression and stigmatisation. The macrosystem encapsulates wider policies, legislation and culture and this can be shaped by war, religion, racism and cultural approaches to issues such as poverty and asylum. With knowledge of where the trauma stems from, professionals can begin to think about how to address issues with the service user. If issues occur within the individual or microsystem stages, then psychoanalytic/

counselling approaches might be worth considering, but as you go further out on the model, consideration needs to be given to interventions that address oppression and empower the individual. The chronosystem recognises that the age and stage of the individual will also shape how trauma is dealt with – the older the individual is at the time of trauma, the better the coping strategies should be, and this is explored further on in this chapter.

- Empower the individual to address issues

This comes as a direct result from the previous stage. Empowerment is about creating awareness of the issues faced by the individual, but needs to be done in conjunction with the individual. It is about working in a holistic manner and helping the individual to recognise the source of their emotional trauma. Cohen and Ainley (2000) stress the importance of adopting a socioecological approach at this stage to facilitate learning, but also to enhance identity. To practice social work in a quality manner, the worker needs to recognise how the individual feels about themselves, how they interact with their family, how their peers influence them, how they are viewed by their community, how society treats them and how politics shapes their life.

EFFECTS OF TRAUMA ACROSS THE LIFESPAN

In short, the most damaging effects of trauma occur in infancy. In Chapter 1, we looked at attachment theory and identified the importance of brain development – in normal situations, the brain will grow and develop in accordance with appropriate experiences, but in traumatic situations the inbuilt 'fight or flight' response becomes challenged. The body will produce chemicals to regulate our emotional state (the sympathetic/parasympathetic systems), but in situations where we can neither flee nor fight, the production of cortisol can become toxic and actually damage healthy growth in the brain. The brain is more susceptible to damage through this toxic chemical production when it is developing fastest and whilst stress responses are still maturing – typically up to the age of three – and this high cortisol exposure can seriously impinge on the ability to appropriately respond to stress in later years (Gerhardt, 2006; Choi et al., 2009). This also exposes the developing infant to the risks of dissociation or hyperarousal. Dissociation results in an individual 'detaching' from reality which might be witnessed in behaviours such as daydreaming, freezing and memory loss, and has also been linked to personality disorders. Hyperarousal exposes an individual to increased levels of tension and stress and feelings of constantly being 'on guard' and can have seriously detrimental effects on sleep patterns, pain tolerance and anxiety levels.

> ## Critical Thinking
>
> *Dissociation* and *hyperarousal* are key reactions to trauma and it is important that social workers understand about these two concepts. It can be useful to view them as opposite ends of a continuum.

This is not to say that trauma at later stages in life is not as detrimental, but the hope would be that the individual may have built up levels of resilience if there have been good building blocks in place throughout the formative years. Adolescence also sees another period of brain development (see Chapter 4), where experiences are reorganised and attachments restructured to facilitate autonomy and independence. During this period, the major changes in the brain occur in the cortex which is responsible for organisation, prioritising and problem solving, which means that the more primitive parts of the brain are relied on to regulate emotions during this reorganisation (www.nonviolenceandsocialjustice.org). This is set against a period of loss, change and transition as the body goes through puberty, and trauma at this stage can impact on brain chemistry at a time when the ability to conceptualise past/present/future thinking is in its infancy. Schore (2003c) warns that experienced trauma left unaddressed can predisposition the developing individual to sociopathic tendencies wherein impulsive reactions, violence and emotional detachment can manifest.

Again, effects of trauma in adulthood may be cushioned by life experiences up to that point, but this can often be the time when the impact of childhood traumas may emerge. An American study into the effects of adverse childhood experiences found that the impact in adulthood can lead to impairments in emotional and cognitive functioning, high increase of risk taking behaviours (including drug and alcohol abuse), health issues, and an increased risk of early death (www.acestudy.org/home). There also exists the risk that trauma is relived and re-experienced within adult relationships when memories from within the subconscious are demonstrated through behaviours as a means of telling stories of past experiences, and as a mechanism of asking for help. Bloom (1999) warns that this can also lead to seeking out relationships where trauma can be experienced through dangerous and maladaptive methods wherein the victim of past trauma seeks out danger because, as bizarre as it might seem, the feeling is familiar to them and offers hope of finding a way through the emotional distress.

APPROACHES TO WORKING WITH TRAUMA

One of the best known trauma-related diagnoses is Post-Traumatic Stress Disorder (PTSD), which is akin to living in a state of constant hyperarousal. There are three main categories which describe the symptoms of PTSD. The first of these involves involuntary re-experiencing of the emotional experience of the traumatic event which can include flashbacks and nightmares and randomly reliving distressing sensations and images. This can include physical and emotional sensations, and feelings of shame and guilt often accompany these experiences. This can directly impact on the second symptom, which involves attempting to avoid any experience which may remind the individual of the original trauma. Distraction techniques are not uncommon but this typically leads to isolation and loneliness, and often emotions are numbed to avoid any risk of unpleasant reminders from the past (www.nhs.uk/Conditions/Post-traumatic-stress-disorder/Pages/Introduction.aspx). Hyperarousal is classed as the third symptom and Liberzon et al. (1999) attribute this to a part of the brain known as the 'amygdala' being in a constant state of arousal because a primitive reflex triggered by earlier experiences of fear keeps the body in a perpetual state of vigilance (Gerhardt, 2006).

PTSD can be triggered immediately after a traumatic event, or lie dormant for years before becoming symptomatic and has been closely linked to childhood abuse (Lindberg and Distad, 1985). Often a diagnosis of PTSD can be a relief for an individual experiencing the symptoms, but medical options tend to treat the symptoms of anxiety and stress through the use of anti-depressants rather than the route of the problem which often remains buried in the subconscious. Talking therapies are a good option to help the individual explore experiences and Giarratano (2004) suggests that this helps service users to develop control over emotions if they are able to explore memories again and again in a supportive environment with an empathetic listener. Similarly, Rothschild (2000) stresses the importance of empathy within the therapeutic relationship when dealing with trauma but she also encourages practitioners to be aware of other triggers within PTSD. Rothschild underlines the power of the physical body to retain information from the past and memories can be released if the body moves in a certain way, a scent or sound can awaken dormant issues, and the sensations caused by a certain breathing pattern can remind the body of physical sensations that occurred during the original trauma. To this end, Rothschild states that practitioners need to be constantly reassessing the situation when working with service users who have experienced trauma to evaluate ways in which the three areas of psychological, emotional and physical sensations can be drawn back into alignment in order to assign the trauma to the past.

Case Study – Part 1

Asal grew up just outside Jalalabad in Northern Afghanistan, close to the Pakistan border on the road to Peshawar. This was a well-established trading route and close to the famous Khyber Pass. She came from a relatively large family and had two older sisters and one older brother. Her father sold textiles and her mother cared for the family at home as Asal was only six.

(Continued)

(Continued)

Asal remembers when things started to go bad. She had been playing with her cousins nearby and returned home in the late afternoon. Her mother was crying and her father was hugging a body. Asal knew immediately that it was her brother. He had been shot.

Neighbours started to shun the family and Asal did not understand what had happened. She remembers army jeeps constantly passing through the area and she has memories of not being able to sleep at night because of the noise of the bangs. One night, the bangs were closer and her mother picked her up from her sleep and carried her outside. She remembers a lot of other people and they began to move towards the mountain pass towards Pakistan.

In the darkness, they were stopped by soldiers and corralled into a shepherd's hut. She remembers crying and not much else. There were screams from some of the women which she had only heard before when people were very sore. Her father was taken from the hut. In the morning, he, along with all of the other men, were executed in front of the women and children.

The next few days were a blur. The survivors were transported by night in trucks. One night, the truck stopped and Asal, her mum and her two sisters slipped out from the side and ran. They were caught and her mother was executed and her eldest sister was sexually attacked and then she disappeared. Asal was left with her other sister and put back onto the truck to continue the journey.

Asal has blanked out a lot of what happened next, but she recalls that she must have been kept in captivity for months. More soldiers came one night and there was a fight, and Asal and her sister ran away. They spent months moving from place to place, hiding during the daytime and moving at night and eventually ended up crossing into Europe. They continued to hide by day and managed to negotiate a passage to the UK. When they arrived, they asked for asylum. Asal's sister was visibly pregnant after her period in captivity.

Asal and her sister remained together whilst the asylum claim was being processed. A doctor refers Asal to you as a social worker because she has been having 'night terrors' and is bed-wetting, and does not speak to any of the male workers at the centre. The doctor thinks that she needs someone to speak to:

- How might you start to work with Asal?
- How much of her behaviour could be linked to PTSD? Are there other theories, such as loss and change or transitions, that would be appropriate?
- Can you use Bronfenbrenner's model to plot where the trauma stems from?

Briere (2004) suggests that a number of techniques need to be incorporated into trauma-based work and advocates a therapeutic approach utilising talking therapies, but also believes elements of cognitive behavioural therapy and behavioural therapy can also be incorporated. Because he focuses on affect tolerance and affect modulation he terms his approach the 'self-trauma model' because he stresses the importance of internal coping strategies to effectively process the experiences. Briere also highlights the importance of looking out for avoidance techniques which fit into the pattern of dissociation. Often the memory is suppressed through the use of substances and this will provide temporary relief from the unpleasant effects of the experiences, but this also entails a multitude of problems in itself and can lead to repeated use, dependence, addiction and death. Therefore, any trauma-based work needs to expose the service user to the memories that they find difficult to deal with, but in a manner whereby they do not become overwhelmed by the experiences. The therapeutic relationship becomes central to the process and the worker has to carefully assess coping strategies at each session.

Every approach to working with trauma underlines the importance of the therapeutic relationship. Saakvitne et al. (2000) echo this but also stress that trauma work will have an impact on the professional who works with the service user. Symptoms of trauma are merely coping strategies that have been developed by the service user, and to unravel these strategies may involve recounting horrific and disturbing events throughout life. As social beings, we can empathise with others and this involves, to a degree, placing ourselves into a situation in our minds and imagining what it would be like, and how we would cope. Service users working through traumatic memories may have issues around trust which could have been impacted on throughout their development (think about Erikson's stages) or their experience of attachment and being continually disappointed or hurt because of relationships. The therapeutic relationship will need to establish trust in the first instance before the narrative of experience can begin.

To this end, it is important that the worker recognises the effects of trauma on themselves. Professional support needs to come from appropriate supervision so the effects of working with trauma can be explored in an appropriate, supportive environment. It is also useful to identify coping strategies out with the workplace and acknowledge which strategies are useful at certain times. General awareness of the impact on the self is encouraged and after particularly stressful sessions a worker should take time to mentally check themselves, be aware of tension in the body and use mindfulness techniques (as outlined in Chapter 7) to try to clear the mind before progressing onto the next bit of work. Resilience also comes into play here and this will be explored in the next section.

Critical Thinking

What outlets do you have for relieving stress? Do you talk to anybody in particular? How do you manage issues of confidentiality? Are there potentially harmful behaviours you engage in to combat stress? If so, how might this impact on your overall health and well-being?

RESILIENCE

What do we mean by 'resilience'?

'Resilience' is a word that is often used within social work, particularly in the context of children, and it can sometimes be misused as a general term meaning that the child can cope. However, it is important to understand what it means to be resilient, and indeed, where resilience stems from. When these areas are understood, workers can identify ways in which resilience can be developed using existing resources, or how it can be built up in areas that might be lacking.

Within social work we often come across service users who have dealt with an incredible amount of loss, pain, grief and trauma, yet still manage to function on a day-to-day basis and 'get by'. Clearly, there are coping strategies at play and it can be easy to dismiss these service users as 'doing okay', but it can be useful to find out where the source of strength is coming from as it can then be maintained, or encouraged, if future issues lay ahead. To do that, we need to think about the concept of resilience and what it means in practice.

Resilience is the ability to rise to challenges and to deal with the issues that they bring. Gilligan (2000) describes resilience as a quality which allows a person to bounce back after periods of adversity, with a continued ability to function despite the fact that there may be ongoing risk within the situation. It is not a rare concept; most of us develop resilience throughout our lives and this is based on the quality of experiences we have throughout the life course, however Maclean (2004) explains that resilience can be dependent on a mixture of nature and nurture. She points out that children who are good academically and have a positive outlook may have more resilience than children who are born with an illness or a disability from the outset, but positive nurturing can enhance other areas of life that impact on resilience. Among the areas which contribute to resilience are: a good sense of self-worth and self-esteem; a belief in the fact that achievements are possible and problems are surmountable which ultimately leads to positive self-efficacy; a sense of initiative which can often manifest within problem situations as looking for ways out of the situation (or ways in which others can be protected from the situation); and the importance of a good attachment – preferably a secure attachment – with the primary caregiver. She also lists qualities such as trust, autonomy, identity and faith as being positive factors in building resilience – which points to the importance of Erikson's psychosocial stages when considering a person's development across time.

Environmental factors play a large part in the development of resilience and we therefore need to view resilience as a process which constantly changes over time depending on age, stage, and experience. It should also be viewed as helping to understand two aspects of behaviour: the ability to manage emotions during difficult times and the ability to adapt in the face of adversity. Because of the view that resilience incorporates both nature and nurture, it is useful to return to Bronfenbrenner's model (Figure 12.1) again to consider risk and protective factors within the process.

RISK AND PROTECTIVE FACTORS

Daniel and Wassell (2002) looked at the extensive range of factors which contribute to the quality of resilience across childhood and they align with Bronfenbrenner's socioecological model in that they begin by focusing on individual qualities, then look at familial influences and then consider wider societal factors.

Beginning at Bronfenbrenner's individual level, they identified that gender plays a role from the outset. Maclean (2004) explains that pre-adolescent girls are more resilient than pre-adolescent boys and benefit from experiences that foster autonomy, appropriate risk taking opportunities and emotional support; whereas boys benefit from routine, structure, appropriate role models (particularly male ones) and outlets for appropriate emotional expression. She goes on to highlight the point that when they reach adolescence the situation is reversed, and males tend to be more resilient. Durlak (1998) also highlights medical issues, such as low birth weight, disability and mental health issues as impacting on resilience. Daniel and Wassell (2002) look at the importance of healthy development contributing towards protective factors and identify qualities such as good problem-solving skills, good concentration skills and a good sense of humour as being advantageous. As the child gets older, these skills should develop into strong values, empathy and good self-efficacy.

Within the microsystem, and into the mesosystem, attachments should contribute towards resilience – the more secure the attachment, the higher the benefits. We have already looked at attachment across the lifespan and identified the risks within insecure attachment styles, and the quality of attachment will impact on trust, autonomy and the ability to be nurtured. Interestingly, an age gap of over two years between siblings enhances resilience, as does family composition with families with four or less children showing higher degrees of resilience. Other factors identified by Daniel and Wassell include a lack of parental issues with mental health and/or substance use, good family ties with extended members of the family (including grandparents), good relationship with siblings and access to finances.

At the mesosystem and exosystem levels (and even extending into the macrosystem), the importance of a supportive community is emphasised. Good links with neighbours and other supportive community members are viewed as being protective, as is encouraging appropriate peer contact across the preschool, primary school and secondary school years. Education itself is viewed as important, and the value of having appropriate adult role models, both inside and outside the family, is advantageous.

Luthar (2003) underlines the importance of viewing resilience as a process, and stresses that we cannot assume that if someone lacks a handful of the protective factors covered above then they will not be resilient. It may be that some of these protective factors are particularly evident in the life of an individual and these might be enough to help them cope in challenging situations, whilst others might have a wide range of them and may be able to draw on a number of resources to help them through situations. For many, these protective factors will develop over time, but if the factors listed are not evident, or worse, are in fact having negative impacts, then they need to be viewed as risk factors and addressed as such.

Critical Thinking

Using the socioecological model to think about protective factors in your life, plot these across the domains of microsystem, mesosystem, exosystem and macrosystem. If you have any, plot risk factors, too. Can you now circle the ones that are most important to you?

Doing this exercise can help to see where resources are strongest, and perhaps identify ones that can be built up, or if they are risks, can they be removed from your life?

RESILIENCE MATRIX

Separating resilience factors into the two different categories of nature and nurture has helped in the formation of a resilience matrix, a tool to help practitioners think about factors affecting the lives of service users, predominantly children, and visualise these in a useful diagram.

'Nature' factors are considered on a continuum, which runs from vulnerability to resilience. Elements attributed to vulnerability include: poor attachment, disability, childhood trauma and neglectful care; whereas elements viewed as placing an individual towards resilience include: good attachment, adaptability and good parenting. These factors are often called *intrinsic* factors as they contribute to internalised emotions, impacting on self-esteem and identity.

These intrinsic factors have been summarised by Daniel et al. (2011) and are as follows:

- There needs to be a secure base within existing relationships. This provides the individual with a sense of belonging, safety and security.
- The individual should have a good sense of self-worth. Self-esteem should also be good as this fosters a sense of competence, and impacts on confidence to master difficult situations.
- The ability to master situations extends into feelings of self-efficacy and the individual should be able to identify their own strengths and their own weaknesses.

'Nurture' factors look at environmental influences and place these on a continuum, which runs from adversity to protective environment. Factors appearing at the end of adversity might include: substance use issues, poverty, asylum status, loss and an unsettled environment at home; whilst factors providing a protective environment include: supportive relationships (with at least one adult), a good education and leisure pursuits. Elements within this domain are often termed *extrinsic* factors.

Daniel et al. (2011) have also summarised the three main building blocks to providing an environment wherein resilience is stronger:

- Attachment theory is recognised as an important element. Secure attachments have been seen to contribute to positive mental well-being, security, effective communication and the ability to take risks with the knowledge that there is safety within relationships.
- Support should also be available from the wider community, particularly from extended family and friends.
- Positive experiences within school, family and life history are advantageous, as is the ability to make sense of the lived experiences and incorporate them into internal working models.

When placed together, these two axes – nature and nurture – form a resilience matrix (Figure 12.2) and can be used alongside traditional assessment tools to consider how resilient a person might be. Daniel and Wassell (2002) do caution that any assessment tool must consider a number of opinions, and when working with children it is important to also elicit views from significant adults within their lives as the child may be stating that they are coping externally, but intrinsic factors might suggest otherwise and be contributing to emotional issues such as stress and anxiety.

The matrix can be used to identify specific factors within the life of the child, and perhaps each factor can be noted individually on the matrix to build up a clearer picture of where the majority of the factors lie. Once this is done, the SHANARRI well-being indicators can be employed to plan possible actions. These indicators look at specific areas of: Safety, Health, Achievement, Nurture, Activity, Respect, Responsibility and Inclusion (hence the acronym SHANARRI), and are often incorporated into assessment tools within social work.

Resilience / vulnerability matrix

| Resilient child High adversity | **Resilience** Good attachment, Good self-esteem, Sociability, Intelligences, Flexible temperament, Problem-solving skills, Positive parenting | Resilient child Protective environment |

Adversity
Life events / crises, Serious illness, Loss / bereavement, Separation / Family breakdown. Domestic violence, Asylum seeking status, Serious parental difficulties – e.g. Substance misuse, Parental mental illness, Poverty

Protective environment
Good school experience, One supportive adult, Special help with behavioural problems, Community networks, Leisure activities, Talents and interests

Vulnerability
Poor attachment, Minority status, Young age, Disability, History of abuse. Innate characteristics in child / challenge development. A loner / isolation, Institutional care, Early childhood trauma. Communication differences, Inconsistent, neglectful care

| Vulnerable child High adversity | | Vulnerable child Protective environment |

Variables:
Timing and age, Multiple adversities, Cumulative protectors, Pathways. Turning points, A sense of belonging

Interventions:
Strengthen protective factors and resilience, Reduce problems and address vulnerability, Achieve initial small improvements

Figure 12.2   The Resilience Matrix

Source: Adapted from *The Child's World: Assessing Children in Need, Training and Development Pack* (Department of Health, NSPCC and University of Sheffield, 2000; available at: www.scotland.gov.uk).

Case Study – Part 2

Asal is now 12. She lives in Glasgow with her sister and her nephew, who is 4. Asal loves her sister and is very close to her. Their asylum process has still not been decided and, as a result, they have limited recourse to public funds which has presented significant financial hardship. They have relied on food banks and charity to help them get by, and they do get a significant amount of support from a local Muslim community centre. Unfortunately, Asal has been caught shoplifting three times, and on all occasions she was stealing food for the family. The police have cautioned her and are aware of her status as an asylum seeker and of the financial situation that the family are in.

Asal has just started secondary school but she does not go that often. She finds language difficult and still presents as very shy and reserved in public. She does like art and design because she can be expressive through creativity, but finds language-based classes very challenging. Because of this, she prefers not to attend these classes and will often go home after telling the school secretaries that she is sick.

In a social education class, the focus of the session was on sex education and Asal got extremely distressed in the class and ran out. She later told her guidance teacher that she did not know why she got so distressed, but it might have something to do with when she was a child. Asal likes her guidance teacher but feels that she does not want to bother her with too many problems.

Asal describes herself as a private person but has spoken to her doctor about ongoing sleep problems. The doctor has prescribed sleeping tablets. Asal has admitted to her guidance teacher that sometimes she thinks about storing up the tablets and taking them all at once so that she can see her Mum and Dad again. The guidance teacher contacted you as the social worker to discuss.

- Using the resilience matrix to help, plot Asal's issues and decide where she might be on the diagram.
- What are the protective factors?
- What are the risk factors?
- How can you work with Asal to improve resilience? And who else do you need to involve?

ASSESSING RESILIENCE THROUGH THE USE OF LANGUAGE

To effectively use the resilience matrix with a child, it is important that a good working relationship elicits appropriate information and that the worker takes time to get to know the child. Once this is established, the use of language can often be a good indicator of how the child feels about themselves and others. Grotberg (2000) looked at resilience across cultures, and her research incorporated information from over 600 interviews across thirty countries. She found that there were common themes that emerged, and many related to how children spoke about their support systems and protective factors. She noted three distinct patterns:

- 'I have …'

Children were able to identify important things in their lives. These elements ranged across a number of areas but she identified the importance of loving and trusting relationships with parents, siblings, peers and education staff; there was an emphasis on structure within the home environment to establish clear boundaries and routines with appropriate reprimands when these were broken; the importance of appropriate role models was noted, as was encouragement towards autonomous behaviour; and environments where health, education and social needs could be met. These qualities tend to link directly to aspects of the secure base.

- 'I am ...'

  Children were able to view themselves in a positive light and identify qualities that were intrinsic to them. These included the belief that they were lovable and had characteristics that appealed to other people which facilitated the forming of relationships; they were also able to return this feeling and give love to others in a reciprocal manner which fostered empathy and sensitivity; there was a sense of pride in their language and a belief that they could achieve within their environment; they could also demonstrate that they could accept responsibility for their actions, and that these actions impacted on other people (both positively and negatively); and there was also belief that the future held hope. Aspects within this domain tend to link into self-esteem.

- 'I can ...'

  Children were able to identify specific skills that contributed to coping strategies which included good communication so that feelings could be expressed appropriately, but also so that assistance could be sought when required, and the ability to listen to others; problem solving so that issues could be tackled with a knowledge of when to involve others; appropriately manage emotions and feelings and recognise emotions within other people; having a good awareness of their own personality traits and when these factors contribute positively and negatively to situations; and the ability to develop trust in other people so that they did not need to go through life feeling self-reliant. Within this domain, these statements indicate how an individual feels about their own self-efficacy.

Grotberg's (2000) research focused on children, but resilience crosses all age ranges, and the use of language will give an insight into these intrinsic and extrinsic factors that shape coping strategies. By listening carefully in the assessment stage to statements relating to 'I have/am/can ...', professionals can elicit quality information and start to address ways to enhance resilience.

HOW TO SUPPORT RESILIENCE

Daniel and Wassell (2002) have identified six specific domains which can be considered when working to assess supporting resilience. These are illustrated in Figure 12.3 and consider the secure base, education, friendships, talents and interests, positive values and social competencies.

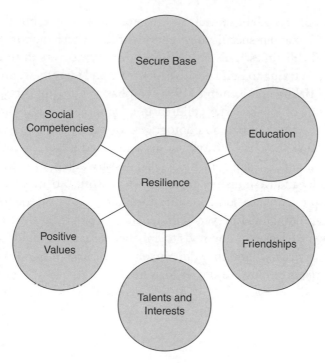

Figure 12.3   'Resilience', adapted from Daniel and Wassell (2002)

This tool allows workers and service users to consider each area in detail to look at the strengths and weaknesses within each. Secure base considers the home environment and parental support; education looks at ability and achievement, but also considers whether there are significant members of staff who provide support (or role modelling) within the environment; friendships consider peer support and issues that might impact on self-esteem such as bullying and other oppressive acts.

Talents and interests are included because research demonstrates that extracurricular activities can be protective factors in helping to prevent school dropout and criminal activity (Mahoney, 2000). Maclean (2004) adds that work experience can also help formulate a sense of confidence and self-efficacy, as long as the experience is appropriate, non-stressful and interesting.

Positive values stem from life experience and upbringing and relate to ways in which the individual views other people in terms of gender, ethnicity, age and general opinions about others which can underpin the ability to form and maintain relationships; social competencies link into communication skills and the ability to verbalise emotions, seek assistance from others and present themselves within society.

Not all six domains will be entirely positive for many people, but the model does facilitate discussion about specific areas and identifies where support can be drawn from during difficult times. This model has informed workers in residential child care settings when trying to build positive identities and identify where connections can be built up. Baldry and Kemmis (1998) emphasised the importance of identity within their study of looked-after children in a London borough and highlighted that a third of the children had no photographs or personal items to remind them of the families that they had left, which demonstrated a lack of elements within the secure base domain. Using this model can assist workers to enhance areas: for instance, in Baldry and Kemmis's example, life-story work, eco-maps or photo-based work could help to enhance some identity formation, and consequently resilience, within this single domain. However, with deficits in domains it should not be up to the social worker to decide on methods to enhance areas – it should involve discussions with the service user and the wider involvement from other professionals and key family members to move strategies forward.

13 VOICES FROM PRACTICE

In this final chapter, you will hear from practitioners about how they have been able to make use of psychosocial theories in their direct practice. The first three examples are provided by student social workers who, at the time of writing, were in the third year of a four-year Scottish BA (Hons) course in Social Work. The other examples have been provided by more experienced practitioners in a variety of settings. In all the cases, the names of service users have been disguised.

AISHA WOODALLY, ROBERT GORDON UNIVERSITY (RGU)

During my practice placement, I encountered several young people who had developed different attachment styles which I understood from teaching at university. Paul had been placed in foster care at the age of two following the death of his father, and had later been adopted by his foster parents. He made no mention of his biological mother at any point during the 12-week period that I worked with him. I undertook a piece of narrative working with Paul in which he described his lifespan through the use of a timeline, and in this way I was able not only to develop a good rapport and working relationship with Paul but I was also able to understand his attachment style from his life's experiences.

I would describe Paul's attachment style as being insecure anxious/ambivalent. This is the title given to an individual who desires to be close to a caregiver, then almost simultaneously is unable to be comforted. This most often stems from the child believing that love is not unconditional and that it has to be fought for in whatever way possible. I gathered this from Paul's explanation of living with several siblings, including one biological sibling. I found it fairly straightforward to apply attachment theory here without meeting Paul's adoptive parents. My teaching had suggested an approach that looked at every individual involved in the service user's childhood, and using methods such as a narrative approach (the timeline), I was able to gather enough information to make my assessment of Paul's attachment style, as he is the expert of his own life and experiences.

Nevertheless, it was at first difficult to apply an attachment style to an individual who was often quite difficult to engage with; some days Paul would fully partake in the group activities, then other days he would not. After two weeks of working with him and undertaking the narrative work, it became clear that my teaching from university was indeed applicable here. Once I had applied attachment theory to my thinking, I could see more clearly how Paul fitted the insecure anxious/ambivalent 'frame' and why he was acting and reacting towards the other group members in the way he was. Another member of the group, Jane, with whom I also worked, had an attachment style which was also insecure anxious/ambivalent. Her father had left the family unit when she was young, and other contributing factors resulted in Jane displaying a need to be cared for and then showing an inability to be comforted.

Attachment theory was accessible and proved to be key in understanding the young people I was working with.

MICHAEL HOGAN, RGU

I had always had an interest in people's behaviour before coming to university, but I did not have the theoretical knowledge to fully understand why people display the behaviours that they do. I found that questioning these behaviours and developing my knowledge of psychosocial theories of development has enabled me to better understand people and has improved my practice greatly.

Having a knowledge of these theories also helps to understand why people find themselves in difficult situations now and how their experience in childhood can impact upon their life chances. One of the young people I worked with on a recent placement had been physically and emotionally abused, in childhood, by his mother, who was a lone parent. I found that by applying attachment theory, I was able to understand that he had an anxious attachment because of the abuse that he had suffered as his mother failed to provide him with consistent loving care.

I found attachment theory in this situation, as well as others, very relevant in its application and find that it is a good way to understand an individual's past experiences and how they impact upon their present behaviour. Having an understanding of an individual's attachment style I find is a good way to gauge how the individual may interact with you on a professional level. Due to the abuse he endured, the service user has experienced great difficulty in forming friendships and relationships and has underachieved in his school years. He therefore now finds himself unemployed and has no educational qualifications which has impacted greatly on his future.

Family systems theory is a theory which I had never applied in practice before but I found it extremely helpful when working with one young person in my recent placement. I discovered that, through its application, I was able to better understand the service user's family situation and also some of the behaviours she displayed.

I found that she was a very quiet individual who rarely became involved in group tasks which were necessary in team-building situations. I explored her reasoning for not taking part and discovered that she has very little interaction with anyone outside of her immediate family. I found that these closed boundaries within the family were a reflection on her everyday behaviour and found that I could apply further psychosocial theory in the form of Erikson's life cycle to explain that she has developed trust within the family through these boundaries but also mistrust in the outside world through lack of familiarity with it.

Additionally, when working with this service user, I applied the theory of marital fit as I found that through the information she divulged, her situation with her own partner mirrored her experience of what a relationship should be like. I found that there was a similar age gap between her and her partner as there was with her mother and father and that her partner and father had similar occupations, both working offshore. I found that by applying marital fit, I was able to understand why she had chosen the partner that she had as she felt safe in the atmosphere and the situations that her partner creates, as her father did when she was a child.

On a personal level, I have found that possessing a knowledge of psychosocial and developmental theory can make parenting more challenging. Whereas a parent without a theoretical knowledge may allow a baby to cry themselves to sleep as a method of self-soothing, I have found great difficulty in doing so as I am aware that the child may be splitting what they feel as an anxiety-provoking situation from their central ego, creating a punitive side in the child.

Additionally, having such an awareness of Erikson's life cycle theory can be problematic as, at times, the natural frustrations of being a parent are more difficult to express as I strive to encourage my children to develop their initiative to undertake tasks rather than have them doubt their ability.

HEATHER CUNNINGHAM, RGU

As a student, I have found it challenging to relate theory to practice because each theory overlaps, and it is impossible to incorporate only one theory during work undertaken with a service user. During my time on placement, I worked in a group setting with young people aged 16–25. Because of the complex needs of each team member, there were a range of theories that I used when working in the team environment to allow me to understand and support the service users.

Object relations theory was extremely relevant to the work I undertook during placement. It allowed me to highlight needs and try to understand, more effectively, the intervention that would best support the team member. I worked with an extremely shy and self-conscious individual on placement, who displayed many personality traits which I was able to understand more clearly when applying object relations theory.

Understanding the split in her personality allowed me to recognise certain behaviours which she displayed when faced with certain uncomfortable situations. This became apparent during team activities when she became punitive or needy towards myself and other staff. When she felt that her needs were not being met, she was unable to see the staff member as a whole being and instead saw them as a rejecting object, often removing herself from the situation or lashing out verbally at staff.

I also found during practice that I was able to relate object relations theory to my own personality. Due to the stress that can occur during a placement setting, I found it extremely useful to use this theory to understand my own behaviour during certain situations. I was able to realise the libidinal and anti-libidinal split in my own personality when becoming frustrated in the team. Understanding this enabled me to critically evaluate the work I undertook and reflect back on the decisions made.

Object relations theory is extremely difficult to apply during practice due to the complexity of the theory and the jargon used. A situation could impact on an individual, producing either a rejecting and confrontational response, or a needy, overly affectionate response. However, I found it particularly useful working with the individuals in a group setting as, understanding the splits in an individual's central ego, helped me in supporting that individual during team tasks. I also found that object relations theory became a lot easier to apply during practice over time, and I was able to use it more effectively with support and the experience gained during my time on placement. When working with any individual in a practice setting, I find it particularly beneficial to allow myself time to consider which theories may be most relevant to the situation and that will enable me to support the individual.

Object relations theory is extremely effective when working with individuals with complex needs as it allows us to gain perspective on the needs of the individual and areas of their personality that should be seen as resilience factors. As many of the service users involved in my practice setting had been through difficult situations from a young age, it was extremely important as a Social Worker in Training to recognise and promote resilience. There were similarities in the resilience factors for each team member which included the relationships developed on team. It was important as a staff member that these were protected as they aided stability and allowed for the young people to develop relationships. I found that, in order to use these theories in practice, it worked more effectively once a therapeutic relationship had been established. This then meant that I was able to discuss possible resilience factors with the team members more efficiently, and they felt more comfortable in doing this.

LEANNE KELLAS, SOCIAL WORKER, MORAY COUNCIL

Since graduating from RGU in 2013, I have worked in various social work settings, expanding and building on my knowledge base all the time. I currently work for a statutory fostering service, supporting foster carers and prospective foster carers, supervising them in their role and ensuring they have the adequate skill set needed to be able to foster children and young people. To give foster carers the best possible support and guidance, it is absolutely essential to have a good understanding of theory that underpins practice.

This particular practice example from my experience in a Children and Families team shows how developmental theory can assist and help us understand the difficulties children can experience and the impact this can have on their behaviour and development.

Jemma, a young girl aged 13 years, became subject to Compulsory Measures of Supervision through the Children's Hearing system, until she was accommodated by the local authority, following significant concerns of emotional and physical neglect. In a matter of several months, Jemma was removed from her mother's care, and subsequently had three placement moves before remaining in a long-term, specialised foster placement, with a view to progressing to a Permanence Order in the near future.

Throughout Jemma's early years and childhood, she observed her mother suffer from bouts of very poor mental health, impacting significantly on her emotional availability to her daughter and her ability to put her daughter's needs before her own. As a result, Jemma learnt to muddle along throughout her childhood with unreliable, sporadic and, quite often, erratic care provided by her mother. Although her mother could, at times, be in good health and manage well, being a child growing up in such an unpredictable environment was very unsettling, resulting in Jemma developing the likelihood of an ambivalent and disorganised attachment.

Jemma displayed quite challenging behaviours in her foster placements and while she was still in her mother's care. She is very demanding of adult attention and can display controlling behaviours with her peers and adults, including fabricating stories and stealing, sometimes items of very little financial value. This behaviour would indicate that there had been a high level of disruption to Jemma's early years, and the behaviours she developed could be a direct result of that longing need for attention and to exert power and control. Developing positive relationships with her peers was also very difficult, which is connected to the lack of nurturing and affection she experienced in her early years.

It is likely that she never gained that basic sense of trust in others, impacting significantly on her emotional development and outlook of the world. Now a teenager, Jemma is in the midst of her adolescent years and should be developing a strong sense of her identity, building from previous developmental stages. Since being accommodated, the focus has been to work alongside Jemma, enabling her to address developmental stages she has been deprived of in her early years. This has given Jemma the opportunity to explore in regressive play in a way which is very subtle and non-direct, given her chronological age, but has allowed for Jemma to explore her inner feelings in a safe environment. Jemma has regressed to playing with dolls and various other children's toys, which is gradually enabling previous developmental needs to be met.

Jemma's experience of separation and loss from her mother and birth family may also be a contributing factor that led to her functioning below her age emotionally and behaviourally and becoming developmentally 'stuck'. Jemma needs time and space in her foster placement to grieve for her feelings of loss. She consistently displayed feelings of anger, guilt and sadness towards her mother; she also blamed herself, lacks self-confidence and self-esteem at times, is unable to empathise, has sleepless nights, controlling food behaviours and feelings of extreme ambivalence and emotional dysregulation.

Providing Jemma with a secure and stable foster placement, offering consistent reliable care, it is hoped Jemma will thrive emotionally, enabling her to establish positive attachments to her carers, furthermore allowing her to go on to form healthy trusting relationships with others in the future.

SUSAN WORKMAN, SOCIAL WORKER, MORAY COUNCIL

I work in an integrated Drug and Alcohol team comprising social work and health. Our client group is adults with alcohol or drug misuse problems. The focus of my work is supporting adults to reduce or stop their substance misuse problem through work on relapse prevention, harm reduction and recovery.

I have been working with Kevin, who is a 43-year-old male who has been involved with my team for a number of years due to his alcohol use. My current involvement has been to make an assessment of his suitability for a place at a residential rehab unit. He has accessed all local supports and previously spent seven weeks at rehab, paid for privately by his family, but at no time has he managed to sustain any significant period of abstinence. Kevin believes that he has been drinking alcohol to excess since he was a teenager, with his alcohol use increasing over the years. He has also started smoking heroin, and although this is not at the stage of becoming a dependent addiction, his use of heroin has been increasing.

As part of my assessment, we talked about his life story and looked to find a possible 'reason' for his addiction. It is common for alcohol or drug misuse to be used as a coping strategy to deal with previous trauma. For someone to fully recover from addiction, they need emotionally to deal with their previous life experiences and find different ways of coping. Kevin described a good childhood, parents who were loving and caring, and he had no experience of abuse or trauma. However, through discussion with him, it became apparent that the breakup of his marriage in 2006 was a major source of trauma for him.

Erikson identifies the importance of identity in *Identity vs Role Confusion*, and Kevin's identity was based on being a *husband, father* and *provider* and he emotionally invested in these heavily. When his marriage ended, he was no longer a *husband* or *provider*. He was still a *father* but was no longer actively involved in his daughters' lives. The loss of this relationship affected his sense of self and identity and has had a massive impact on him. This resulted in a steady increase of his alcohol misuse.

As Marris describes, for someone to adapt to a new sense of identity, they need to go through the process of mourning. Kevin needs to mourn his marriage and the loss of the role that he had in order to enable him to create a new identity. However, it is difficult to deal with a loss if trying to mourn an idealised vision of the reality. Kevin remembers his marriage in a more positive light than it clearly was. He was sacked a number of times due to his alcohol use, was drinking heavily throughout his marriage and was unreliable for both his wife and daughters. For mourning to be complete, the lost object needs to become a meaningful internal part of the past. Kevin has not been able to think of his marriage as part of his past as he has been unable to accept that his marriage is over.

When someone experiences loss or change, they often go through a five-stage process, as described by Colin Murray Parkes. People can sometimes get stuck at one stage or move between stages. The five stages are: *Shock and Alarm, Anger and Guilt, Searching, Mitigation and Gaining a New Identity*. Kevin's marriage ended eight years ago, and he has been unable to progress through all these stages and accept and understand the loss of his marriage. Kevin will often move between *Anger and Guilt* and *Searching*. He has lots of feelings of anger and bitterness towards his ex-wife for ending the marriage, although he knows that it was not really a happy relationship. However, his feelings of anger often become internalised and he feels guilty for the way he behaved during and immediately after his marriage ended. He is still *Searching* as he often tries to re-establish connections with his ex-wife, offering to support her, asking to be reconciled and trying to keep her in his present life, but these attempts always fail as she has no desire to maintain any contact with him.

He has been unable to move to the *Mitigation* stage as he feels the pain of the loss each day and is unable to focus on futures and making new plans. While his ex-wife's life has improved and she has a new child and is planning to remarry, he has become alcohol dependent, started misusing heroin and is long-term unemployed.

He has not been able to form a new identity as he has not completed the process of grief and loss. Unfortunately, he currently has no positive identity as he does not wish to identify with being an alcoholic or drug user.

While Kevin's alcohol use was most likely at a problem level before and during his marriage, his inability to move through the process of loss and change has effectively resulted in him being 'stuck' in the grieving process, and to cope with those feelings he has increased his use of alcohol and heroin to a dependent level.

For Kevin to move forward in his life, he has to accept the end of his marriage and needs to form a new identity, finding what is important to him and in which he can emotionally invest. To support him, my role has been to refer him for residential rehab to get his alcohol addiction under control and to support him in his long-term recovery by giving him a focus for the future and to help him re-enter the job market so that he can finally create a positive new identity for himself.

KENNY O'BRIEN, SOCIAL WORK SERVICE MANAGER, ABERDEEN CITY

I still remember being a Social Worker in Training and being delighted whenever an essay question or assignment would want you to talk about 'loss and change'. Everyone studying social work knew that theories of change and loss were the easy ones to get your head around. Let's face it, no one wanted to spend the time getting their heads around CBT [cognitive behavioural therapy] or psychodynamic theory if they could get away with it. Jot down 'all change involves loss', 'Marris' and 'assumptive world' and you'll pass … that was the plan amongst all of us on the Social Work course back then.

If I could go back and talk to my lanky, somewhat poorly dressed student self now, I'd give him a gentle slap in the face and tell him to pay more attention (and buy better-fitting clothes). I'd also tell him to show some respect for a set of theories that, 12 years into professional practice, are the most relevant, useful and encompassing of anything I was ever taught. In a career that has so far encompassed children's homes, GP surgeries and Adult Protection/Safeguarding Units, the theories surrounding loss and change have underpinned my professional work.

So let's talk about Joe, one of my first cases in my first fieldwork job as a Care Manager in an integrated Health and Social Care team. Joe had been a sailor for many years and after leaving the boats had drifted from odd job to odd job, all the while cultivating a growing alcohol problem. Joe had gotten older, and the alcohol (and poor diet) had begun to take its toll on him physically, which meant that Joe was really starting to struggle. He had neglected his personal hygiene for a long time, but now even if he wanted to give himself a wash, he couldn't.

Joe lived in a council bedsit and had managed to ignore/avoid the housing officers for so long that he'd missed at least three refurbishments of the council house estate. If you ever wanted to see what council housing departments were fitting in kitchens and bathrooms in the 1960s, Joe's flat was the place to be. That was, if you could see the fixtures and fittings underneath the empty cans, bags and papers. The boiler had been condemned a long time ago, so Joe relied on dirty blankets and an unsafe electric-bar heater to keep himself warm.

Striding into Joe's life to rescue him from such squalor was my newly qualified self. Filled with desire to be helpful and support Joe, I offered him respite care, a clean-up of his house, a link with the housing department to upgrade his bedsit and to get the heating sorted. I also talked about lots of plans to have support workers in once the bedsit was clean to ensure that he had ongoing help and support. All good, crunchy, task and outcome focused work.

You can imagine how put out I was when the first word of Joe's rather passionate response to my well-thought-out plan of intervention rhymed with 'duck'. Going back to the office, I couldn't work out how a man with apparently so little (and with so much apparently to gain from the support being offered), was not willing to work with me. It was at this point that the apparently 'easy answer' of my training came to the fore. It is a cliché that 'all change involves loss' – but how often had I actually considered the depth and breadth of that concept? It is easy to link loss and change with events that are universally recognised as negative like acute/sudden disability or bereavement. Indeed, a lot of the theories and strategies focus on acute loss in their examples. It is not so easy to keep at the forefront of your mind that even a change which appears overwhelmingly positive can (and will) result in losses as well – and all that goes alongside that.

Joe was being offered a clean and warm place to live, with better food and care, plus, he could have central heating and hot water. However, these things weren't Joe's priority. Joe had gotten on just fine, thank you very much, with his blankets and his bar heater. Joe's priority at the moment was to still be able to keep himself to himself. The *loss* that Joe felt he would face from going into a respite service and then having all kinds of strangers poke their noses into his life was far greater than any benefit he could immediately see.

Once I had finally realised that, I was able to approach Joe's situation in a way that actually worked for him while getting some positive changes made as well.

Going back to visit Joe, I started with a blank piece of paper and worked out with Joe what, if anything, he wanted out of our working relationship. The list was small and (at least to my eyes) did not address many of the risks and concerns. However, it was a start. There was no way that Joe was going to go to respite – but he would take in emergency radiators from housing to give him more heat and let them take the bar heater away. There was also no way that Joe was letting anyone help him with a wash – but he would let the district nurse take a look at the bad rash he had. Joe wasn't going to let me (or anyone else) gut and clear out his bedsit – but he would let a support worker come in once a week to go through some of his things with him as it had started to 'get on top of him'.

Two years later, Joe's flat was clean, he had a working boiler, and with the combination of better nutrition and a freshly fitted bathroom, he didn't need help to wash – just a little seat in his new bath from the occupational therapist who sat next to me in the office.

Joe's assumptive world was threatened by my original plans of immediate respite, care and marked changes to his environment. He interacted with the world in his own way, and in his own time. Joe's bedsit was something he could control – both in terms of who he allowed access, and also as a base where he could retreat to. The threatened loss of that control mechanism was just too much for him, even if there were other gains to be made. By working more slowly with Joe, he was able to adjust and reconcile his own schema and understanding of his way of life that then allowed for incremental change over an extended period. Interestingly, apart from going into respite, we eventually got to the stage with Joe that almost everything I had originally proposed in my first meeting with him had been accomplished.

Joe's story is one of so many I could tell where understanding the theories of loss and change have been key to a successful outcome. My message to future practitioners is simple – if you want to be equipped to meet your client's needs – pay attention, and don't treat loss and change as the easy option. The simplest of concepts can have the greatest depths when explored … and the greatest utility in the real world.

MOIRA WATSON, MENTAL HEALTH SUPPORT WORKER AND INDEPENDENT PRACTICE TEACHER, MSC COMMUNITY CARE, SOCIAL WORKER, PRACTICE TEACHER, REGISTERED MENTAL HEATH NURSE (RMN)

Lou was a 37-year-old woman who experienced anxiety and depression. She had low self-esteem and self-confidence and felt that her life was meaningless. Lou felt lonely and isolated and later admitted that she had thought about suicide.

Lou is an only child of older parents who had little social contact outside their church. Her mother was also an only child, and her father was not in touch with his family after a family row. She found it difficult to make friends at school, and her best friend emigrated to Canada in her teens. Working in the local supermarket after leaving school, Lou always felt that she would like to do something else but had little confidence to change her job. She met Alan, a colleague of her father's, through her father's and Alan's shared interest in cars.

Three years on, Lou and Alan became an item and her parents were thrilled to think that their daughter would marry a nice 'safe' man like Alan. Lou described her relationship with Alan as 'like having a brother', and he continued to spend time with his father-in-law at weekends, leaving Lou to her own devices.

Lou heard about the mental health project through a contact at the church and came along to the Woman's Group. She was very nervous and almost didn't come, but felt she was getting very low and had been tearful at home and at work. Alan offered little support, telling her she was very lucky and that there was 'nothing coming over her'. Likewise, her parents were at a loss and tended to change the subject if Lou mentioned how she was feeling, so she stopped talking about how she felt.

Lou was very quiet for the first few weeks, and we suspected she might not come back, but she made a good connection to one of the other women, Linda, who suggested they meet up to come together, as this would help them both. This mutual arrangement was a big step for Lou, and the group became the first thing she had looked forward to for some time.

Opportunity-Led Work is an intervention based on using the opportunities presented by this kind of work with individuals and within groups. Relationships are formed and trust built up which can enable people to start to open up about their lives, and in Lou's situation, about her feelings of worthlessness and hopelessness.

Peer Support is the notion that other people with mental health problems are in a very good position to offer support and empathy. Linda, for example, thanked Lou for meeting up and said she looked forward to their walk together from the bus stop. Lou was surprised by this but smiled in a way that lit up her face, the first time this had been seen in the group.

The Woman's Group was encouraged to think about any subjects that might be of interest and have a 'therapeutic' outcome. This is distinct from 'therapy' per se, which can be a more formal and possibly more threatening approach which did not fit in with the idea of encouraging growth and development in an informal way. Some of the suggested topics were: Assertiveness, Confidence-Building and Managing Anxiety, and three sessions were planned looking at those topics. These ran every two weeks to allow a Woman's Group session to run in-between.

Group Work can enable people to explore issues in a supportive yet potentially dynamic way, and the facilitator's role is central in helping to set the scene and the tone of the sessions. Preparation and planning of the sessions, considering content, timings and the needs of individuals within the group, are vital.

Lou was very interested in the sessions and attended every one of them. She started to be able to recognise when she had not been assertive for example, and listened to how others had dealt with situations. Her confidence increased as she tried some of the 'techniques' suggested in the sessions, and became more vocal in supporting other members of the group. Lou and Linda also started going to the cinema together and took up walking at the weekend, when both reported being very lonely.

Lou also started to talk about a change of job, and the mental health worker was able to offer information and a contact to college offering short courses. Choosing 'Computing for the Terrified', Lou became a regular at her local library, where she could access a computer and practice her newfound skills. Her mental health improved, and she obtained an office role in the supermarket, having plucked up the courage to tell her manager that she was attending college. They agreed to support her in this and offered her day-release to a course with a qualification.

Resilience can be built up in adults and linked back to earlier skills and the development of new ways of thinking and therefore doing. Increasing confidence also assists in this process and 'practicing' in advance of situations. Sharing experiences in the group also helps individuals to explore their reactions and speculate about how they might deal with situations in the future.

John Henry Newman said 'growth is the only evidence of life', and Lou was a good example of someone who had been almost paralysed by her poor mental health, and stuck in a rut in her job and her relationship. New assertiveness and peer support enabled her to recognise that she had skills and abilities that could be put to use to improve her quality of life. She felt that she had more purpose, more possibilities and meaning, and that she had hope for better mental health, recognising her growing resilience.

Lou continued to be friends with Linda, but decided not to continue with the Woman's Group as she was busy with work and college and had suggested to her husband that they went to counselling about their relationship.

GARY DAWSON, COMMUNITY COORDINATOR, ADJUST, ABERDEEN

I am the Community Coordinator of a local pilot project called ADJUST. This is an acronym for Aberdeen Delivering Joined-Up Service Transitions. Our aim is to create and facilitate a multi-agency framework between agencies working in the field of Criminal Justice in the Aberdeen area. As a result of this framework, enhanced services and support mechanisms have been created to help meet the needs of ex-prisoners who wish to refrain from further offending behaviour.

The name ADJUST also supports the ethos of the work that we do in that we ask agencies who wish to support our work to 'adjust' their practices to more effectively meet the needs and reduce risks for prisoners pre-release. We also encourage prisoners and service users post-release to 'adjust' their behaviour and to engage with the opportunities created through meeting their needs in a person-centred way.

I have worked in the Criminal Justice field for over twenty years as both a Social Worker and Community Worker. From the social work perspective, I have always valued the various theories to hand, as tools and guides to help the practitioner and service user make progress, when journeys of change can often look daunting and dubious.

Over the years, I have been guided through the mechanics of change by many theorists, initially, by Peter Marris looking at the psychological principles of loss and change. Working with people struggling with substance misuse led me to the enlightening and simple concepts of James Prochaska and Carlo DiClemente's stages of change (Prochaska et al.,1994), where they identify the rolling process of supporting service users into their contemplation of the need to change, supporting these changes, being aware of the risks of relapse and having systems in place to start the process again if needs be. Working through change is supported by theoretical inputs using Motivational Interviewing techniques such as eliciting 'change talk' through review and reinforcement of positive movement forwards (Miller and Rollnick, 1991). Research carried out by Saarni and Lewis (1993) supported the view that people going through change need to keep the integrity of two beliefs and assumptions concerning their own actions in order to move forward psychologically. The first is the belief that 'I'm a good person,' and the second assumes 'I am in control most of the time.' Believing in these two assumptions is critical in both protecting and enhancing our mental health and self-belief in achieving change.

For me, this is about valuing the input and engagement of the service user. Change should not be imposed by practitioners, but making use of aspects of theories should meet person-centred needs and help empower someone to make the change process smoother and more effective for themselves.

Peter is in his late twenties and was a prolific offender, having spent most of his adult life in prison with only a matter of weeks in the community between sentences. He was a heroin user, had lost two tenancies due to his drug use and antisocial behaviour and had Hepatitis C, amongst other ailments. He had little contact with his family, apart from his mother, and had only worked briefly as a slater some years ago.

When we first met Peter, it looked like he had a mountain to climb. He had the above issues to face but equally was tired of his previous lifestyle and wanted to change. Previously, as with many in similar circumstances, he found it easier in many regards to acquire and take drugs, forget about problems and take it from there. His previous experience of minimal housing support and lack of money through benefits, amongst other issues, made his expectations for positive change minimal.

This time, however, after acknowledging and discussing his support needs, more realistic housing supports were put in place through a Short Assured Tenancy. Penumbra linked with him and the Local Authority via a Support Worker to make sure his tenancy was supported. He accessed Employment Support Allowance and created good personal links with a Job Centre Plus contact. This meant that he could embark on a prolonged course of treatment for his Hepatitis without fear of feeling pressured to seek employment. He met regularly with a Community Psychiatric Nurse (CPN) to look at his previous drug use and to help reduce risks through prescribing methadone for his opiate addiction and other medications to help stem anxiety and stresses faced from taking these new positive steps forwards.

Peter has now been out of prison for almost two years. His previous norm was two weeks. He has his own tenancy in a beautiful flat overlooking the sea, which he has decorated and furnished himself. He no longer needs one-to-one support from Penumbra or from his CPN.

This past Christmas was the first one since childhood where he has sat down for Christmas dinner with his wider family. It is also the first time that he has had gifts for everyone. His Hepatitis is gone and he is planning to come off methadone soon and has been working with the Foyer, a charitable organisation which aims to prevent and alleviate youth homelessness and unemployment, towards securing a job in the near future.

Despite the happy ending, it has not all been plain sailing for Peter. He has gone through the three phases of Bridges's transition model with various aspects of his journey of change. His 'ending' phase meant that he had to turn his back on the vast majority of his acquaintances there and then, and also to have the strength to cross the street away from them in future, too. Peter struggled with this period in the 'neutral zone' initially on his release. He got into some scrapes that luckily he could walk away from and had the supports in place to help him reflect on his experiences and capitalise on the positive opportunities he had at hand and the progress he had made.

He very much values his 'new beginning' and takes great strength from his achievements and the benefits that these have brought. So much so, that he has stated that he would like to mentor other prisoners or somehow pass on his experiences to others coming behind him on their own journeys of transition and change.

GEORGE ROBERTSON, SOCIAL WORKER AND PRACTICE TEACHER, ABERDEENSHIRE COUNCIL

Fiona is a 10-year-old service user of a Children and Families team and was in foster care due to her parents' disabilities, which meant that they were not in a position to care for her. Contact was facilitated monthly with the biological parents, and Fiona has an older sibling, also in care, who has supervised contact every two weeks. There were ongoing issues with the foster parents and Fiona: there were two other children in long-term care with the family and often conflict would arise as a result of their relationships and the attachments they had with the foster care family.

Fiona had previously had four foster placements which had broken down due to her behaviour deteriorating. All the placements were terminated. Her behaviour deteriorated with her current family, to the stage that an emergency meeting was called and a new foster family were identified to take Fiona into their care.

This case was assigned to a social work student on placement, who initially had to apply some Crisis Interventions with Fiona on their first meeting to keep her safe and reduce risky behaviour. Follow-up work was identified for the student to undertake Life Story work with Fiona to explore her current situation and try to assist with understanding issues from her past which were still impacting on her.

However, these unresolved issues were having an effect on Fiona's behaviour, which would deteriorate to the extent that she would put herself in risky situations. The student engaged Fiona in the life-story process by promoting a good value base, offering Fiona choice, respecting her decisions and being respectful of the situation she was currently in. Through working in collaboration with Fiona on the life-story book, the student was then able to use professional supervision to discuss Fiona's attachments and the impact they were having on her, as well as the resultant negative behaviours being displayed. By analysing the attachments which Fiona had in her life, the student and practice teacher went on to identify that Fiona had an avoidant attachment with her parents from information gathered from Fiona, previous parenting assessments and social work involvement in the past. Avoidant attachment results in the child finding it hard to display feelings and emotions, which was a key feature reported by the student working with her.

Another aspect of attachment identified by the student was ambivalence in relation to her relationship with her foster carers. The student assessed that because Fiona was not in a permanent placement, though she wanted to be close to and loved by the foster carers, the uncertainty of where she would be living made her unable to accept this. Fiona has been seeking to form attachments, but due to inconsistent care this had not been possible for her.

The understanding gained by the student on attachment and how this was affecting Fiona allowed them to discuss this together and get Fiona's view that she would like to be in a long-term foster placement. The student was then able to report this at the Children's Hearing shortly after Fiona had moved in with her new foster carers. This was accepted by the Hearing and Fiona's biological parents and deemed to be in Fiona's best interests.

The student reported that in the final weeks of the placement, Fiona had begun to open up. She was able to discuss her feelings and thoughts and their impact on her.

REFERENCES

The Adverse Childhood Experiences (ACE Study) (2014) Home Page. Available at: www.acestudy.org/home (accessed 20 October 2014).

Ainsworth, M.D.S., Blehar, M.C., Waters, E. and Wall, S. (2014) *Patterns of Attachment: A Psychological Study of the Strange Situation*. Hove: Psychology Press.

Ainsworth, M.S. (1989) 'Attachments beyond infancy', *American Psychologist*, 44 (4): 709–16.

Allan, G. (2014) 'Cognitive behavioral therapy: Its practice and its place in social work', in J. Lishman et al. (eds), *Social Work: An Introduction*. London: Sage, pp. 255–68.

Allen, J.P. and Land, D. (1999) 'Attachment in adolescence', in J. Cassidy and P.R. Shaver (eds), *Handbook of Attachment: Theory, Research, and Clinical Applications*. New York: Guilford, pp. 319–35.

Atchley, R.C. (1989) 'A continuity theory of normal aging', *Gerontologist*, 29: 183–90.

Baldry, S. and Kemmis, J. (1998) 'Research note: What is it like to be looked after by a local authority?', *British Journal of Social Work*, 28: 129–36.

Baltes, P.B. (1987) 'Theoretical propositions of life span developmental psychology: On the dynamics between growth and decline', *Developmental Psychology*, 23: 611–26.

Baltes, P.B. (1993) 'The aging mind: Potential and limits', *Gerontologist*, 33: 580–94.

Bandura, A. and Walters, R.H. (1963) *Social Learning and Personality Development*. New York: Holt.

Banks, S. (2006) *Ethics and Values in Social Work*. Basingstoke: Palgrave Macmillan.

Barker, P. and Chang, J. (2013) *Basic Family Therapy*. Chichester: John Wiley and Sons.

Bartholomew, K. and Horowitz, L.M. (1991) 'Attachment styles among young adults: A test of a four-category model', *Journal of Personality and Social Psychology*, 61: 226–44.

Beckett, C. and Taylor, H. (2010) *Human Growth and Development*. London: Sage.

Bennett, R. (2014) 'Go on, have a blazing row – it's good for the kids', *The Times*, 7 November.

Bernard, K. and Dozier, M. (2010) 'Examining infants' cortisol responses to laboratory tasks among children varying in attachment disorganization: Stress reactivity or return to baseline?', *Developmental Psychology*, 46: 1771–8.

Bertin, E. (1993) 'Prologue', in C. Clulow (ed.), *Rethinking Marriage: Public and Private Perspectives*. London: Karnac. pp. 1–8.

Bloom, S.L. (1999) *Trauma Theory Abbreviated*. Available at: www.sanctuaryweb.com/Documents/Trauma%20theory%20abbreviated.pdf (accessed 7 October 2014).

Bloom, S.L. (2013) *Creating Sanctuary: Toward the Evolution of Sane Societies*. Abingdon: Routledge.

Bolger, J. and Walker, P. (2014) 'Models of assessment', in J. Lishman et al. (eds), *Social Work: An Introduction*. London: Sage, pp. 69–83.

Bowen, M. (1993) *Family Therapy in Clinical Practice*. Lanham, MD: Jason Aronson.

Bowlby, J. (1969) *Attachment and Loss, Vol. 1: Attachment*. London: Hogarth Press.

Bowlby, J. (1972) *Attachment and Loss, Vol. 2: Separation: Anxiety and Anger*. London: Hogarth Press.

Bowlby, J. (1979) *The Making and Breaking of Affectional Bonds*. London: Tavistock.

Bowlby, J. (1980) *Attachment and Loss, Vol. 3: Loss: Sadness and Depression*. New York: Basic Books.

Bowlby, J. (2008) *Attachment*. New York: Basic books.

Bowlby, J. and Parkes, C.M. (1970) 'Separation and loss within the family', in E.J. Anthony (ed.), *The Child in his Family*. New York: J. Wiley, pp. 197–216.

Brazelton, T.B. and Greenspan, S.I. (2001) *The Irreducible Needs of Children: What Every Child Must Have to Grow, Learn, and Flourish*. Cambridge, MA: Da Capo Press.

Brearley, J. (2007) 'A psychodynamic approach to social work', in J. Lishman (ed.), *Handbook for Practice Learning in Social Work and Social Care: Knowledge and Theory*, 2nd edn. London: Jessica Kingsley, pp. 86–98.

Breuer, J. and Freud, S. (1957) *Studies on Hysteria*. New York: Basic Books.

Bridges, W. (2004) *Transitions: Making Sense of Life's Changes*. Cambridge, MA: Da Capo Press.

Bridges, W. (2009) *Managing Transitions: Making the Most of Change*. Cambridge, MA: Da Capo Press.

Briere, J. (2004) 'Treating the long-term effects of childhood maltreatment: A brief overview', *Psychotherapy in Australia*, 10: 12–19.

Brim, O. (1976) 'Theories of the male mid-life crisis', *Counselling Psychologist*, 6: 2–9.

British Association of Social Workers (BASW) (2014) *BASW Code of Ethics*. Available at: www.basw.co.uk/codeofethics/ (accessed 13 October 2014).

Brodie, S. and Swan, C. (2014) 'Human growth and development', in J. Lishman et al. (eds), *Social Work: An Introduction*. London: Sage, pp. 98–110.

Brody, J. (1983) 'Influential theory on bonding at birth is now questioned', *New York Times*. Available at: www.nytimes.com/1983/03/29/science/influential-theory-on-bonding-at-birth-is-now-questioned.html (accessed 19 September 2014).

Brody, Y. and Rosenfeld, B. (2002) 'Object relations in criminal psychopaths', *Journal of Offender Therapy and Comparative Criminology*, 46: 400–11.

Bronfenbrenner, U. (1986) 'Ecology of the family as a context for human development: Research perspectives', *Developmental Psychology*, 22: 723–42.

Bronfenbrenner, U. (1992) *Ecological Systems Theory*. London: Jessica Kingsley.

Bronfenbrenner, U. and Bronfenbrenner, U. (2009) *The Ecology of Human Development: Experiments by Nature and Design*. Cambridge, MA: Harvard University Press.

Brown, J.A.C. (1961) *Freud and the Post-Freudians*. Harmondsworth: Pelican.

Burnham, J.B. (1968) *Family Therapy: First Steps Towards a System Approach*. London: Tavistock.

Byng-Hall, J. (1998) *Rewriting Family Scripts: Improvisation and Systems Change*. New York: Guilford Press.

Caldwell, J.G. and Shaver, P.R. (2014) 'Promoting attachment-related mindfulness and compassion: A wait-list-controlled study of women who were mistreated during childhood', *Mindfulness*, 5 (2): 1–13.

Caplan, G.E. (1961) *Prevention of Mental Disorders in Children: Initial Explorations*. New York: Basic Books.

Carr, A. (2003) *The Handbook of Child and Adolescent Clinical Psychology: A Contextual Approach*. Abingdon: Routledge.

Carter, B. and McGoldrick, M. (1988) *The Changing Family Life Cycle: A Framework for Family Therapy*. New York: Gardner Press.

Carter, E.A. and McGoldrick, M. (1999) *The Evolving Family Life Cycle: Individual, Family, and Social Perspectives*. New York: Allyn & Bacon.

Caruth, C. (1995) *Trauma: Explorations in Memory*. Baltimore, MD: JHU Press.

Caspers, K.M., Cadoret, R.J., Langbehn, D., Yucuis, R. and Troutman, B. (2005) 'Contributions of attachment style and perceived social support to lifetime use of illicit substances', *Addictive Behaviors*, 30: 1007–11.

Cassidy, J. and Shaver, P.R. (1999) *Handbook of Attachment: Theory, Research, and Clinical Applications*. New York: Guilford Press.

Center for Nonviolence and Social Justice (2014) Home Page. Available at: www.nonvio lenceandsocialjustice.org (accessed 15 October 2014).

Choi, J., Jeong, B., Rohan, M.L., Polcari, A.M. and Teicher, M.H. (2009) 'Preliminary evidence for white matter tract abnormalities in young adults exposed to parental verbal abuse', *Biological Psychiatry*, 65: 227–34.

Christiano, D. (2008) *A Baby's View of Birth*. Available at: www.parents.com/pregnancy/ giving-birth/labor-and-delivery/a-babys-view-of-birth/ (accessed 2 August 2014).

Clulow, C. (2001) *Adult Attachment and Couple Psychotherapy*. London: Brunner Routledge.

Cohen, P. and Ainley, P. (2000) 'In the country of the blind?: Youth studies and cultural studies in Britain', *Journal of Youth Studies*, 3: 79–95.

Creemers, D. (2014) *Implicit and Explicit Self-Attitudes in Relation to Adolescent and Young Adult Depression, Stress and Treatment*. Radboud University of Nijmegen. Available at: http://repository.ubn.ru.nl/bitstream/handle/2066/127777/127777.pdf (accessed 14 November 2014).

Crittenden, P.M. (2008) *Raising Parents: Attachment, Parenting and Child Safety*. Portland, OR: Willan Publishing.

Crittenden, P.M. and Ainsworth, M.D.S. (1989) 'Child maltreatment and attachment theory', in D. Cicchetti and V. Carlson (eds), *Child Maltreatment: Theory and Research on the Causes and Consequences of Child Abuse and Neglect*. Cambridge: Cambridge University Press.

Cumming, E. and Henry, W. (1961) *Growing Old: The Process of Disengagement*. New York: Basic Books.

Daniel, B. and Wassell, S. (2002) *Assessing and Promoting Resilience in Vulnerable Children: Adolescence*. London: Jessica Kingsley.

Daniel, B., Gilligan, R. and Wassell, S. (2011) *Child Development for Child Care and Protection Workers*. London: Jessica Kingsley.

Davis, A. (2007) 'Structural approaches to social work', in J. Lishman (ed.), *Handbook for Practice Learning in Social Work and Social Care: Knowledge and Theory*, 2nd edn. London: Jessica Kingsley, pp. 27–38.

Deacon, S.A. and Piercy, F.P. (2001) 'Qualitative methods in family evaluation: Creative assessment techniques', *American Journal of Family Therapy*, 29: 355–73.

Department of Health, National Socicty for the Prevention of Cruelty to Children (NSPCC) and University of Sheffield (2000) 'The Resilience Matrix', *The Child's World: Assessing Children in Need, Training and Development Pack*. Available at: www.gov.scot/ resource/doc/1141/0109967.pdf

Deresiewicz, W. (2014) *Excellent Sheep: The Miseducation of the American Elite and the Way to a Meaningful Life*. New York: Free Press.

Dicks, H.V. (1967) (reprinted 1993 Karnac Books) *Marital Tensions: Clinical Studies towards a Psychological Theory of Interaction*. London: RKP.

Donellan, M.B., Conger, R.D., Bryant, C.M. (2004) 'The big five and enduring marriages', *Journal of Research in Personality*, 38: 481–504.

Dunn, J. (1993) *Young Children's Close Relationships: Beyond Attachment*. London: Sage.

Durlak, J.A. (1998) 'Common risk and protective factors in successful prevention programs', *American Journal of Orthopsychiatry*, 68: 512–20.

Duvall, E. (1977) *Marriage and Family Development*, 5th edn. Philadelphia, PA: Lippincott.

Erikson, E. (1959) *Identity and the Life Cycle*, Psychological Issues Monograph 1. New York: International Universities Press.

Erikson, E. (1965) *Childhood and Society*. Harmondsworth: Penguin.

Fahlberg, V.I. (2012) *A Child's Journey through Placement*. London: Jessica Kingsley.

Fairbairn, W.R.D. (1952) (reprinted 1986) *Psychoanalytic Studies of the Personality*. London: Routledge/Kegan Paul.

Feeney, J.A.A. and Noller, P. (1996) *Adult Attachment*. London: Sage.

Feeney, J.A., Noller, P. and Hanrahan, M. (1994) 'Assessing adult attachment', in M.B. Sperling and W.H. Berman (eds), *Attachment in Adults: Clinical and Developmental Perspectives*. New York: Guilford Press, pp. 128–52.

Feilberg, F. (2014) 'Counselling in social work', in J. Lishman et al. (eds), *Social Work: An Introduction*. London: Sage, pp. 348–60.

Finkelstein, L. (1988) 'Psychoanalysis, marital therapy and object relations', *Journal of the American Psychoanalytic Association*, 36: 905–31.

Finkenauer, C., Kerkhof, P., Righetti, F. and Branje, S. (2009) 'Living together apart: Perceived concealment as a signal of exclusion in marital relationships', *Personality and Social Psychology Bulletin*, 35: 1410–22.

Fonagy, P. (2003) 'The development of psychopathology from infancy to adulthood: The mysterious unfolding of disturbance in time', *Infant Mental Health Journal*, 24: 212–39.

Fraley, R.C. and Shaver, P.R. (2000) 'Adult romantic attachment: Theoretical developments, emerging controversies, and unanswered questions', *Review of General Psychology*, 4: 132–54.

Freud, S. (1933) *New Introductory Lectures on Psychoanalysis*. New York: W.W. Norton.

Freud, S. (1957 [1917]) 'Mourning and melancholia', *The Standard Edition of the Complete Psychological Works of Sigmund Freud*, Vol. 14 (1914–16). London: Hogarth Press.

Freud, S. (2001) *The Complete Psychological Works of Sigmund Freud*. New York: Random House.

Fyffe, C.-M. (2014) 'Psychological approaches: Their application and relevance to social work', in J. Lishman et al. (eds), *Social Work: An Introduction*. London: Sage, pp. 83–97.

Gaskill, R.L. and Perry, B.D. (2012) 'Child sexual abuse, traumatic experiences and their effect on the developing brain', in P. Goodyear-Brown (ed.), *Handbook of Child Sexual Abuse: Identification, Assessment, and Treatment*. New York: Wiley & Sons, pp. 29–49.

George, C. and West, M. (1999) 'Developmental vs. social personality models of adult attachment and mental ill health', *British Journal of Medical Psychology*, 72: 285–303.

George, C. and West, M. (2001) 'The development and preliminary validation of a new measure of adult attachment: The Adult Attachment Projective', *Attachment and Human Development*, 3: 30–61.

George, C., Kaplan, N. and Main, M. (1985) 'The Berkeley adult attachment interview', unpublished protocol, Department of Psychology, University of California, Berkeley.

George, C., Kaplan, N. and Main, M. (2011) *Adult Attachment Interview Protocol*. Available at: www.psychology.sunysb.edu/attachment/measures/content/aai_interview.pdf (accessed 13 August 2014).

Gerhardt, S. (2006) *Why Love Matters: How Affection Shapes a Baby's Brain*. London: Routledge.

Giarratano, L. (2004) *Clinical Skills for Treating Traumatised Adolescents: Evidence-Based Treatment for PTSD*. Mascot, NSW: Talomin Books.

Gibson, A. (2007) 'Erikson's life cycle approach to development', in J. Lishman (ed.), *Handbook for Practice Learning in Social Work and Social Care: Knowledge and Theory*, 2nd edn. London: Jessica Kingsley, pp. 74–85.

Gilligan, R. (2000) 'Adversity, resilience and young people: The protective value of positive school and spare time experiences', *Children and Society*, 14: 37–47.

Gilligan, R. (2004) 'Promoting resilience in child and family social work: Issues for social work practice, education and policy', *Social Work Education*, 23: 93–104.

Gilligan, R. (2009) *Promoting Resilience*. London: British Association for Adoption and Fostering (BAAF).

Gordon, R.M. (1982) 'Systems-object relations view of marital therapy: Revenge and reraising', in L.R. Wolberg and M. Aronson (eds), *Group and Family Therapy*. New York: Brunner-Mazel. Available at: www.mmpi-info.com/psychology-publications-systems-object-relations-marital-therapy (accessed 28 April 2015).

Gottman, J.M. (2014) *What Predicts Divorce? The Relationship between Marital Processes and Marital Outcomes*. Hove: Psychology Press.

Grotberg, E.H. (2000) 'The International Resilience Research Project', in A.L. Comunian and U. Gielen (eds), *International Perspectives on Human Development*. Vienna: Pabst Science Publishers, pp. 379–399.

Gutmann, D. (1976) 'Individual adaptation in the middle years: Developmental issues in the masculine mid-life crisis', *Journal of Geriatric Psychiatry*, 9: 41–59.

Haley, J. (1967) 'Toward a theory of pathological systems', in G. Zuk and I. Nagy (eds), *Family Therapy and Disturbed Families*. Palo Alto, CA: Science and Behavior Books, pp. 11–27.

Hawkins, A.J., Willoughby, B.J. and Doherty, W.J. (2012) 'Reasons for divorce and openness to marital reconciliation', *Journal of Divorce and Remarriage*, 53: 453–63.

Hazan, C. and Shaver, P. (1987) 'Romantic love conceptualized as an attachment process', *Journal of Personality and Social Psychology*, 52: 511–24.

Hazan, C. and Zeifman, D. (1994) 'Sex and the psychological tether', in K. Bartholomew and D. Perlman (eds), *Attachment Processes in Adulthood: Advances in Personal Relationships*, Vol. 5. Philadelphia, PA: Jessica Kingsley, pp. 151–78.

Heidkamp, B. (1994) '"Angels of death": The Lainz Hospital murders', in H. Birch (ed.), *Moving Targets: Women, Murder and Representation*. Berkeley, CA: University of California Press, pp. 218–40.

Helms, H.M. (2013) 'Marital relationships in the twenty-first century', in G.W. Peterson and K.R. Bush (eds), *Handbook of Marriage and the Family*, 3rd edn. New York: Springer, pp. 233–54.

Hesse, E. and Main, M. (2006) 'Frightened, threatening, and dissociative parental behavior in low-risk samples: Description, discussion, and interpretations', *Development and Psychopathology*, 18: 309–43.

Holmes, T.H. and Rahe, R.H. (1967) 'The social readjustment rating scale', *Journal of Psychosomatic Research*, 11: 213–18.

Howe, D. and Campling, J. (1995) *Attachment Theory for Social Work Practice*. London: Macmillan.

Humphrey, D. (2014) 'Task-centred intervention', in J. Lishman et al. (eds), *Social Work: An Introduction*. London: Sage, pp. 269–81.

Huston, T.L. (2000) 'The social ecology of marriage and other intimate unions', *Journal of Marriage and Family*, 62: 289–320.

James, K.R. and Gililand, B.E. (2001) *Crisis Intervention Strategies*. Belmont, CA: Wadsworth/Thompson.

Janzen, C. and Harris, O. (1986) *Family Treatment in Social Work Practice*. Itasca, IL: FE Peacock Publishers.

Kassel, J.D., Wardle, M. and Roberts, J.E. (2007) 'Adult attachment security and college student substance use', *Addictive Behaviors*, 32: 1164–76.

Kaufman, J. and Zigler, E. (1989) 'The intergenerational transmission of child abuse', in D. Cicchetti and V. Carlson (eds), *Child Maltreatment: Theory and Research on the Causes and Consequences of Child Abuse and Neglect*. Cambridge: Cambridge University Press, pp. 129–50.

Kobak, R.R., Sudler, N. and Gamble, W. (1991) 'Attachment and depressive symptoms during adolescence: A developmental pathways analysis', *Development and Psychopathology*, 3: 461–74.

Kubler-Ross, E. (1970) *On Death and Dying*. London: Tavistock.

Liberzon, I., Taylor, S.F., Amdur, R., et al. (1999) 'Brain activation in PTSD in response to trauma-related stimuli', *Biological Psychiatry*, 45: 817–26.

Lindberg, F.H. and Distad, L.J. (1985) 'Post-traumatic stress disorders in women who experienced childhood incest', *Child Abuse and Neglect*, 9: 329–34.

Lindsay, T. (ed.) (2009) *Social Work Intervention*. Exeter: Learning Matters.

Lishman, J. (ed.) (2007) *Handbook for Practice Learning in Social Work and Social Care: Knowledge and Theory*, 2nd edn. London: Jessica Kingsley.

Loewenthal, D. (2013) *Phototherapy and Therapeutic Photography in a Digital Age*. Abingdon: Routledge.

Luthar, S.S. (2003) *Resilience and Vulnerability: Adaptation in the Context of Childhood Adversities*. Cambridge: Cambridge University Press.

Maclean, K. (2004) 'Resilience: What it is and how children and young people can be helped to develop it'. Available at: www.cyc-net.org/cyc-online/cycol-0304-resilience. html (accessed 2 November 2014).

Mahoney, J.L. (2000) 'School extracurricular activity participation as a moderator in the development of antisocial patterns', *Child Development*, 71: 502–16.

Main, M. and Morgan, H. (1996) 'Disorganization and disorientation in infant strange situation behavior', in L. Michelson and W. Ray (eds), *Handbook of Dissociation: Theoretical, Empirical, and Clinical Perspectives*. New York: Springer, pp. 107–138.

Main, M. and Solomon, J. (1986) 'Discovery of an insecure-disorganized/disoriented attachment pattern', in T. Berry Brazelton and M.W. Yogman (eds), *Affective Development in Infancy*. Norwood, NJ: Ablex Publishing, pp. 95–125.

Main, M., Kaplan, N. and Cassidy, J. (1985) 'Security in infancy, childhood, and adulthood: A move to the level of representation', *Monographs of the Society for Research in Child Development*, 50 (1–2, Serial No. 209): 66–104.

Malekpour, M. (2007) 'Effects of attachment on early and later development', *British Journal of Development Disabilities*, 53: 81–95.

Mallon, B. (2008) *Dying, Death and Grief: Working with Adult Bereavement.* London: Sage.

Manassis, K., Bradley, S., Goldberg, S., Hood, J. and Swinson, R.P. (1994) 'Attachment in mothers with anxiety disorders and their children', *Journal of the American Academy of Child and Adolescent Psychiatry,* 33: 1106–13.

Marris, P. (1986) *Loss and Change,* revd edn. London: Routledge & Kegan Paul.

Marron, D., Buckley, R. and Leece, J. (2011) 'Social inequality and social class', in C. Yuill and A. Gibson (eds), *Sociology for Social Work: An Introduction.* London: Sage, pp. 26–44.

Marsden, C. (2014) 'Methods of intervention of working with individuals with substance problems', in J. Lishman et al. (eds), *Social Work: An Introduction.* London: Sage, pp. 377–91.

Maslow, A.H. (1943) 'A theory of human motivation', *Psychological Review,* 50: 370–96.

Masten, A.S. and Coatsworth, J.D. (1998) 'The development of competence in favorable and unfavorable environments', *American Psychologist,* 53: 205–20.

Merz, E.-M. and Consedine, N.S. (2012) 'Ethnic group moderates the association between attachment and well-being in later life', *Cultural Diversity and Ethnic Minority Psychology,* 18: 404–15.

Mikulincer, M. and Florian, V. (2001) 'Attachment style and affect regulation: Implications for coping with stress and mental health', in G.J.O. Fletcher and M.S. Clark (eds), *Blackwell Handbook of Social Psychology: Interpersonal Processes.* Malden: Blackwell Publishers, pp. 535–57.

Mikulincer, M. and Shaver, P.R. (2008) 'Adult attachment and affect regulation', in J. Cassidy and P.R. Shaver (eds), *Handbook of Attachment: Theory, Research, and Clinical Applications.* New York: Guilford Press, pp. 503–31.

Millar, J. (2014) 'Working in the life space', in J. Lishman et al. (eds), *Social Work: An Introduction.* London: Sage, pp. 282–94.

Miller, W.R. and Rollnick, S. (1991) *Motivational Interviewing: Preparing People For Change.* New York: Guilford Press.

Minuchin, S. (1974) *Families and Family Therapy.* Cambridge, MA: Harvard University Press.

Moretti, M.M. and Peled, M. (2004) 'Adolescent–parent attachment: Bonds that support healthy development', *Paediatrics and Child Health,* 9: 551–5.

Morrison, B. (1997) *As If.* London: Granta.

Napoli, E.A., Breland, E.A. and Allen, R.S. (2013) 'Staff knowledge and perceptions of sexuality and dementia of older adults in nursing homes', *Journal of Aging and Health,* 25: 1087–1105.

The Observer (2014) 'British sex survey, 2014', 28 September.

Orth, U., Trzesniewski, K. and Robins, R. (2010) 'Self-esteem development from young adulthood to old age: A cohort sequential longitudinal study', *Journal of Personality and Social Psychology,* 98: 645–58.

Paley, V.G. (2004) *A Child's Work: The Importance of Fantasy Play.* Chicago, IL: University of Chicago Press.

Parad, H.J. and Caplan, G. (1960) 'A framework for studying families in crisis', *Social Work,* 5: 3–15.

Parker, J. and Bradley, G. (2007) *Social Work Practice: Assessment, Planning, Intervention and Review.* Exeter: Learning Matters.

Parkes, C.M. (1988) 'Bereavement as a psychosocial transition: Processes of adaptation to change', *Journal of Social Issues*, 44: 53–65.

Parkes, C.M. and Prigerson, H.G. (2010) *Bereavement Studies of Grief in Adult Life*. London: Penguin.

Parkes, C.M., Stevenson-Hinde, J. and Marris, P. (2006) *Attachment Across the Life Cycle*. Abingdon: Routledge.

Payne, S., Horn, S. and Relf, M. (1999) *Health Psychology: Loss and Bereavement*. Buckingham: Open University Press.

Perry, B.D. (2001) 'The neurodevelopmental impact of violence in childhood', in D. Schetky and E.P. Benedek (eds), *Textbook of Child and Adolescent Forensic Psychiatry*. Washington, DC: American Psychiatric Press, pp. 221–238.

Phung, T.-C. (2014) in 'Relationship-based social work', J. Lishman et al. (eds), *Social Work: An Introduction*. London: Sage, pp. 229–40.

Piaget, J. (1926) *The Language and Thought of the Child*. New York: Meridian Books.

Pincus, L. and Dare, C. (1978) *Secrets in the Family*. London: Faber and Faber.

Pomerantz, A. (2014) *Clinical Psychology: Science, Practice and Culture*, 3rd edn. Thousand Oaks, CA: Sage.

Prochaska, J.O., Norcross, J.C. and DiClemente, C.C. (1994) *Changing for Good*. New York: Morrow.

Rapaport, L. (1970) 'Crisis intervention as a mode of brief treatment', in R.W. Roberts and R.H. Nee (eds), *Theories of Social Casework*. Chicago, IL: University of Chicago Press, pp. 265–312.

Rholes, W.S. and Simpson, J.A. (2006) *Adult Attachment: Theory, Research, and Clinical Implications*. New York: Guilford Press.

Ringel, S. and Brandell, J.R. (2011) *Trauma: Contemporary Directions in Theory, Practice, and Research*. London: Sage.

Robinson, L. (1995) *Psychology for Social Workers: Black Perspectives*. London: Routledge.

Rosenstein, D.S. and Horowitz, H.A. (1996) 'Adolescent attachment and psychopathology', *Journal of Consulting and Clinical Psychology*, 64: 244–53.

Roth, E.G., Keimig, L., Rubinstein, R.L., et al. (2012) 'Baby boomers in an active retirement community: Comity interrupted', *The Gerontologist*, 52: 245–54.

Rothschild, B. (2000) *The Body Remembers: The Psychophysiology of Trauma and Trauma Treatment*. New York: W.W. Norton.

Ryan, R.M. and Lynch, J.H. (1989) 'Emotional autonomy versus detachment: Revisiting the vicissitudes of adolescence and young adulthood', *Child Development*, 60 (2): 340–56.

Saakvitne, K.W., Gamble, S., Pearlman, L.A. and Lev, B.T. (2000) *Risking Connection: A Training Curriculum for Working with Survivors of Childhood Abuse*. Brooklandville, MD: Sidran Press.

Saarni, C. and Lewis, M. (1993) 'Deceit and illusion in human affairs', in M. Lewis and C. Saarni (eds), *Lying and Deception in Everyday Life*. New York: Guilford Press.

Schaffer, H.R. and Emerson, P.E. (1964) 'The development of social attachments in infancy', *Monographs of the Society for Research in Child Development*, 29 (3), serial no. 94: 1–77.

Schore, A.N. (2000) 'Attachment and the regulation of the right brain', *Attachment and Human Development*: 2: 23–47.

Schore, A.N. (2001) 'Effects of a secure attachment relationship on right brain development, affect regulation, and infant mental health', *Infant Mental Health Journal*, 22: 7–66.

Schore, A.N. (2003a) *Affect Regulation and Disorders of the Self*. New York: W.W. Norton.

Schore, A.N. (2003b) *Affect Regulation and the Repair of the Self*, Norton Series on Interpersonal Neurobiology. New York: W.W. Norton.

Schore, A.N. (2003c) 'Early relational trauma, disorganized attachment, and the development of a predisposition to violence', in M.F. Solomon and D.J. Siegel (eds), *Healing Trauma: Attachment, Mind, Body and Brain*. New York: W.W. Norton, pp. 107–67.

Schweitzer, J., Zwack, J., Nicolai, E., Weber, G. and Hirschenberger, N. (2007) 'Family systems psychiatry: Principles, good practice guidelines, clinical examples, and challenges', *American Journal of Orthopsychiatry*, 77: 377–85.

Sharry, J. (2004) *Counselling Children, Adolescents and Families: A Strengths-Based Approach*. London: Sage.

Shaver, P.R., Hazan, C. and Bradshaw, D. (1988) 'The integration of three behavioral systems', in R.J. Sternberg and M.L. Barnes (eds), *The Psychology of Love*. New Haven, CT: Yale University Press.

Shaver, P.R., Lavy, S., Saron, C.D. and Mikulincer, M. (2007) 'Social foundations of the capacity for mindfulness: An attachment perspective', *Psychological Inquiry*, 18: 264–71.

Shemmings, D. and Shemmings, Y. (2011) *Understanding Disorganized Attachment: Theory and Practice for Working with Children and Adults*. London: Jessica Kingsley.

Shirran, A. (2014) 'Motivational interviewing', in J. Lishman et al. (eds), *Social Work: An Introduction*. London: Sage, pp. 320–33.

Skynner, A.C. (1976) *Systems of Family and Marital Psychotherapy*. New York: Brunner/Mazel.

Skynner, R. and Cleese, J. (1983) *Families and How to Survive Them*. London: Methuen.

Sutherland, J.D. (1980) 'The British object relations theorists', *Journal of the American Psychiatric Association*, 28 (4): 829–60.

Sutherland, J.D. (1989) *Fairbairn's Journey into the Interior*. London: Free Association Books.

Toman, W. (1993) *Family Constellation: Its Effects on Personality and Social Behavior*. New York: Springer.

Tweed, R.G. and Dutton, D.G. (1998) 'A comparison of impulsive and instrumental subgroups of batterers', *Violence and Victims*, 13: 217–30.

Veroff, J. (1978) 'Social motivation', *American Behavioral Scientist*, 31: 709–30.

Vygotsky, L.S. (1962) *Thought and Language*. Cambridge, MA: MIT Press.

Walker, J. and Crawford. K. (2014) *Social Work and Human Development*. Exeter: Learning Matters.

Whishman, M.A., Uebelacher, L. and Weinstock, L.M. (2004) 'Psychopathology and marital satisfaction: The importance of evaluating both partners', *Journal of Consulting and Clinical Psychology*, 72: 830–8.

Winek, J.L. (2009) *Systemic Family Therapy: From Theory to Practice*. London: Sage.

Winnicott, D.W. (1960) 'The theory of the parent–infant relationship', *International Journal of Psychoanalysis*, 41: 585–95.

Winnicott, D.W. (1964) *The Child, the Family and the Outside World*. London: Pelican.

Winnicott, D.W. (1971) *Playing and Reality*. New York: Basic Books.

Winnicott, D.W. (1974) 'Fear of breakdown', *International Review of Psycho-Analysis*, 1: 103–7.

Worden, J.W.A. (2008) *Grief Counselling and Grief Therapy: A Handbook for the Mental Health Practitioner*. New York: Springer.

Wortman, C.B. and Silver, R.C. (2001) 'The myths of coping with loss revisited', in M.S. Stroebe, R.O. Hannsson, W. Stroebe and H. Schut (eds), *Handbook of Bereavement Research: Consequences, Coping and Care*. Washington, DC: American Psychological Association, pp. 405–429.

Wu, Z., Schimmele, M.A. and Chappell, N.L. (2012) 'Aging and late-life depression', *Journal of Aging and Health*, 24: 3–28.

Yuill, C. and Gibson, A. (eds) (2011) *Sociology for Social Work: An Introduction*. London: Sage.

Zimmermann, P. and Iwanski, A. (2014) 'Emotional regulation from early adolescence to emerging adulthood: Age differences, gender differences, and emotion-specific developmental variations', *International Journal of Behavioural Development*, 38: 182.

INDEX